D0419773

Fashion and Modernity

Edited by
Christopher Breward
and
Caroline Evans

Oxford • New York

First published in 2005 by
Berg
Editorial offices:
1st Floor, Angel Court, 81 St Clements Street, Oxford OX4 1AW, UK
175 Fifth Avenue, New York, NY 10010, USA

Berg is the imprint of Oxford International Publishers Ltd.

Supported by
A · H · R · B
arts and humanities research board

Library of Congress Cataloging-in-Publication Data
Fashion and modernity / edited by Christopher Breward and Caroline Evans.
p. cm.
Includes bibliographical references.
ISBN 1-84520-027-6 (cloth) -- ISBN 1-84520-028-4 (pbk.)
1. Fashion--History. 2. Fashion--Psychological aspects. 3. Clothing and dress--Symbolic aspects. 4. Modernism (Aesthetics) I. Breward, Christopher, 1965- II. Evans, Caroline.

TT515.F297 2005
391'.001--dc22

2004023161

British Library Cataloguing-in-Publication Data
A catalogue record for this book is available from the British Library.

ISBN 1 84520 027 6 (Cloth)
1 84520 028 4 (Paper)

Typeset by JS Typesetting Ltd, Porthcawl, Mid Glamorgan
Printed in the United Kingdom by Biddles Ltd, King's Lynn

www.bergpublishers.com

Contents

Part II Performing Bodies

Part III Processes of Modernity

General Acknowledgements

The editors would like to thank the Arts and Humanities Research Board whose funding of the 'Fashion and Modernity Project' involving staff at Central Saint Martins College of Art and Design and London College of Fashion (both University of the Arts London) supported the publication of this book. The project could not have succeeded without the enthusiasm and good will of all the contributors and we are grateful for their hard work and understanding during the editing process. Jane Rapley and Central Saint Martins hosted the symposium that brought early versions of the following chapters together for the first time, expertly chaired by Andrew Stephenson. This event, together with its development into a coherent, illustrated manuscript were very ably co-ordinated by Marketa Uhlirova. All the contributors are particularly grateful to her for her expert picture research for this publication. Peter Close, Gerard Dufrene, Martin Durrant, Kathryn Earle and her team at Berg, Arabella Hayes, Steve Hill and Ken Jackson have also worked hard to ensure in their different ways that the book reached a state of satisfactory completion. Every effort has been made to trace copyright holders of images, but if any have not been properly credited, please contact the publishers, who will be happy to rectify the omission in future editions. Where appropriate individual contributors have acknowledged further support in their own chapters.

Notes on Contributors

Andrew Bolton trained as an art historian and anthropologist. Currently Associate Curator at The Costume Institute of The Metropolitan Museum of Art, New York, he is the author of *The Supermodern Wardrobe* (V&A Publications 2002), *Bravehearts: Men in Skirts* (V&A Publications 2003) and the forthcoming *WILD: Fashion Untamed* (to be published by The Metropolitan Museum of Art).

Christopher Breward is Deputy Head of Research at the Victoria and Albert Museum, London and is a Visiting Professor at London College of Fashion (University of the Arts London). He has a background in art and design history and has previously published *The Culture of Fashion* (Manchester University Press 1995), *The Hidden Consumer* (Manchester University Press 1999), *Fashion* (Oxford University Press 2003) and *Fashioning London* (Berg 2004). He is co-author of *The London Look: Fashion from Street to Catwalk* (Yale University Press 2004) and co-editor of *Material Memories* (Berg 1999) and *The Englishness of English Dress* (Berg 2002). His current research relates to the history of fashion and consumer cultures in London and other world cities.

Dr Jamie Brassett gained his PhD in Philosophy from the University of Warwick in 1993. He is Senior Lecturer and Programme Leader in Contextual Studies for Product Design at Central Saint Martins College of Art and Design (University of the Arts London). He is currently writing a book for I.B.Tauris on the philosophical considerations of the design of intimate technology.

Adam Briggs is Principal Lecturer in Cultural and Historical Studies at the London College of Fashion (University of the Arts London). He is currently researching the relationship between production and consumption in the British Fashion Industry in the period 1945–70. Recent publications include *The Media: An Introduction* (co-edited with P. Cobley, Longman, 2nd edition 2002).

Dr Becky E. Conekin is Principal Lecturer and Senior Research Fellow in Historical and Cultural Studies and Course Director of the MA in the History and Culture of Fashion at the London College of Fashion (University of the Arts London). She received her PhD in History from the University of Michigan, Ann Arbor in 1998. In 2004–05 she will be Postdoctoral Fellow at the Illinois Program for Research in the Humanities at the University of Illinois, Urbana-Champaign, where she is researching a cultural history of the notion of 'taste' in the US and Britain from ca 1860 to the present. She is the author of '*The Autobiography of a Nation': The 1951 Festival of Britain* (Manchester University Press 2003) and the co-editor of *Moments of Modernity: Reconstructing Britain 1945–64*, (Rivers Oram 1999) and *The Englishness of English Dress* (Berg 2002).

Barry Curtis is Professor of Visual Culture at Middlesex University. He has recently published essays on architecture and urbanism and is currently working on a book on film and architecture.

Dr Caroline Dakers is Professor of Cultural History at Central Saint Martins College of Art and Design (University of the Arts London). She is currently writing a book for Yale University Press on the Morrisons of Fore Street. Her most recent publications are *Clouds. The Biography of a Country House* (Yale University Press 1993) and *The Holland Park Circle. Artists and Victorian Society* (Yale University Press 1999).

Caroline Evans is Reader in Fashion Studies at Central Saint Martins College of Art and Design (University of the Arts London). She is the author of *Fashion at the Edge: Spectacle, Modernity and Deathliness* (Yale University Press 2003) and the co-author of *Women and Fashion: A New Look* (Quartet 1989) and *The London Look: Fashion from Street to Catwalk* (Yale University Press 2004). She is currently working on a history of early-twentieth-century fashion shows and their relation to industrial aesthetics and Taylorism.

Kitty Hauser is a Research Fellow at Clare Hall, Cambridge University, and an Honorary Associate of Sydney University. Her research interests revolve around the relationship between photography and the activities of forensic scientists, detectives and archaeologists. She is writing a book about the archaeologist O.G.S. Crawford, entitled *Bloody Old Britain*, to be published by Granta. Another version of her contribution to this volume, entitled 'A Garment in the Dock', was published by the *Journal of Material Culture* (Sage 2004), which awarded it the inaugural Alfred Gell Memorial Prize.

Ben Highmore is a Senior Lecturer in Cultural Studies at the University of the West of England, Bristol. He is the author of *Everyday Life and Cultural Theory: An Introduction* (Routledge 2002) and *Cityscapes: Cultural Readings in the Material and Symbolic City* (Palgrave Macmillan 2005). He is also the editor of *The Everyday Life Reader* (Routledge 2002). His *Michel de Certeau: Analysing Culture* is forthcoming from Continuum in 2006.

Andrew Hill is a Junior Research Fellow in the School of Media and Performing Arts at the University of Ulster. He has written on various aspects of popular culture, and is currently researching the media in Northern Ireland, and the 'war on terror'.

Esther Leslie teaches in the School of English and Humanities, Birkbeck, University of London. Her writings include *Walter Benjamin: Overpowering Conformism* (Pluto 2000) and *Hollywood Flatlands, Animation, Critical Theory and the Avant Garde* (Verso 2002). Her next book is a study of the German chemical industry in relation to the Romantic philosophy of nature, and the politics and poetics of modernity. She is actively involved in editing three journals – *Historical Materialism: Research in Critical Marxist Theory*, *Radical Philosophy* and *Revolutionary History*, and has also edited and contributed to a collection called *Mad Pride: A Celebration of Mad Culture*.

Lynda Nead is Professor of History of Art at Birkbeck College, London. Her most recent book is *Victorian Babylon: People, Streets and Images in Nineteenth-Century London* (Yale University Press 2000). In 2002 she was awarded a Leverhulme Senior Research Fellowship to work on a new book called *The Haunted Gallery* which looks at relationships between painting, photography and cinema and will be published by Yale University Press.

Susan North is Curator of seventeenth- and eighteenth-century fashion at the Victoria and Albert Museum, London. She has an MA in the History of Dress from the Courtauld Institute and is co-author of *Fashion in Detail: The 17th and 18th Centuries* (V&A Publications 1998).

Alistair O'Neill is a Research Fellow and Lecturer in Historical and Cultural Studies at London College of Fashion (University of the Arts London). His articles have appeared in *Fashion Theory, Radical Fashion* (V&A Publications 2001) and *More Dirty Looks* (British Film Institute 2004). As a curator his exhibitions include 'Philip Castle: A Clockwork Orange Poster Design' (Sho Gallery 2000) 'Queernation02' (Elms Lester 2002) and 'The Harry Jacobs Archive' (LCF 2003). His first book considers the relation between fashion and London in the twentieth century and will be published by Reaktion in 2005.

Andrea Stuart is currently a Visiting Lecturer at Central Saint Martins College of Art and Design (University of the Arts London). Her research interests include historical studies, film, literature, sexuality, race and gender. She has contributed to numerous anthologies and journals. Her first book, *Showgirls*, was published by Jonathan Cape in 1996. *The Rose of Martinique* (2003), a biography of Napoleon's Josephine, is published by Macmillan in the UK and Grove Press in the US.

John Styles is Research Professor in History at the University of Hertfordshire, responsible for the V&A/RCA MA Course in the History of Design, and associate director of the AHRB Centre for the Study of the Domestic Interior. He has published extensively on design, manufacturing and crime in eighteenth-century Britain. He was historical advisor to the new British Galleries at the V&A which opened in 2001, co-author of *Design and Decorative Arts: Britain, 1500–1900* (V&A Publications 2001), and is currently writing a book on clothes, fashion and the plebeian consumer in England, 1660 to 1830.

Carol Tulloch is a Senior Research Fellow in Black British Visual Culture at Chelsea College of Art and Design (University of the Arts London) and the Victoria and Albert Museum. She is co-curator of the Victoria and Albert Museum exhibition 'Black British Style' and editor of the accompanying book *Black Style* (V&A Publications 2004). Her main area of study is the dress and style practices of people from the African diaspora.

Elizabeth Wilson is Visiting Professor in Cultural and Historical Studies at the University of the Arts London. Her recent work includes *Bohemians: The Glamorous Outcasts* (I B Tauris 2000), *Adorned in Dreams: Fashion and Modernity* (I B Tauris 2000) and 'Magic Fashion', in *Fashion Theory*, forthcoming. She is currently working on glamour, celebrity and the uncanny.

Illustrations

Introduction

Christopher Breward and *Caroline Evans*

The key intellectual concern of this book is to examine the role, importance and meaning of fashion in relation to modernity. The term 'modernity' is largely confined, for this project, to the development of consumer culture in the wake of eighteenth- and nineteenth-century industrialisation. Like fashion its effects are intimately concerned with the relationship between the two processes of production and consumption. Definitions of modernity are, however, as many as they are contradictory, particularly in terms of the meaning of the concept as it has been discussed by the social sciences and the humanities traditions. Like all such interpretations, modernity is thus a term in an abstract classificatory system, invented by scholars to make sense of the world. A number of historians, for whom the idea of modernity is bound up with an analysis of industrial capitalist society as a form of rupture from preceding social systems, have used the term to designate the enormous social and cultural changes which took place from the mid sixteenth century onwards in Europe.[1] In contrast to this fairly neat sense of periodisation, for the sociologist Max Weber, the origins of capitalism, and thus of modernity, lay in the Protestant ethic; its leitmotifs were modernisation and rationalisation but also, and crucially, ambiguity (Turner 1990: 1–13)

Sitting somewhere between these two positions Marshall Berman used the term 'modernity' as one of a triumvirate of terms: modernisation, modernity and modernism (Berman 1983: 16–17). 'Modernisation' refers to the processes of scientific, technological, industrial, economic and political innovation that also become urban, social and artistic in their impact. 'Modernity' refers to the way that modernisation infiltrates everyday life and permeates sensibilities. And 'Modernism' refers to a wave of avant-garde artistic movements that, from the early twentieth century onwards, in some way responded to, or represented, these changes in sensibility and experience.[2]

More recently, cultural theorists have embraced the Baudelairean notion that the pivotal moment of modernity was located in the flux of the nineteenth-century city. In 'The Painter of Modern Life' Baudelaire famously described the experience of modernity in the Paris of 1863 as incorporating 'the ephemeral, the fugitive, the contingent' (1964: 12). In comparable vein, Simmel related fashion to the fragmentation of modern life and discussed modern life's neurasthenia, that is, the overstimulation and nervous excitement that came with the growth of the metropolis (Simmel 1971: 324–39). He associated fashion with the middle classes and with the urban, as well as with the stylisation of everyday objects (for him the Jugendstil movement in Germany), and he pointed to a close relation between art, fashion and consumer culture. It is this connection, drawing on both Baudelaire and Simmel, which became topical again in the 1980s and 1990s as the field of cultural studies returned to the world of fashion and consumer culture for inspiration (Chambers 1985a and 1985b; Calefato 1988; Turner 1990; Featherstone 1991; Lash and Friedman 1992; McRobbie 1992; Featherstone and Burrows 1995).

This new literature of modernity also drew on the interwar work of Walter Benjamin. He described a change in the structure of experience whereby modern life was characterised by violent jolts and dislocations (a feature also shared by many accounts of postmodern experience at the close of the twentieth century, for example, ICA 1986; Jameson 1991). Benjamin cites Baudelaire's description of the crowd as 'a reservoir of electric energy'; the man who plunges into it is 'a kaleidoscope equipped with consciousness' (Benjamin 1973: 177). Urban encounters with telephones, cameras, traffic and advertising are experienced as 'a series of shocks and collisions' and the fractured and dislocating experience of modernity is made formal in the principle of montage in early modernist cinema. Both Simmel and Benjamin, in their writing on modernity, suggest the idea of rupture with the past, a sense that could also be said to have characterised the last twenty years of the twentieth century. Hal Foster suggested that, by the mid 1990s, Baudelaire's 'shock' had become electronic, and he argued that we are '*wired* to spectacular events' and 'psycho-techno thrills' (1996: 221–2).

While the key texts of modernity by Baudelaire, Simmel and Benjamin have focused on the process and context of modern life in the form of the nineteenth- and twentieth-century city, the term 'modernity' has also been used more generically to describe the experience of 'feeling modern' or up to date. The term was first used in English by the philosopher and divine George Hakewill in the mid seventeenth century to describe the quality or condition of being 'in the present' rather than part of a decaying past. Interestingly Samuel Pepys referred to Hakewill's work when he noted on 3 February 1667 that he 'fell to read a little' of it 'and did satisfy myself mighty fair in the truth of the saying that the world do not grow old at all' (*Dictionary of National Biography* 1973: 890–2). In the nineteenth century Arthur Rimbaud's 'il faut être absolument moderne' reprised the theme (Rimbaud 2003: 502).

In more recent academic discourse Anthony Giddens has identified reflexivity, or self-scrutiny, as a central aspect of modernity (Giddens 1991). This is where fashion as a process comes in to play as a useful mechanism for interrogating the subjective experience of modern life. Fashion is a process in two senses: it is a market-driven cycle of consumer desire and demand; and it is a modern mechanism for the fabrication of the self. It is in this respect that fashion operates as a fulcrum for negotiating the meeting of internal and external worlds. As Marx suggested, 'men make their own history, but they do not make it just as they please; they do not make it under circumstances chosen by themselves, but under circumstances directly encountered, given and transmitted from the past' (1954: 10). If fashion is a paradigm of the capitalist processes which inform modern sensibilities, then it is also a vibrant metaphor for modernity itself.

Many writers have paid lip service to the role of fashion in modernity, but only Elizabeth Wilson and Ulrich Lehmann have addressed the relationship in any detail. Both assert the continuing relevance of nineteenth-century modernity to the present, Lehmann in general terms and Wilson in more specific ones (Lehmann 2000: 401; Wilson 2003: 10). Lehmann has noted that the etymologies of the French words for fashion and modernity, *la mode* and *modernité*, (the modernity of Baudelaire and Benjamin), are the same (2000: xv and 5–19). Wilson, writing in 1985, pinpointed the moment of dissonance in the modern city as being key to twentieth-century style; the 'hysteria and exaggeration of fashion' expressed 'the colliding dynamism, the thirst for change and the heightened sensation that characterise the city societies particularly of modern industrial capitalism [that] go to make up this "modernity"' (Wilson 2003: 10). Building on Wilson's ground-breaking work it is the ambition of this book to extend some of her ideas to a consideration of other moments and contexts in which the discourses of fashionable modernity are further illuminated.

More specifically, the book scrutinises the relationship of fashion to technology, industrialisation and consumption from the court masques of seventeenth-century London to the forensic laboratories of late-twentieth-century Washington. The book considers how that relationship affects appearances and subjectivities, soliciting questions about the nature of identity, the body, nationality and gender. These issues are located in specific historical, geographic and cultural contexts, with the aim of producing a materialist examination of fashion as both a social and a spatial practice, and also as both image and artefact. We do not propose to present a single, continuous history but, rather, a series of interlocking studies deploying diverse approaches. These are organised into three sections: 'Producing Identities', 'Performing Bodies' and 'Processes of Modernity'.

Elizabeth Wilson opens the book with a chapter offering further reflections on the broad concepts of modernity and fashion which we have only sketched out in this introduction. In the first section, 'Producing Identities', the chapters foreground the way in which the fashion industry shapes subjectivities. In her study of the early-nineteenth-century retail entrepreneur James Morrison, Caroline Dakers paints a picture of a new incarnation of the London merchant mediating between the factory and the market place. She portrays him analysing markets, judging fashion trends, and assessing the viability of retail outfits as he made his meticulous observations on the state of business in contemporary Europe. Becky Conekin moves from the business of fashion to its representation in her study of the model turned photographer Lee Miller. Conekin looks at Miller's life as she moved between the roles of model, muse, war photographer, hostess, wife and mother both before and after the Second World War. The ambiguities of these overlapping roles enable a discussion of the paradoxes of modernity, biography and identity. By way of contrast, Andrew Hill's literary reflections on late-twentieth-century consumer culture present a wry critique of the assumption that modern consumption has opened up creative opportunities for making and remaking the self. A disillusioned *flâneur* in a modern mall, he argues instead for the flatness and banality of modern life as represented by the everyday clothes of everyday people.

The chapters in 'Performing Bodies' are concerned with the staging of modern fashions and identities in the public sphere. Andrea Stuart takes the elaborate set pieces of seventeenth-century court masques and argues that the reactionary court etiquette of an absolutist monarchy, and the fantastical designs of artists such as Inigo Jones, were not incompatible with the emergence of new philosophical and scientific paradigms at a time when Western Europe was forming its colonial ambitions. Indeed, it was this broader context that informed the extreme modernity of the masques' presentations. In his study of the late-nineteenth-century London actress Christopher Breward addresses the issue of modernity through the themes of parasexuality, celebrity and democratisation. He suggests that the performance of the actress both on and off stage radically shifted the moral and aesthetic direction of fashion at the fin de siècle. Continuing with the theme of woman as spectacle of modernity, Caroline Evans looks at the ambiguous figure of the fashion mannequin in the early twentieth century, and argues that her representation was a cipher of many of the contradictions present in the French and American fashion industries during the period.

In the final section, 'Processes of Modernity', the tropes of identity and performance are pulled together and rearticulated in a consideration not so much of the material realities of fashion and its cycles, as of the idea of fashion as something that has insinuated itself stealthily into modern modes of being. Kitty Hauser looks at the startling appearance of blue jeans in forensic science. The chapter examines ways in which worn clothing can be seen as an index of the wearer. It shows how recent FBI research on the identification of denim trousers from surveillance film effectively reveals the hidden history of objects that is occluded in everyday commodity culture. Alistair O'Neill considers collage as a core practice of modernity. Taking as its starting point a magazine project by contemporary fashion designers Viktor & Rolf, and tracing a fascination with bricolage in the work of Schiaparelli, Schwitters and Richard Prince, his chapter locates the ephemeral and the superficial as indices of modern meaning. Jamie Brassett uses Guattari and Deleuze to argue that fashion can not only provide points for closing a system and promoting entropy but also for enhancing connectivity, multiplicity and emergence. He suggests, however, that the latter may need a new type of fashion, one which blurs distinctions, thereby enhancing connectivity between subjects, designed objects and the world. On this note the book concludes with a version of modernity that prioritises the imaginative, the utopian and the speculative. Having commenced with the history of fashion, the book closes with a notion of the physics of fashion that has challenging implications for its future practice and interpretation.

Each of the nine chapters is followed by a short response by an academic who has a shared interest in the topic under discussion but who does not necessarily come from the same disciplinary background. This was the format of the symposium where they were first given, and the book is intended to preserve this order in published form, suggesting that the subject area can be fruitfully developed through dialogue and discussion. These focused, historically specific case studies and their responses counter the risk of making overarching assertions about fashion and modernity. At the same time, rather than settling fine historical points, we believe that the format of proposition and response fosters a lively variety of approaches and topics and generates new debates. We do not claim that the collection offers a coherent or finite account of fashion and modernity, nor do we believe that it would be possible to do so, given that modernity itself is not so much a historical 'fact' as a category of historical interpretation. However, we are committed to an interpretation of fashion that values a multiplicity of voices and approaches. Thus contributors to this volume come from a range of disciplinary backgrounds including history, sociology, art and design history, philosophy, literature and cultural studies. In this sense the collection is as much multidisciplinary as it is interdisciplinary. It uses a variety of methods, from the empirical to the theoretical. This range and variety is what the contemporary study of fashion and dress requires. For, as one of our respondents has previously suggested:

> Postmodern priorities have worked to move the history of dress from the wings to the centre stage ... broader intellectual developments have propelled the history of dress to its new respectability and have brought with them new ways of conceptualising that history ... [interdisciplinarity] underpins its new prominence ... it requires from those who study the subject a commitment to a mode of enquiry combining elements of both conceptual and empirical work. (John Styles, 1998: 387–8)

Notes

1. Turner (1990) discusses the major debates and cites key texts.
2. The schematic nature of these terms belies the very real difficulties of definition and distinction that they raise, particularly in relation to modernity and modernism. Lisa Tickner (2000: 184–214) provides a very useful discussion,

and gathers together many relevant sources, in her 'Afterword: Modernism and Modernity'. As she points out, the distinction has spawned its own interdisciplinary journal, *Modernism/Modernity*, Johns Hopkins University Press. For another overview, with bibliographic references, also cited by Tickner, see Smith 1996. There is also a large body of design history writing on these themes, for example Greenhalgh 1990 and Thakara 1988.

References

Baudelaire, C. (1964 [1854]) 'The Painter of Modern Life', in *The Painter of Modern Life and Other Essays*, trans. J. Mayne. London: Phaidon Press.

Benjamin, W. (1973 [1955]) 'On Some Motifs in Baudelaire', in *Illuminations*, trans. H. Zohn. London: Fontana/Collins.

Berman, M. (1983) *All that is Solid Melts into Air: The Experience of Modernity*, London: Verso.

Calefato, P. (1988) 'Fashion, the Passage, the Body', *Cultural Studies*, 2(2) May: 223–8

Chambers, I. (1985a) *Metropolitan Culture.* London: Macmillan.

—— (1985b) *Urban Rhythms: Pop Music and Popular Culture.* London: Macmillan.

Dictionary of National Biography (1973) vol. 8. Oxford: Oxford University Press.

Featherstone, M. (1991) *Consumer Culture and Postmodernism.* London: Sage.

—— and R. Burrows (eds) (1995) *Cyberspace/Cyberbodies/Cyberpunk.* London: Sage.

Foster, H. (1996) *The Return of the Real: The Avant Garde at the End of the Century.* Cambridge, MA: MIT Press.

Giddens, A. (1991) *Modernity and Self-Identity: Self and Society in the Late Modern Age.* Cambridge: Polity Press.

Greenhalgh, P. (ed) (1990) *Modernism in Design.* London: Reaktion Books.

ICA (1986) *ICA Documents 4: 'Postmodernism'.* London: ICA.

Jameson, F. (1991) *Postmodernism, or the Cultural Logic of Late Capitalism.* London: Verso.

Lash, S. and J. Friedman (eds) (1992) *Modernity & Identity.* Oxford: Blackwell.

Lehmann, U. (2000) *Tigersprung: Fashion in Modernity.* Cambridge, MA: MIT Press.

Marx, K. (Third revised edition 1954 [1852]) *The Eighteenth Brumaire of Louis Bonaparte,* translated from the German. Moscow: Progress Publishers.

McRobbie, A. (1992) 'The *Passagenwerk* and the Place of Walter Benjamin in Cultural Studies: Benjamin, Cultural Studies, Marxist theories of art', *Cultural Studies,* 6(2) May: 147–69.

Simmel, G. (1971 [1903]) 'Fashion' and 'The Metropolis and Mental Life', in *On Individuality and Social Forms*, ed. and with an intro. by D.N. Levine. Chicago: University of Chicago Press.

Smith, T. (1996) 'Modernism' and 'Modernity', *The Dictionary of Art*, 21: 775–7 and 777–9. London: Macmillan.

Styles, J. (1998) 'Dress in History: Reflections on a Contested Terrain', *Fashion Theory,* 2(4).

Rimbaud, A. (2003 [1873]) *Une saison en enfer*, reprinted in *Rimbaud Complête*, trans. ed. and with an intro. by W. Mason. New York: Modern Library.

Thakara, J. (ed) (1988) *Design After Modernism: Beyond the Object.* London: Thames & Hudson.

Tickner, L. (2000) *Modern Lives and Modern Subjects*. New Haven: Yale University Press.

Turner B.S. (ed) (1990) *Theories of Modernity and Postmodernity*. London: Sage.

Wilson, E. (2003 [1985]). *Adorned in Dreams.* London: I.B. Tauris.

Fashion and Modernity

Elizabeth Wilson

Definitions of Modernity

How is modernity to be defined? It is an imprecise, yet all-embracing concept. Modernity, rather than being like, say, the Newtonian law of gravity, a clear-cut *thing*, concept, theory or proposition, is an umbrella term used to indicate everything about the period since the industrial and French revolutions. Indeed it can be extended further back to a period of 'early modernity' that equates with the rise of mercantile and agricultural capitalism. Either way, however, whether originating in the late sixteenth or the eighteenth century, the term modernity effectively refers more to a zeitgeist than a clearly distinct epoch. It is a general term or label for an epoch, the parameters of which are highly elastic.

On the one hand, therefore, we might object to it as being so all-embracing as to be vacuous; on the other hand, the term may simply be brought into play as a more politically neutral term for capitalism, and to that extent can be seen as ideological and mystifying. Yet it does always suggest something more precise than simply 'everything', and something less narrow than a mere mask for capitalism. It refers to things both intangible and undeniably material: the atmosphere and culture of a whole epoch, its smell, its sounds, its rhythm. While an economic analysis may ultimately explain our society more objectively than any other, the use of the term 'modernity' makes possible the exploration of our subjective experience of it.

Central to modernity is a paradox: the seventeenth and eighteenth century Enlightenment values of Reason and Science and the defeat of tradition, obscurantist superstition and the perils of what was then termed religious 'Enthusiasm', emerged in tandem with, or as a precursor of, the headlong development of industrial capitalism, which has proved so irrational, so out of control, so unstoppable. For modernity is not defined by Reason, but by speed, mobility and mutability. And, while it always contains the idea of progress and continual forward movement, Theodor Adorno, for example, asserted that it is not chronological at all – although he also objected to the view that it has something to do with zeitgeist (Adorno 1984).

Weber, one of the most influential interpreters of modernity, believed that by the end of the nineteenth century industrialisation – machine production – dominated and determined the lives of all those living in industrialised society. That is to say, machine production affected not only the economic, but every aspect of life, with the advent of the rational bureaucratic structures of domination. Weber's famous metaphor for this was the 'iron cage'. However, Derek Sayer has suggested that a better translation for his wording might be 'a casing or housing, as hard as steel' (quoted in During 2002: 38). In this translation it is not so much an iron cage as a shell on a snail's back: a burden, yet something impossible to live without – a translation that captures the ambivalence of the modern condition better than the metaphor of a cage.

Aside from speed, change and novelty, modernity is characterised by the advance of mass production into every area of life. Raphael Samuel, in an autobiographical account of his youth in the British Communist Party, recalled the mass leisure pursuits of the 1940s: the dance halls, the cinemas, the football grounds, the holidays in Blackpool (Samuel 1985). For Patrick Brantlinger (1990), there was on the one hand the mass leisure of the works outing or holiday, and the crowds of shoppers in the burgeoning metropolis, on the other the mass of factory workers, and proletarian opposition to capital's domination organised into the mass trades unions and political parties.

There is a further dimension to that which we term modernity: what Tony Giddens (1991) refers to as reflexivity. The moderns, he says, continually re-appraise and reconsider their activities in every sphere. No longer dependent on traditional ways, we anxiously scrutinise handbooks and consult experts and gurus, but far from resulting in certainty, this leads only to continually changing practices and fads – fashions in other words. Reflexivity destroys certainty. Scientific and technological advances create anxiety rather than reassurance; for there is no longer one unchallenged source of authority: namely the Church. Progress is continually sought, yet constantly questioned and undermined.

More paradoxically still, the unstoppable trajectory forwards results in nostalgia and, if not overt longing for the past, then a formless regret and a melancholy feeling that the magic of the world has been lost. Indeed, modernity repeatedly clothes itself in reconstructions of the past, a theme much dwelt on by modernist architects between the two world wars, when they complained about the 'fancy dress' of pseudo-traditional architecture, whether of the Beaux Arts or suburban Tudorbethan variety.

Matei Calinescu (1977) has looked at this in a slightly different way. He claims that at some point in the immediately pre-industrial period the idea of beauty loses its connotations of classical transcendence and becomes a historical and therefore changing category. Beauty itself becomes a question of changing fashion. He also claims that in the nineteenth century there occurs what he terms an 'irreversible split' – between modernity as a product of scientific and technical progress, including the Industrial Revolution and 'the sweeping economic and social changes wrought by capitalism', and (Calinescu 1977: 41) modernity as an aesthetic concept, something closer, presumably, to modernism. He argues that the relations between these two are permanently hostile. In other words, in the industrial capitalist period, the world of the arts and aesthetic production provides an 'enraged critique' of the economic and social order. While this may be overstated and oversimplified, it does account for what I term modernity's Other.

Modernity's Other

The spectre of the past: this is modernity's 'Other', the 'dark side' of modernity – or one aspect of it. How strange that the scientific rationality of the modern produces the irrational, often in new forms. Even as tradition and superstition are consigned to the past, they resurrect themselves in the culture of modernity: in Gothic literature, in the Romantic movement with its protest against mechanical modernity, in a whole literature of vampirism, ghost stories, the detective novel and the thriller. The cinema, above all, provides a vast field for the exploration/exploitation of magic and the irrational, for an exploration of the passions and terrors that Enlightenment thinking so signally failed to eradicate. Indeed Nicholas Royle (2003) goes so far as to say that the cinema per se is inherently uncanny: in other words that an art form perhaps most typical of or appropriate to the industrial period is, in its essence, the opposite of the scientific and rational that industrial society was supposed to produce and to be.

On the contrary: we find that contemporary society is riddled from top to bottom with irrational beliefs of all kinds, and while Cherie Booth, wife of the British Prime Minister, has been frequently mocked for her reliance on crystals, rebirthing ceremonies and the like (especially since she is simultaneously a devout Roman Catholic), she is no more than typical of a contemporary sensibility that takes refuge with incredible credulity in all manner of superstitious and unscientific beliefs, quite apart from adherence to organised religions. Which of us fails to read our horoscope? How many of us have never sought help from alternative therapies?

Numerous writers, notably Thorstein Veblen (1957), but there are many others, have criticised fashion precisely on the grounds that it is irrational. Such critics have demanded of 'modern dress' that it be as rational and scientific as the age is, or was, supposed to be. The British Dress Reform Society spoke openly of 'rational dress' and the exaggerated and restrictive forms of nineteenth-century women's dress were especially rejected on these grounds. In fact, the irrational aspect of fashion is very important; fashion provides a field for the expression of fetishistic and magical impulses and beliefs (Wilson 2004). The Surrealists' interest in garments is relevant here.

Elizabeth Wilson

Fashion and Modernity

This short article originated as a brief introductory paper at a conference entitled 'Fashion and Modernity'. The organisers of the conference stated that the rationale for such a conference was that fashion directly reflects the mobility and mutability of modernity itself. It has often been pointed out that in the period of monopoly capitalism, it is no longer the use-value of things that is being consumed, but rather their exchange value. Consequently the reciprocal and fixed relations between social groups are dismantled, and commodities function increasingly as signs organising value and desire (During 2001).

Fashion is commonly held to be a crucial medium for the construction of signs for changing desires and consumption patterns. It would also, following Calinescu, articulate the endlessly changing notions of beauty characteristic of culture in modernity.

Yet, in other respects, fashion appears to articulate quite other impulses. Throughout the industrial period, fashionable dress, women's in particular, has been at least as likely to express a longing for the past of tradition and stability destroyed by industrial turmoil as an enthusiasm for the shock of the new. The New Look is a major example – although perhaps not all that typical – of a sartorial attempt to turn back the clock, and the various retro fashions that have been recycled, in some cases several times, since the 1970s, provide further examples. Often, these days, explained as examples of postmodern parody and pastiche, they may actually be saying something rather different.

Then there is the case of men's dress. Mark Wigley (1994) has demonstrated exhaustively the engagement of architects of the modern movement with fashion, even as they obsessively disavowed it, condemning fashion as the antithesis of the modern. Le Corbusier and a number of his contemporaries in the worlds of art and architecture, while rejecting the frivolity of feminine dress, idealised the modernity of the masculine suit with its white shirt as the epitome of modern dress: a uniform ideally adapted to the streamlined speed and minimalist interiors of the twentieth century, and moreover, an unchanging, utopian one.

Quentin Bell (1947) also foresaw the future of fashion as its abolition over fifty years ago when he predicted that with the coming of democracy there would be no further place for fashionable dress. This was because, following Veblen, he saw fashion as expressing social status and distinction; once these were abolished, fashion's function would disappear.

He wrote this at the height of Britain's 'age of austerity', when Clement Atlee's postwar Labour government was battling with a catastrophic economic crisis that necessitated the continuation of wartime controls, including rationing of food and clothing, and when many (largely but not exclusively on the political right) feared that this drab world was socialism in action. In fact, the sad truth is that modernity does not necessarily equate with democracy, any more than austerity equated with socialism. Today's political system is closer to a marketocracy than a genuine democracy. Nor did Bell anticipate that democracy might fail to equate with social equality. Today, moreover, celebrity, one of the main forms of expression of the spirit of the marketocracy, is just as undemocratic as the old aristocratic systems, for more often than not celebrity resides in gifts, such as beauty or a talent in the entertainment field, that are in large part the product of birth.

And yet I often feel as if Bell's prediction has come to pass, for an interesting feature of contemporary dress is what I at least anecdotally perceive as a tendency towards increasing standardisation and uniformity. It is true that 'postmodern' eclecticism and diversity are evident in the proliferation of styles produced by designers every season, but when these are boiled down to a more limited range of trends to be reproduced at every level of quality from the diffusion line to the high-street knock-off, the end result is more uniform and in any case does nothing to dislodge the pre-existing uniform of jeans, combats (or similar), trainers and fleeces. The idea that one's dress might express one's unique identity seems naïve these days.

Asserting that modernity is not chronological, Adorno said that it answered rather to Rimbaud's view that 'in relation to its own time, art [must] be the most advanced consciousness where sophisticated technical procedures and equally sophisticated subjective experience interpenetrate. Rooted in society, these procedures and experiences are critical in orientation' (Adorno 1984: 49).

I thought of this, perhaps inappropriately, when I visited the 'Radical Fashion' exhibition at the Victoria and Albert Museum in 2001 (Wilson 2002). The garments by Gaultier, Westwood and Alexander McQueen were not the most innovative garments in the show (and in any case I found Margiela's use of recycled garments more interesting than the technical innovations of some of the other designers), but what struck me so forcibly about them was the exquisite craftsmanship and materials of the work displayed. This was the epitome of haute couture – and surely in the words of French *Vogue*, as anachronistic and dream-laden as a sailing ship, an astonishing debauchery of efforts to produce a minimum of garments, an *acte gratuit*, an extravagant adventure that cannot be logically justified.

It was Baudrillard who found this quotation, and he uses it to develop the idea that the universal denigration of fashion results from its futility and artificiality, qualities that constitute a taboo in a utilitarian society. 'In our culture, futility plays the role of transgression and fashion is condemned for having within it the force of the pure sign which signifies nothing' (Baudrillard 1993: 95).

This comes close to Adorno's defence of art as a protest against bad reality. Whether fashion is to be aligned with art, and whether it can bear so heavy a load of significance, I leave as questions unanswered.

References

Adorno, T. (1984) *Aesthetic Theory*. London: Routledge.

Baudrillard, J. (1993) *Symbolic Exchange and Death*. London: Sage.

Bell, Q. (1947) *Of Human Finery*. London: The Hogarth Press.

Brantlinger, P. (1990) 'Mass Media and Culture in *fin-de-siècle* Europe', in M. Teich and R. Porter (eds), *Fin de Siècle and its Legacy*. Cambridge: Cambridge University Press: 98–114.

Calinescu, M. (1977). *Faces of Modernity: Avant Garde, Decadence, Kitsch*. Bloomington: Indiana University Press.

During, S. (2002) *Modern Enchantments: The Cultural Power of Secular Magic*. Cambridge, MA: Harvard University Press.

Giddens, A. (1991) *The Consequences of Modernity*. Cambridge: Polity Press.

Royle, N. (2003) *The Uncanny*. Manchester: Manchester University Press.

Samuel, R. (1985) 'The Lost World of British Communism', *New Left Review*, 154, November/December.

Veblen, T. (1957) *The Theory of the Leisure Class*. London: Allen & Unwin.

Wigley, M. (1994) *White Walls, and Designer Dresses*. Princeton: Princeton University Press.

Wilson, E. (2002) 'Review: Radical Fashion at the Victoria and Albert Museum, 2001', *Feminist Review*, Special Issue: Fashion and Beauty, 71.

—— 2004 'Magic Fashion', *Fashion Theory*, 8(4). Oxford: Berg.

Part I
Producing Identities

–1–

James Morrison (1789–1857), 'Napoleon of shopkeepers', Millionaire Haberdasher, Modern Entrepreneur

Caroline Dakers

> The technical marvels of steam engines and spinning-machines are more striking than the mundane activities of merchants and shopkeepers who left fewer visible remains and records, but they are not necessarily of greater economic significance. After all, the greatest fortune in the textile trades was not made by Richard Arkwright in the production of yarn; it was accumulated by James Morrison, the 'Napoleon of shopkeepers', whose textile warehouse in the City of London supplied the inland trade with its handkerchiefs, ribbons, braids, and fabrics.
>
> Daunton 1995: 318.

James Morrison's fortune was largely made early in the nineteenth century, between the Battle of Waterloo and the coronation of Queen Victoria. However, the vast scale of his mercantile operations; his commitment to free trade, political reform and self-help; his understanding of the power of communication, advertising and packaging and of nurturing a faithful workforce, make him a very modern entrepreneur. This essay examines the 'mundane activities' attached to a haberdashery business which not only dominated the British wholesale market in dress fabrics and accessories, but also provided Morrison with the means to acquire a considerable portfolio of properties. While the wholesale operation influenced consumer choice throughout the middle and lower levels of the market, Morrison's personal purchases of land (including the Pavilion, Fonthill, see fig. 1.4) and houses and the necessary goods with which to fill them, made individuals rich. Bankers, lawyers, architects, surveyors, furniture makers, interior decorators, dealers in art and antiquities, landscape gardeners, land agents, tailors, dressmakers, painters and sculptors benefited from his largesse.

When Morrison joined the Fore Street haberdashery warehouse of Messrs Todd & Co in 1809, his salary as a shopman was £40 per annum. The turnover of the company was £13,234 and its stock valued at £9,217. In 1824 Morrison became sole owner of the business which he renamed James Morrison & Co. Turnover

Figure 1.1 James Morrison, 1839–40, by Sir Francis Chantrey (1781–1841). (Private Collection)

was £1,533,656 and his annual income over £17,000. By 1830, turnover reached £1,883,391; 150 hands were employed, their combined salaries amounting to £11,000; Morrison's capital investment had risen to £300,000 and his annual income was £72,500 (Gatty 1976; Morrison).

From 1830, Morrison extended his business activities, forming a merchant bank, lending large amounts of money to members of the aristocracy, investing heavily in North America (particularly in canals and railways), and buying works of art, country estates and property in London. He also became an MP, joining the radical Whig group led by Joseph Hume. He helped to found London University, the School of Design at Somerset House and the Reform Club. The Fore Street warehouse continued to provide him with a steady income of about £60,000 per annum; his investments gradually increased his income to about £120,000 per annum. In 1836 Morrison assessed he was worth over £1 million. When he died in 1857, his property was valued at some £4 million. He was the richest commoner in nineteenth-century Britain (Rubinstein 1981).

Morrison's story is no simple 'rags to riches' tale even though he transformed himself from the son of a village innkeeper to a millionaire merchant. He was born in 1789 at the George Inn, Middle Wallop, in Hampshire. His parents' hostelry was a flourishing concern, strategically positioned on the turnpike road between London and Salisbury. In 1763 there were only six coaches a week from London to Salisbury; by 1795, fifty-two coaches passed through Middle Wallop. 'Improvements in the mail shot London news, gossip and fashions into the shires' (Porter 1996: 135).

Morrison's experience in the George Inn of the commercial impact of a faster communications system would influence his approach to the operations of Fore Street; the George also provided him with the skills for dealing with a wide range of customers as well as up-to-date information about politics, war with France, trade and fashion. Much of the business passing through Middle Wallop was connected with textiles. Far-sighted investment by Morrison's father (another valuable lesson – Morrison regularly borrowed, usually from his banker friend Samuel Gurney, to fund improvements in Fore Street) enabled the George to provide pens for up to 3,000 sheep and accommodation for the sheep-drovers en route from Scotland to markets at Wilton and Salisbury (the first Morrison to settle in Middle Wallop at the beginning of the eighteenth-century was reputedly a Scottish drover). There was also stabling for sixty horses, good quality bedrooms for passing gentry and more modest accommodation for the travelling lacemen and drapers supplying village shops and market stalls. The national network of private and common carriers expanded dramatically at the end of the eighteenth century, providing services to London and most provincial towns. They made use of inns like the George, collecting goods and making exchanges (Daunton 1995: 307). Many serviced Salisbury's textile industry (the city was ten miles to the south-west), which experienced a short revival in its fortunes between 1780 and 1810, producing flannels and linseys (linen and wool) and fancy cloths using imported silk and Spanish wool (Chandler 1983: 91). The fictional William Simmons, a carrier connected with a large stage-coaching establishment in Hounslow, took Martin Chuzzlewit from his 'little Wiltshire village' up to London – they would have passed through Middle Wallop (Dickens, 1912c: 171).

> Joe Toddyhigh had never been in the capital of Europe before, and he wandered up and down the streets that night amazed at the number of churches and other public buildings, the splendour of the shops, the riches that were heaped up on every side, the glare of light in which they were displayed, and the concourse of people who hurried to and fro, indifferent, apparently, to all the wonders that surrounded them. (Dickens, 1912d: 441)

After the death of his parents, Morrison chose to seek his fortune in London while his elder brother Samuel remained in Middle Wallop. Before he joined the

Figure 1.2 Fore Street and Cripplegate Church, 1830, by T.H. Shepherd (1793–1864). Engraving on paper. (Guildhall Library and Art Library © Corporation of London)

Fore Street (see fig. 1.2) warehouse as shopman in 1809, he spent at least two years, probably an apprenticeship, working for retail and wholesale haberdashery businesses in Holborn and in the City of London. Though Britain was still at war with France, Morrison had chosen a particularly fortuitous time to pursue a commercial career in textiles. 'There was no sector of British trade growing faster than textiles. City merchants, through their considerable working capital, enjoyed a control of credit and marketing denied to the disintegrated textile manufacturers of the north; this aspect of the square mile, linked closely to British industry, was more important than has tended to be recognised' (Kynaston 1994: 58).

His impact on Joseph Todd's business was immediate. Turnover virtually doubled between 1809 (£13,234) and 1810 (£24,339). His method was twofold: first, to locate cheap sources of goods in large quantities in Britain and Europe and, second, to seek small profits and quick returns. He described his approach to his friend and business associate Sir John Bowring:

> Morrison told me that he owed all his prosperity to the discovery that the great art of mercantile traffic was to find sellers rather than buyers; that if you bought cheap, and satisfied yourself with only a fair profit, buyers – the best sort of buyers, those who have money to buy – would come of themselves. He said he found houses engaged with a most expensive machinery, sending travellers about in all directions to seek orders, and to effect sales, while he employed travellers to buy instead of to sell, and, if they bought well, there was no fear of his effecting advantageous sales. So, uniting this theory with another, that small profits and quick returns are more profitable in the long run than long credits with great gains, he established one of the largest and most lucrative concerns that has ever existed in London. (Chapman 1992: 175–8)

The work was hard. One account of the Fore Street regime survives. It was written in 1812, when Morrison still lodged in the warehouse with the other employees and members of Todd's family.

> We open shop before seven in the morning and never shut up before nine in the evening and sometimes twelve o'clock, and we have to sleep in the shop. Every night there is five of us, and a son and daughter [presumably Mary Ann Todd, Morrison's future wife], three young women and several boys; and six of us sleeps in the shop. Most of the houses have so little room in them. I cannot speak much in favour of London so far. I never get out except on Sunday. (Gatty 1976: 11)

Todd was quick to recognise Morrison as being responsible for the dramatic increase in turnover, offering him a partnership in 1812. Two years later, Morrison married Todd's daughter, Mary Ann, and the turnover rose to almost £90,000. Morrison was on his way to becoming the 'kingpin' of textiles (Kynaston 1994: 58). Morrison's business acumen coincided with a massive expansion in textile goods and, in 1815, the end of war with France.

> [F]actory production of textiles in England between 1760 and 1850 was associated with an increasingly diverse range of final products... During the late years of the eighteenth century, for example, the range of pure cotton fabrics expanded dramatically. Similarly, in the second quarter of the nineteenth century, cheap cotton yarn and changes in women's fashion encouraged the creation of a whole new range of mixed worsted and cotton fabrics, as well as the use of new animal fibres like alpaca wool. Moreover, variety in the appearance of the final product was further increased by the enormous expansion of textile printing, particularly on cotton. (Styles 1993: 530–1)

The heart of the haberdashery trade was still the City of London but concerns were opening up and expanding throughout the West End. In 1812 Stags and Mantle's opened in Leicester Square and George Swan opened on the north side of Piccadilly; the following year, Flint and Clark of Wigmore Street, a ready-made concern selling to the wealthy clientele moving to new houses in and around

Cavendish Square, became Clark and Debenham. As Napoleon was transported to his final home on St Helena, the turnover of the Fore Street warehouse reached £243,052.

Morrison was not the only young man to seek a fortune in Fore Street and as he became increasingly powerful, he offered partnerships to his colleagues, many of whom stayed in the business all their working lives. George Crow joined in 1812, and became an expert in French lace. When he retired in 1838 he engaged Morrison's architect J.B. Papworth to design his country house in Yorkshire. Richard Pearson's specialism was mercery. He joined in 1813 and, with his wife, was managing three departments with sales in the 1820s of some £400,000 per annum. He was also superintendant of the warehouse and shop so allowed 'sufficient meat drink and private apartments in or about the said shop and premises in Fore St area' rent free (Morrison). John Dillon, 'lover of art and friend of Macready the tragedian' (Papworth 1879: 58), had intended a career as a playright but joined the warehouse in 1818 after his play *Retribution, or the Chieftain's Daughter* ran for only nine nights in Covent Garden. He and Morrison met at the nonconformist Freethinking Christians (Morrison's limited education in Middle Wallop was probably obtained at the nonconformist Sunday school). A young solicitor, William Ashurst, was also a member. Dillon became senior partner in the Fore Street warehouse, renamed Morrison, Dillon & Co in 1838; the firm of Ashurst, Morris and Crisp served three generations of the Morrison family (Slinn 1997).

Samuel Gurney, the Quaker banker and philanthropist, completed Morrison's team. His bank, Overend, Gurney & Co, was the greatest discounting house in the world in the first half of the nineteenth century; when Gurney died in 1856 the house had deposits of £8 million (DNB). Morrison regularly borrowed money from Gurney for capital investments but always paid his debts on or before time. During the period 1827 to 1831, for example, when he was carrying out extensive building works in Fore Street (see figs 1.3 and 1.5), he still managed to repay Gurney £150,000. Overend, Gurney & Co was used as an alternative to the Bank of England, Morrison and other merchants often depositing surplus money. While travelling on the continent in 1826, Morrison heard from Dillon of an unexpectedly high monthly return so immediately wrote back 'if you are rich you will of course, & as a matter of course, give the surplus to Gurneys' (Morrison).

Sales in the warehouse exceeded £1 million during the period 1818 to 1819. The highest monthly sales after 1809 regularly fell during the months of April, May and June, coinciding with the beginning of the London Season. In April 1819, for example, £115,464 goods were bought in and £149,813 were sold. These comprised 'mercery', 'haberdashery', 'lace', 'fancy', 'hosiery', 'gloves', 'ribbons', 'Norwich' (including 'bombazine', 'shawls', 'bandanas', 'barcelonas') and a little 'Yorkshire' ('kersey'). Of the total monthly sales for April, mercery accounted for £38,255 and ribbons, sold by the piece, £30,897.

The scale of the operation is breathtaking. It undoubtedly encouraged Morrison to begin investing in more property. In 1820 and 1821 he purchased four houses in Grub Street (renamed Milton Street in 1831 and at right angles to Fore Street), for a total of £5,000. He also made improvements to the Fore Street warehouse:

> parts were in a ruinous state ... repairs were necessary to the health and comfort of the servants, and the preservation of the stock ... the roof of the shop was raised, a new skylight added, and a few bed rooms for the shop-women erected, at a part of the premises distinct from those of the men, it being for the interest of the business that board and lodging should be found for all the servants on the premises. (Morrison)

A library was built and books were purchased for the staff, including copies of expensive limited editions such as Britton's *Graphical and Literary Illustrations of Fonthill Abbey Wiltshire*. Morrison's own education had been slight – perhaps he was determined to help others in search of knowledge. By 1822, when he became seven-eighths partner with personal capital in the company of £50,000, forty shophands were employed, insurance taken out on the buildings and stock totalled £100,000 and sales exceeded £1,500,000.

Morrison's attention to the appearance and facilities of the Fore Street property was not unique. Dickens noted the 'epidemic' among haberdashers in *Sketches by Boz*:

> Six or eight years ago the epidemic began to display itself among the linen-drapers and haberdashers. The primary symptoms were an inordinate love of plate-glass, and a passion for gas-lights and gilding. The disease gradually progressed, and at last attained a fearful height. Quiet dusty old shops in different parts of town were pulled down; spacious premises with stuccoed fronts and gold letters were erected instead; floors were covered with Turkey carpets; roofs supported by massive pillars; doors knocked into windows; a dozen squares of glass into one; one shopman into a dozen. (Dickens 1912e: 134)

When Morrison became sole owner of the business in 1824 the premises extended across four 'houses' in Fore Street (numbers 103, 104, 105 and 106), an area behind 105 and 106 Fore Street called Green Lettuce Court which comprised fourteen houses, and 31 to 34 Milton Street. He immediately approached the architect John Buonarroti Papworth to work on the Milton Street properties. Papworth was in considerable demand to design shops in the City of London and the West End, including premises for a glass manufacturer (John Blade), and a wholesale tea warehouse (Sparrow & Co), both in Ludgate Hill; silk mercers (Sewell & Cross, Frith Street, and Howell & James, Regent Street); paper hanging manufacturers

(Duppa & Collins, Oxford Street); Tattersalls, the horse auctioneers (Grosvenor Place) and Ackermanns, suppliers of frames and prints, in the Strand. He also designed the premises of Thompson & Fearon, wine merchants, Holborn Hill (Fearon was another Freethinking Christian); W. & E. Snell of Albermarle Street and the Grosvenor Basin and G. & T. Seddon in the Gray's Inn Road would supply Morrison with furnishings for all his homes. Papworth made particular use of both glass and gas. Plate glass replaced the small squares of 'best Newcastle Crown Glass' and the 'new invention Gas' 'enabled a larger display to be effected' (Papworth 1879: 66).

Papworth's first development in Milton Street (the left half of fig. 1.3) unified the four houses (numbers 31, 32, 33 and 34), creating a dignified establishment five storeys high, five bays wide, with three single doors. The right hand door led into Dillon's counting house designed with different sized desks (Dillon's was the largest), a gallery and bookcases. Gas lamps were fitted half inside and half outside the single panes of the windows (to give light but not obscure the appearance of goods for sale). The effect was probably similar to that noted by Charles Knight when visiting the premises of George Hitchcock & Sons, silk mercer and haberdasher, in St. Paul's Churchyard, in 1851.

Figure 1.3 Milton Street premises of James Morrison & Co, J.B. Papworth (1775–1847). The drawing shows the 1824 elevation (five bays to the left) to which is affixed the plan and elevation of the 1831 extension (four bays to the right). (RIBA Drawings Collection, [89] 45)

> Here, too, we see on a winter's evening a mode of lighting recently introduced, by which the products of combustion are given off in the street, instead of being left to soil the goods in the window: the lamps are fixed outside the shop, with a reflector so placed as to throw down a strong light upon the commodities in the window. (Adburgham 1981: 96)

The new property was fireproofed. Kitchen, scullery, porter's room, laundry and diningroom were on the first floor; water closets and bedrooms on the second, third and fourth floors. John Sylvester, civil engineer, submitted plans in 1826 for the kitchen and scullery (£135), and for heating and ventilation (£260). The total cost of the building was some £20,000; it would have been worthy of the Cheerybles, the kindly cloth merchants in *Nicholas Nickleby*:

> The old gentleman got out with great alacrity when they reached the Bank, and once more taking Nicholas by the arm, hurried him along Threadneedle Street, and through some lanes and passages on the right, until they at length emerged in a quiet shady little square. Into the oldest and cleanest-looking house of business in the square he led the way. The only inscription on the door-post was 'Cheeryble Brothers'; but from a hasty glance at the directions of some packages which were lying about, Nicholas supposed that the Brothers Cheeryble were German-merchants... Everything gave back, besides, some reflection of the kindly spirit of the brothers. The warehousemen and porters were such sturdy, jolly fellows that it was a treat to see them. (Dickens 1912a: 350 and 364)

Before he became an MP, Morrison's trips through Britain and Europe, with his wife and any number of children and servants, combined tourism (he called it 'seeing lions') and business. He kept careful notes of retail shops (whether or not they were buying from Fore Street), evidence of flourishing or depressed trade, unusual practices and products and new sources of goods for the warehouse. Senior staff also travelled through Europe purchasing goods (skins for gloves, brandy, olive oil, straw hats); Morrison encouraged their proficiency in French, Spanish and Italian: 'use well your long evenings in gaining the languages – *you can do nothing without them* – and especially the french' (Morrison). His tactics paid off: foreign sales rose from £28,223 in 1823 to £253,694 by 1835.

Touring Britain, he was particularly gratified at the sight of cleanliness, of well-conducted shops, decent and bustling, 'pushing in business', with handsome fronts and fine goods. Of Hythe, which he visited in June 1823, he noted: 'Hythe is a pretty Town & tho small is composed mostly of decent houses it has a small market & the Artillery Barracks still kept up. 2 shops Packham, mostly drapery & Hammond & Fritton a clean well conducted looking shop & customers we ought to do all we can with' (Morrison). In Dover he encountered Henry Dicks, formerly of Fore Street: 'Dicks is exactly what a pupil of Fore Street should be – leading cheap goods. Handkerchiefs, hose, braces, caps, etc. hung along the front of the house with large tickets; and cotton-lace and cheap thread-lace ticketed in the window. He is full of bustle and will keep his head above water' (Morrison). Deal, however, offered 'a painful exhibition of the effects of a transition from War to Peace', its suburbs 'half empty'. None of its nine shops were 'respectable looking', four in particular appeared to be 'blackguard concerns, ticketing, puffing & lying, here to day & gone tomorrow' (Morrison).

The letters written to his staff during his longest continental tour, which lasted from July 1826 to July 1827, reveal his range of interests: culture and self-education, including mastering foreign languages; European trade and commerce, transport, fashion and food; openings for Fore Street and the welfare of his family. He wrote to Dillon from Bern on 12 August 1826:

> My last was (I think) from Zurich & stated that I had purchased a few samples of Hdkfs & which I intended to send home by Miss Todd [his sister-in-law] ... the silk trade ... completely the old system in Switzerland – you *must* (especially at this season) give an order 3 or 4 months beforehand the goods are made chiefly by the peasants, when they cannot work or have nothing to do in the fields – The masters both at Zurich & Basle are among the 'Magrets' of the places and I suspect have no idea of quick returns & small profits – the little check Hdkfs about 10/- & 12/- pr dozen are sold in great quantities all over the Continent. (Morrison)

On 27 September, the Morrisons were in Geneva. Morrison wrote to Dillon:

> I do not forget business – Mrs M [Mary Ann Morrison] will send patterns & prices of all the things she has bought – The 'Sisters Soupat' one of them a clever woman & the best shop here I have given the address of our house to this morning & she may write or order her 'Commissioner' to call – Switzerland I have already told you enjoys a perfect freedom in trade & in the same shop you see the competition of different countries always in full play ... scarcely any thing but english [stuffs] is sold all over the continent – what a field for Pearson ... we ought to do a great lace trade for Frankfort [sic] & Holland that we have not done it, is disgraceful to the House – Cant Croft [Fore Street employee] assist you? ... among the things bought by Mrs M is a beautiful broad gauze Ribbon French of course. (Morrison)

And the next day:

> In Haberdashery we ought to sell largely for the continent & perhaps buy some things ... a free trade – *really* a free trade would give to England the market of the whole continent – Except silks, Toys, Perfumery & perhaps one or two other articles – there is nothing manufactured articles good, & few cheap, *except English* ... you see I am a gleaner of all things & always with an eye to the Shop. (Morrison)

Morrison was an advocate of free trade in his own business practices and in parliament. Travelling through Italy he was struck by the absence of the flourishing middle class which ensured his vast profits in Britain. He could buy goods (in particular skins for gloves) for the British market, but there was little scope for selling Fore Street textiles to the Italians. He wrote to Dillon from Rome on 24 December:

> you must recall it is only in capitals or largest purely commercial towns (of which there are only 3 or 4 in Italy) that any thing could be done – the peasants here *as in all other countries* mear [mere] home made things the men for the want of native cloth mear principally sheep skins – there is no gentry, scarcely any thing worthy to be calld a middle class – except the merchants & priests – Even in the principal towns, such as Ferrara, you look in vain for a decent shop & in Rome the very best is not equal to a very middling very inferior one in London – indeed more business can be done in Exeter or Plymouth than in all the papal dominions in our way. (Morrison)

Though letters might take several weeks to reach Fore Street, Morrison kept a careful watch on political events at home which could have commercial implications for his business. The poor health of the Duke of York was just such a topic. Members of the royal family were dying almost annually (Princess Charlotte in 1817, Queen Charlotte in 1818, Queen Caroline in 1821), to the enormous benefit of haberdashery businesses dealing in funeral crape. The Fore Street warehouse was no exception, so Morrison wrote to Crow from Naples on 7 January 1827:

> On the subject of stock I have no doubt you have done right. The D of Y [Duke of York] will go off I expect either on or before the spring, but this will not perhaps make much difference unless it should fall in March or April – of course after threatening so long every one will have a good stock of black. (Morrison)

A week later, Morrison wrote with satisfaction to Dillon 'the D of Y has died most conveniently – I hope 2 days after you had no black left' (Morrison).

Sales reached their highest level in 1829 to 1830 – £1,883,391. During the preceding decade the pattern of sales had changed slightly: the London Season continued to boost sales in the spring but there was now a second wave of high sales during September and October as textiles appropriate for winter came into the warehouse. More Yorkshire cloth was sold (broad, kersey, pelisse and stuffs) through the specialist 'cloth' warehouse in the Milton Street complex. Ribbons and mercery continued to be strong (in April 1830 £42,347 worth of ribbons were sold). But the highest turnover was in Manchester goods; sales in March reached almost £50,000. New items were also beginning to be noted separately in the accounts, for example umbrellas, parasols and stays which had formerly been included in fancy.

From 1828 to 1830 Papworth was engaged on the 'up-grading' of the Fore Street buildings; in 1831 he designed new premises to form an extension to the Milton Street block (see fig. 1.3). This very large and complex network of retail and wholesale, living and working accommodation can be seen as a prototype department store.

> The most important technique used by eighteenth-century retailers was the creation of an identity for the shop to signal the quality and quantity of goods consumers sought. It is this element that is distinctive about eighteenth-century retailing. In the nineteenth century these techniques of enticement using design and display were further amplified, particularly imaginatively and capital-intensively in the case of the department store. (Walsh 1995: 175)

Papworth created an imposing and confident front to Morrison's textile empire, which also managed to convey the stability, reliability and, above all, the vast size of the business. William Whiteley, who joined Morrison mid century, reworked the approach when he established his emporium in Westbourne Grove.

The developments in Fore Street and Milton Street should also be viewed in relation to other work by Papworth. In 1829 Morrison took a lease on the Pavilion at Fonthill in Wiltshire (se fig. 1.4), his first country property, just twenty miles

Figure 1.4 The remaining wing or pavilion, Fonthill, in Rutter 1823.

west of Middle Wallop. The Pavilion was all that survived of Fonthill Splendens, the grand mansion built by Alderman Beckford out of income from his West Indian sugar plantations. It had been mostly demolished by his son, William Beckford, to provide materials for Fonthill Abbey which famously rose and fell on the hillside nearby.

After spending a summer in the Pavilion, Morrison decided to buy the house and surrounding land; Papworth was brought in to carry out improvements at the same time as he was working in Fore Street. While discussing decorative schemes for Fonthill, he was creating, in Fore Street, a 'business-like unpretending façade' which exhibited 'great taste in the details and in the difficulties attending the arrangement of the doors and windows' (Papworth 1879: 68). Looking at images of the properties, it would appear Morrison would have felt 'at home' in both.

> Seest thou a man diligent in his business? He shall stand before kings.
>
> Proverbs XXII, 29

Morrison could have been a Merdle, the wealthy businessman in Dickens' novel *Little Dorrit.* He was very possibly a prototype for the character, as he was known

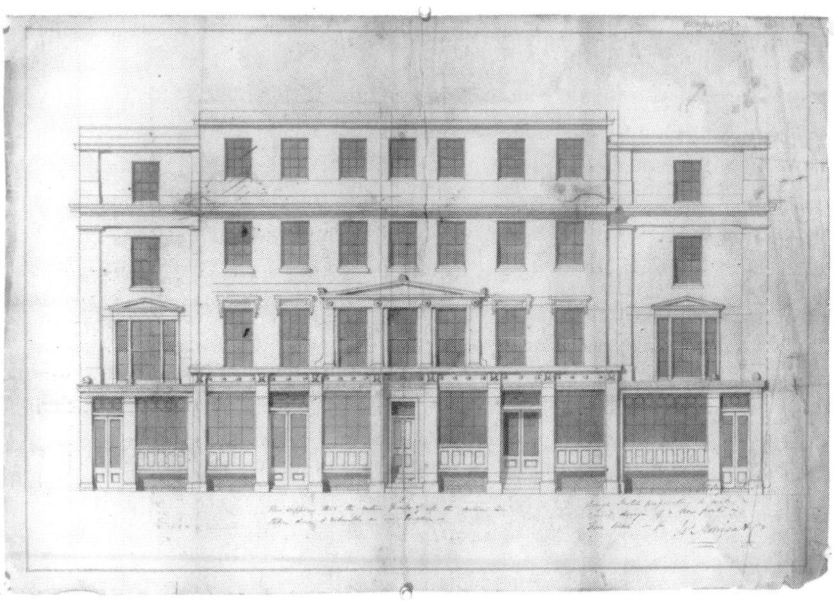

Figure 1.5 Fore Street premises of James Morrison & Co, by J.B. Papworth. The drawing shows the elevation of the proposed new front of 103–7 Fore Street, 1829–30. (RIBA Drawings Collection, [109] 4)

to Dickens through parliament and by reputation. Both Morrison and Merdle took town houses in Harley Street (Morrison acquired 57 Upper Harley Street in 1831). Merdle was 'immensely rich': 'a man of prodigious enterprise; a Midas without the ears, who turned all he touched to gold. He was in everything good, from banking to building. He was in Parliament of course. He was in the City, necessarily. He was Chairman of this, Trustee of that, President of the other' (Dickens 1912b: 195). But Merdle was also a liar and a forger; he slit his throat with his daughter-in-law's tortoiseshell-handled penknife in the warm baths. Morrison continued to make money and to buy property like a case study in Max Weber's *The Protestant Ethic and the Spirit of Capitalism*: 'Capitalism is identical with the pursuit of profit, and forever *renewed* profit, by means of continuous, rational, capitalistic enterprise' (1992: xxxi–xxxii). He extended his estate at Fonthill; he bought the Basildon estate in Berkshire in 1838 for £98,000; the Hole Park estate in Kent in 1849 for £76,400; the Hillesden estate in Buckinghamshire in 1850 for £106,000; the Malham Tarn estate in Yorkshire in 1851 for £90,250 and last, but not least, the island of Islay in 1853 for £400,000. He became Deputy Lord Lieutenant of Wiltshire, he and his wife were presented at court and he sat for Sir Francis Chantrey (see fig. 1.1) for his portrait bust. He acquired a portfolio of stocks and shares in the US and Canada valued at almost £1 million and a collection of paintings which included work by Turner and Constable (whom he knew personally), Rembrandt, Titian, Parmigiano and Van Dyck. Though his annual income after 1840 was substantially increased by rents, mortgage repayments and dividends, textiles remained his principal and most reliable source of wealth, unaffected by the failure of harvests or banks. Morrison's eldest son, Charles, his only son to follow him into business (he was worth some £12 million when he died in 1909), realised as much when he tried to safeguard their American investments in the early 1840s. He wrote to his father from Wheeling on 5 December 1842: 'we must take care of Fore St. All my experiences here [US] tend to increase my affection for that. We never can expect to find elsewhere such an opportunity of combining a high rate of profit on a great scale with complete security' (Morrison).

Through his application of 'small profits and quick returns' to the middle and lower levels of an expanding haberdashery market, Morrison's 'complete security' was assured – at least within his lifetime. 'Mundane activities' reaped huge rewards, but only for an individual with a very modern vision which he applied to all aspects of his life.

Acknowledgements

My thanks to the descendants of James Morrison for allowing me access to their family papers; to Charles Hind and his staff for their assistance in the Drawings

Collection of the Royal Institute of British Architects; to the AHRB for awarding me a 'Changing Places' research grant to work at the RIBA; to the AHRB for awarding me research expenses within the 'Fashion and Modernity' research grant; to the Paul Mellon Foundation and the Scouloudi Foundation for small research grants for travel; to Central Saint Martins College of Art and Design for research support.

References

Adburgham, A. (1981) *Shops and Shopping 1800–1914*. London: Allen & Unwin.

Chandler, J. (1983) *Endless Street. A History of Salisbury and its People*. Salisbury: Hobnob Press.

Chapman, S. (1992) *Merchant Enterprise in Britain: From the Industrial Revolution to World War I*. Cambridge: Cambridge University Press.

Daunton, M. (1995) *Progress and Poverty. An Economic and Social History of Britain 1700–1850*, Oxford: Oxford University Press..

Dickens, C. (1912a) *The Life & Adventures of Nicholas Nickleby*. London: Gresham.

—— (1912b) *Little Dorrit*. London: Gresham.

—— (1912c) *Martin Chuzzlewit*. London: Gresham.

—— (1912d), *Master Humphrey's Clock*. London: Gresham.

—— (1912e), *Sketches by Boz*. London: Gresham.

Dictionary of National Biography.

Gatty, R. (1976) *Portrait of a Merchant Prince: James Morrison, 1789–1857*. Northallerton: author.

Kynaston, D. (1994) *The City of London Volume I: A World of Its Own 1815–1890*. London: Chatto & Windus.

Morrison, unpublished family papers.

Papworth, W. (1879) *John B. Papworth, Architect to the King of Wurtemburg*. London: privately published.

Porter, R. (1996) *London: A Social History*. London: Penguin.

Rubinstein, W.D. (1981) *Men of Property. The Very Wealthy in Britain since the Industrial Revolution*. London: Croom Helm.

Rutter, J. (1823) *Delineations of Fonthill and its Abbey*. London: Charles Knight et al.

Slinn, J. (1997) *Ashurst Morris Crisp: A Radical Firm*. Cambridge: Granta.

Styles, J. (1993) 'Manufacturing, Consumption and Design in Eighteenth-century England', in J. Brewer and R. Porter (eds) *Consumption and the World of Goods*. London: Routledge.

Walsh, C. (1995) 'Shop Design and the Display of Goods in Eighteenth-Century London', *Journal of Design History*, 8(3): 157–76.
Weber, M. (1992) *The Protestant Ethic and the Spirit of Capitalism*. London: Routledge.

Response

John Styles

I would like to exercise the privilege of being the first respondent by beginning with some general reflections on modernity. As someone who trained as a historian and has worked for most of my professional life on the history of Britain in the eighteenth century, I have always been bemused by the ways my colleagues who trained as art and cultural historians and work on the late nineteenth and twentieth centuries can use the words 'modern', 'modernity' and 'modernism' almost interchangeably. The most telling instance of this for me was on one occasion when I was using the term 'early modern' – the historian's shorthand for the sixteenth and seventeenth centuries – and was assumed by some of my colleagues to be referring to a period sometime in the 1870s or 1880s when it is possible to identify the early glimmerings of Modernism (with a capital 'M') as a cultural movement. It is a trivial example, but it points to an important issue. For most historians, especially those who work on periods before the late nineteenth century, 'modern' as a temporal label is used most frequently (although often unreflectively) to refer to the period from the fifteenth century to the present – in other words, that which is neither ancient nor medieval. Of course, the tripartite scheme of ancient, medieval, and modern was itself a late nineteenth century formulation, one that gave explanatory and therefore chronological primacy to Burckhardt's Renaissance and Seeley's global expansion of European power. It was defined in terms of key issues, including most prominently (1) subjectivity – the rise of individualism, (2) technology – the 'scientific revolution', and (3) geopolitics – Columbus, Vasco Da Gama and the expansion of Europe.

Chronologies are not innocent. Every grand cultural and social theory – from Vico to Foucault – carries more or less explicitly within it a chronology of historical change. Any critical engagement with theory necessitates a critical engagement with chronology. But, curiously, the three issues I have just listed – subjectivity, technology and geopolitics – continue to play key roles in discussions of modernity, even in its most uncompromisingly presentist guise. So when was modernity? Well, as we all know, there is no one answer to that question, but to address it I think we need to interrogate two assumptions which, it seems to me, underlie many recent discussions of the subject. First, and this is an issue I shall not address in detail here, we need to question the notion that the moment of modernity was the moment when intellectuals decided humankind should stop taking cultural lessons from the past. Second, we need to question the notion we inherit from the modernisation theory of the 1950s and 1960s that at some point in the nineteenth century Industrial Revolution remade unchanging traditional societies into endlessly self-transforming modern ones. And, of course, it is this second issue that takes us directly to James Morrison, the subject of Caroline's paper.

Morrison was perhaps the single most successful businessman of the era of the classic Industrial Revolution. Yet he was not a factory owner. He represented a much older kind of entrepreneur – the London merchant, dealer and financier – who had been at the cutting edge of economic innovation in Britain since the sixteenth century. But does that mean he and his activities as a businessman should be judged un-modern? I think not. Morrison was more characteristic of those who made great fortunes in nineteenth-century Britain than any factory owner. We know from Rubinstein's work (1981) that the great fortunes were made much more readily in trading and finance – the activities we now associate with the City of London – than in manufacturing. Nineteenth-century modernity was imperial as much as it was carboniferous; as much about communications, global trade and high finance as it was about coal mines, factories and furnaces.

Of course the imperial and the carboniferous were linked. The fact that by the 1830s cotton goods comprised something close to a half of British exports is testimony to the transforming power of steam applied to manufacturing industry. Morrison himself judged modernity by the spread of steam power in his comments on other European countries during his travels. Ironic then that Morrison's fortune was based less on dealing in the factory-made cotton fabrics we inextricably associate with the notion of Industrial Revolution, and more on products that went on being largely made by hand into the second half of the nineteenth century, well after his death – silks, haberdashery, ribbons, gloves, lace.

But then we have learnt in the last twenty years to question those kinds of economic history that privileged a single, all-transforming Industrial Revolution and the rise of mass production. That narrative has been challenged by a new emphasis on the continuing and indeed growing importance of flexible and artisanal forms of production, forms of production of exactly the kinds that generated much of Morrison's turnover (Sabel and Zeitlin 1985 and 1997). This loss of faith in a single economic and technological teleology has been reinforced by important changes in the modern world – in particular, the rise of flexible production systems in manufacturing, most notably in the immensely successful Japanese export industries of electrical consumer goods and automobiles.

Dress, despite all the links that scholars have made between it and a variety of modernities, never fitted easily into those narratives of economic history whose culmination was Fordist mass production. Economic historians wrote extensively about how clothing materials were manufactured, but with few exceptions their histories concluded at the textile factory gate. The production of clothing itself was too fragmented, too small-scale, too primitive to incorporate into their grand narratives of industrial progress. But with the undermining of those grand narratives and the reassertion of the importance of the small-scale, the flexible and the diverse, the distinctive, fashion-driven features of the way clothes are made appear less a historical backwater than one of the main currents in the history of modern manufacturing (Styles 1998).

If by fashion we mean the regular annual or seasonal manipulation of appearances through dress, then James Morrison emerges as a characteristic figure in its history – the commercial intermediary who bestrides what Fine and Leopold (1993) have termed the system of provision, who intervenes and arbitrates between producers and consumers, using capital and information to effect a profitable reconciliation between the capacity to produce and the desires (I hesitate to say needs) of the consumer. But the role of merchant wholesaler is not intrinsically modern, in any sense of the word. So what was new about the way Morrison performed this role? Well, as Caroline has demonstrated, the scale on which he operated was unprecedented, although he was not the first to bring cheap cotton prints, silk handkerchiefs and the like to working-class consumers (Styles 2003). His attention to detail was remarkable. His concern with display is striking, although, as Caroline emphasises echoing Finn (2001), we must beware of Richards' (1990) mistaken assumption that commercial spectacle began with the Great Exhibition and the department store. Morrison emerges as in some respects the characteristic Weberian capitalist – particularly in his obsessive, almost religious, attention to work. In religious affiliation he was a nonconformist – so his work ethic was in a sense a puritan one – but how self-denying was he? To what degree did he, like some of the Victorian manufacturers Tosh (1999) has studied, sacrifice consumption to accumulation? And it remains unclear precisely how he resembled or differed from the wider community of nineteenth-century City of London merchants discussed by Chapman (1992), as well as the merchant princes of earlier generations, like the immensely wealthy Samuel Fludyer in the 1750s, who performed a similar role (Smail 1999: 55–60).

I also want to know more about the nature of Morrison's engagement with fashion. But what should we understand by fashion in this context? Do we simply mean (1) regular changes in visual appearance of any type of good to stimulate sale? We should remember that this is the way economists and economic historians usually employ the term fashion. Used in this way, it is a phenomenon that can be identified in fifteenth-century Florence as much as nineteenth-century England. Or do we mean (2) the annual or seasonal manipulation of normative appearance specifically through dress? Or do we mean (3) the self-consciously extreme/exclusive innovation in dress pursued as a form of cultural and economic self-promotion by a narrow élite – court fashion, haute couture, runway fashion?

Morrison was undoubtedly aware of fashion in this third, narrow sense, but it bore only a tenuous relationship to his business. For Morrison, dealing predominantly in dress fabrics and accessories, it was fashion in the second sense of annual or seasonal changes that concerned him, as his sensitivity to the superior colours of French goods shows. Insofar as he was concerned with fashion in this sense it was with its reinterpretation as products for the middle and lower levels of the market, not for the fashionable elites of London and Paris. Yet we should remember that Morrison was a wholesaler who, as Caroline has pointed out, made his money by buying cheaply. His whole success as a businessman was based on squeezing his suppliers. This was a characteristic business strategy of an age of deflation like that after 1815, one which we can observe both in textiles (Edwards 1967) and in other industries at the time like ceramics (Hunter and Miller 2001: 222–3). It is one that we are all too aware of today in another age of deflation. It required attention to changes in fashion, but not necessarily by the careful manipulation of design in advance of public taste in what we might term the Wedgwood strategy, as described by McKendrick (1982). Rather, manufacturers and wholesalers simply flooded the market with a vast range of designs at the cheapest possible prices to see which ones sold. No wonder that by the 1840s a Lancashire cotton printer was reported to have complained that 'the creation of new patterns was an endless stream. The very instant his hundred new patterns were out he began to engrave others. His designers were working like mill-horses' (Kusamitsu 1991: 119).

So was this scattergun approach to selling fashion, so characteristic of the early nineteenth century, an index of modernity? Certainly not if by modernity we mean it was unprecedented. But it contributed to the Victorians' distinctive sense of their own modernity, their belief (right or wrong) that humanity's ever-growing power over nature was remaking their world in ways that seemed to have no historical precedent. A crucial element in that sense of modernity was the Victorian crisis of choice, the fear that public taste had come to be dominated by an endless search for novelty, a willful striving merely to be different, an aesthetic restlessness that paid little heed to proper notions of beauty or morality. It was by inflicting constant pressure on manufacturers to multiply the range of cheap products by means of endless new designs that men like Morrison were decisive in linking fashion with modernity, or at least modernity as the Victorians understood it (Snodin and Styles 2001: ch. 15).

References

Chapman, S. (1992) *Merchant Enterprise in Britain from the Industrial Revolution to World War I*. Cambridge: Cambridge University Press.

Edwards, M.M. (1967) *The Growth of the British Cotton Trade, 1780–1815*. Manchester: Manchester University Press.

Fine, B. and E. Leopold (1993) *The World of Consumption*. London: Routledge.

Finn, M. (2001) 'Sex and the City: Metropolitan Modernities in English History', *Victorian Studies*, 44: 25–32.

Hunter, R. and G.L. Miller (2001) 'All in the Family: A Staffordshire Soup Plate and the American Market,' in *Ceramics in America 2001*. Milwaukee: Chipstone Foundation.

Kusamitsu, T. (1991) '"Novelty, Give us Novelty": London Agents and Northern Manufacturers', in M. Berg (ed.) *Markets and Manufacture in Early Industrial Europe*. London: Routledge.

McKendrick, N. (1982) 'Josiah Wedgwood and the Commercialisation of Potteries', in N. McKendrick, J. Brewer and J.H. Plumb, *The Birth of a Consumer Society*. London: Europa.

Richards, T. (1990) *The Commodity Culture of Victorian England: Advertising and Spectacle, 1851–1914*. Stanford: Stanford University Press.

Rubinstein, W.D. (1981) *Men of Property: The Very Wealthy in Britain since the Industrial Revolution*. London: Croom Helm.

Sabel, C. and J. Zeitlin (1985) 'Historical Alternatives to Mass Production: Politics, Markets and Technology in Nineteenth-Century Industrialisation', *Past and Present*, 108: 133–76.

—— (eds) (1997) *World of Possibilities. Flexibility and Mass Production in Western Industrialization*. Cambridge: Cambridge University Press.

Smail, J. (1999) *Merchants, Markets and Manufacture. The English Wool Textile Industry in the Eighteenth Century*. London: Macmillan.

Snodin, M. and J. Styles (2001) *Design and the Decorative Arts. Britain, 1500–1900*. London: V&A Publications.

Styles, J. (1998) 'Dress in History: Reflections on a Contested Terrain', *Fashion Theory*, 2: 383–90.

—— (2003) 'Custom or Consumption? Plebeian Fashion in Eighteenth-Century England', in M. Berg and E. Eger (eds) *Luxury in the Eighteenth Century: Debates, Desires and Delectable Goods*. London: Palgrave.

Tosh, J. (1999) *A Man's Place. Masculinity and the Middle-Class Home in Victorian England*. New Haven: Yale University Press.

–2–

Lee Miller and the Limits of Post-war British Modernity: Femininity, Fashion, and the Problem of Biography

Becky E. Conekin

> How can one make a life out of six cardboard boxes full of tailors' bills, love letters, and old picture postcards?
>
> Woolf (1980)

This line, written by Virginia Woolf when she was contemplating her biography of Roger Fry, is an important caution to every historian embarking on any form of biographical work. Unfortunately, the historian attempting to write on Lee Miller is faced with an even bigger challenge than Woolf's six cardboard boxes. There are thousands of photographs taken by Lee Miller and probably almost as many taken of her, but she was not a serious letter writer or journal keeper. So, while we have far more than six cardboard boxes of material relating to her life, to try to say something meaningful about Miller's complex biography is to do so primarily through her photographic work. Her life spans the remarkably turbulent period between 1907 and 1977 and is marked by discontinuities at every level. Existing narratives of her biography to date have responded to this complexity by constructing a simple dichotomy between her life before and after the Second World War, in which the disconsolate domesticity of the 1950s, 1960s and 1970s serves as a foil for the luminescence of the 1920s, 1930s and 1940s.[1] The purpose of this chapter is to ask if it is possible to construct an account of Miller's post-war 'retreat' into domesticity that is both more positive and more consistent with our new understandings of mid-twentieth-century Britain and its culture.[2]

Lee Miller – Modern Woman

Lee Miller was a quintessential 'modern woman'.[3] According to the established biography, she was born in 1907 in Poughkeepsie, New York; at the age of seven she was sexually assaulted by a relative and contracted venereal disease, which necessitated an excruciating medical treatment in the days before penicillin.[4] Miller was expelled from numerous schools by the time she was eighteen, and therefore managed to convince her parents to send her to Paris with two older female chaperones. Her parents 'grudgingly' paid her fees at the new Ecole Medgyes pour la Technique du Théâtre, run by stage designer Ladislas Medgyes and the architect Erno Goldfinger. But, in the winter of 1926, her father, an 'engineer-inventor and accomplished amateur photographer', went to Paris and brought her back home to Poughkeepsie (Penrose 2002: 13–15; Calvocoressi 2002: 7).

She continued her studies in lighting, costume and theatre design at the Art Students' League in New York City. The story goes that she was saved from being run over in the street by Condé Nast, who was immediately impressed by her looks, her European style and her babbling in French. He offered her modelling work at *Vogue*; at the age of twenty, she was the cover girl for American *Vogue*'s March 1927 issue. Edward Steichen often photographed her. In 1929, with a letter of introduction from Steichen to Man Ray and another from Condé Nast to George Hoyningen-Huene, the photographer for French *Vogue*, Miller returned to Paris with her best friend from art college, Tanja Ramm. Also thanks to Condé Nast, Miller had a small job for an American fashion designer. That job led to Miller's first foray into photography.

She had been employed to sketch buckles, bows and lace in Renaissance paintings in Florence for use in contemporary fashion designs. Miller found the work so tedious that she decided to attempt to photograph the paintings instead, using a folding Kodak and a spindly tripod. The results seem to have satisfied her American designer employer and galvanised in Miller the idea of becoming a photographer. She went to Paris to meet Man Ray (Penrose 2002: 22). She later recounted meeting Man Ray in a café near his apartment:

> He kind of rose up through the floor at the top of a circular staircase. He looked like a bull, with an extraordinary torso and very dark eyebrows and dark hair. I told him boldly that I was his new student. He said he didn't take students, and anyway, he was leaving Paris for his holiday. I said, I know, I'm going with you – and I did. We lived together for three years. I was known as Madame Man Ray, because that's how they do things in France (Keenan 1977: 136; Penrose 2002: 22).

What Miller failed to mention was, of course, that Man Ray was living with Kiki de Montparnasse at the time, but that matter was somehow resolved. Miller was Man Ray's student, model, muse and lover for the next three years.[5] (Kiki de Montparnasse was a cabaret artist immortalised by Man Ray in *Le Violin d'Ingres* (1924) in which he satirised cubism and Ingres by making a photographic collage that turned Kiki's naked back into a musical instrument.)[6] By the summer of 1932 she had her own apartment and studio in Montparnasse and regularly

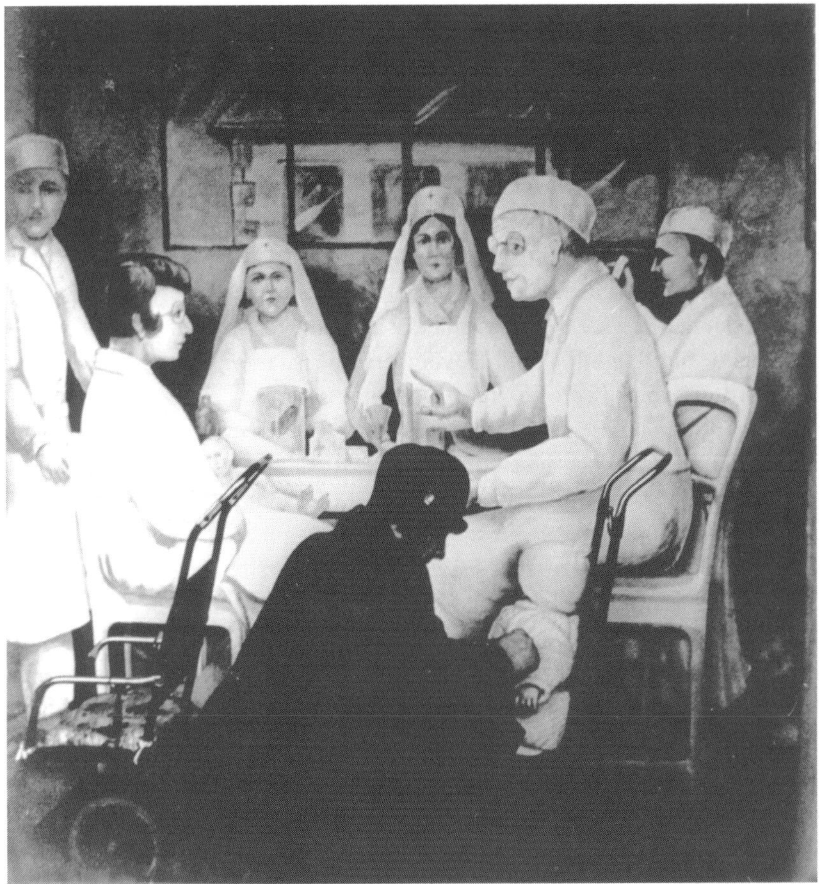

Figure 2.1 *Woman and child at Clinic,* by Lee Miller, Paris Studio, c. 1930. Max Ernst wrote that the surrealist 'procedure' was 'the exploitation of the fortuitous meeting of two distant realities on an inappropriate plane' (1934). The surrealist influence on Miller's photography here seems undeniable. (© Lee Miller Archives)

landed assignments from leading Paris designers, including Patou, Schiaparelli and Chanel (Penrose 2002: 32 and 37). She was young, female, cosmopolitan, fashionable, sexually liberated, and involved in one of Modernism's most important art movements – surrealism (fig. 2.1). She was subject and object, photographer and model, artist and muse. She played the lead female role as a statue in Jean Cocteau's film, *Blood of a Poet*. A famous version of Man Ray's piece, *Object of Destruction*, features a photograph of her eye attached to a metronome, and a glass manufacturer designed a champagne goblet inspired by the shape of her breast (Penrose 2002: 41–2 and 32).

Judith Kerr and Katherine Ware have explained that through photography, new women or 'flapper types' 'found an accessible tool that required minimal training with which they might produce original images and, quite possibly, earn a living (Kerr and Ware 1994: 219). This is an important point. Lee Miller may have been young, beautiful and talented, but she was not of independent means. Remaining unmarried meant that she needed to earn her living and photography provided her with money and independence, as well as a creative outlet. She was apprentice to Man Ray and Hoyningen-Huene. She said in 1975 that Man Ray had 'taught her everything in her first year [with him]: "...fashion pictures ... portraits ... the whole technique of what he did" (Miller, as quoted by Amaya 1975: 55). And then she studied studio lighting with Hoyningen-Huene, as he photographed her for *Vogue*. According to Penrose, 'these modelling sessions with Hoyningen-Huene were rather like a privileged tutorial, allowing Lee to experience the work on both sides of the camera at the same time' (2002: 29).

While she was still in Paris, in the winter of 1932, Julien Levy, one of the few collectors and gallery owners to take surrealist photography seriously at the time, featured Miller's work in a show of twenty artists in New York City, which included Man Ray, Peter Hans, and Moholy-Nagy. Early the following year, after Miller had returned to New York, Levy gave her the only solo show of her life (Penrose 2002: 45). And in May of 1934, *Vanity Fair* listed her alongside Cecil Beaton, amongst others, as one of 'the most distinguished living photographers' (*Vanity Fair*, 1934: 51, as cited by Burke 2001: 130). At the height of this stage of her career, on 19 July 1934, Miller seems rather impetuously to have married a wealthy Egyptian businessman, Aziz Eloui Bey, and moved to Cairo.

Miller in the 1940s: Photographer for British *Vogue*

While in Egypt, Miller took stunning photographs of the surrounding desert, but she found the 'black satin and pearls set', with whom she was expected to socialise, stultifying (Miller, as quoted by Penrose 2002: 78). And in 1939 she and Eloui parted amicably. She left to be with Roland Penrose, British surrealist painter and collector, first travelling, but when Hitler invaded Poland and it became clear war was upon the world, settling in Hampstead, North London (Penrose 2002: 93–8). By 1940, Miller was a staff photographer for British *Vogue* and she took many impressive photos of the homefront, published as *Grim Glory: Pictures of Britain Under Fire*.

At the end of 1942, thanks to her citizenship, Miller became an accredited US Forces War Correspondent. Throughout the war she submitted extraordinary photojournalism to *Vogue* in London. Lee Miller was the photographer who supplied pieces for British *Vogue* on everything from Henry Moore working as an official war artist in underground air-raid shelters to the liberation of the concentration camps at Dachau and Buchenwald, as well as herself being photographed in Hitler's bathtub at his deserted Munich residence in 1945. After years of involvement, Miller married Roland Penrose and had a son with him at the age of forty in 1947. Miller continued to work for *Vogue* until the mid-1950s, but then gave it up, choosing instead to focus on gourmet cooking, competitions, classical music and an odd sort of entertaining, primarily at the family home, Farley Farm in East Sussex (Penrose 2002).

Peter Palmquist, independent historian and founder and curator of the Women in Photography International Archive, has explained that many photographers began as print journalists and moved into photography, especially when faced with the events of the Second World War (1994: 248). But Lee Miller did the opposite. She was a photographer who was often frustrated by what she deemed to be the ineffectual text that publishers put next to her photographs. So, in 1944, in the words of her son and biographer, Tony Penrose, she 'badgered' British *Vogue*'s editor, Audrey Withers, into allowing her to write stories, as well as photograph them. The resulting articles were generally shocking, direct and frequently witty. In the summer of 1944, instead of fulfilling her assignment to produce a small picture story on nurses working in Normandy's US Army field hospitals, Miller filed a hard-hitting piece, along with fourteen photographs on two tent hospitals and a front-line casualty clearing station. British *Vogue* published the article in full in two double-page spreads. Audrey Withers described it as 'the most exciting journalistic experience of my war. We were the last people one could conceive having this type of article, it seemed so incongruous in our pages of glossy fashion' (quoted by Penrose 2002: 118). And clearly Withers revelled in this incongruity because Miller photographed and wrote on the joy of the liberation of Paris, the horrors of the concentration camps (fig. 2.2), the destruction of Hitler's 'Eagle's Nest', and the execution of the fascist former prime minister of Hungary. Miller's wartime photography has been the subject of an exhibition and book, but her writing has gone virtually undiscussed.[7]

How genuine Withers was when she asserted that no one would have expected such work in *Vogue* is somewhat questionable, since, as early as 1940, *Vogue* had published photos by Therese Bonney of refugee women and children fleeing the fighting in France. We also know that *Ladies Home Journal* had its own war correspondent, Cecelia Jackie Martin, while American *Vogue*'s staff photographer from 1931–42, Toni Frissell, became an American Red Cross photographer in 1943 (Hall 1985 and Palmquist 1994: 247–55). But perhaps what Withers really meant was that it was surprising that *Vogue* published Lee Miller's articles and photos, in particular, because of their uniqueness or strangeness.

British *Vogue*'s coverage of the war before Miller began writing, as well as photographing, for them focused primarily on the domestic scene in England.

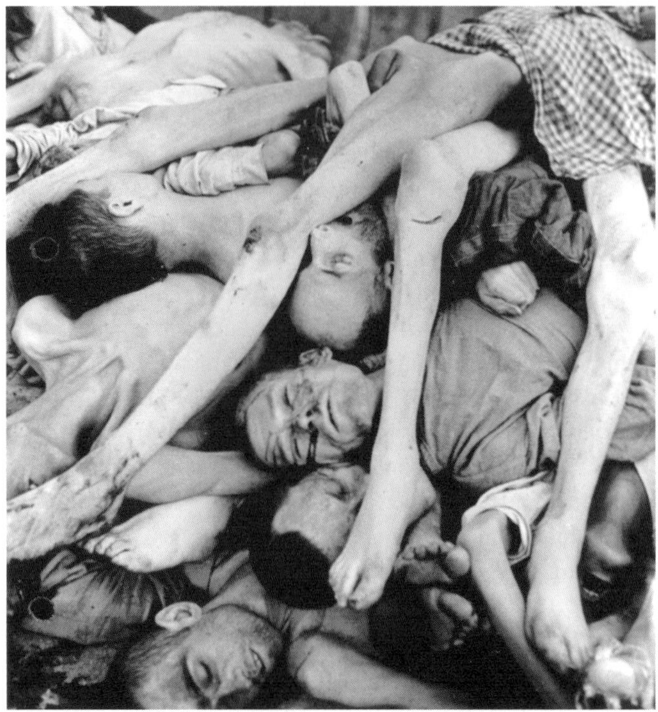

Figure 2.2 *Pile of Dead Prisoners*, by Lee Miller, Buchenwald, Germany, April 1945. (© Lee Miller Archives)

There were articles on how to 'make good meals' from 'simple foods' with 'imagination' and spices (British *Vogue*, 1940). And there was *Vogue*'s own, more elegant version of 'Make Do and Mend',[8] in which readers were encouraged in one article to stretch their wardrobes and coupons by doing things 'the American way' and buying separates (British *Vogue*, August 1944: 76), and in another they were told how to 'camouflage' 'a languishing afternoon dress' with a 'well-draped shawl: lace, wool or fringed Spanish' (British *Vogue*, March 1942). The October 1940 issue featured a piece on the assorted amenities available in the London department stores' bomb shelters, which included everything from books and magazines to hairdressing and manicures (p. 47 and passim). 'General Economy' in May of 1942 'issued his orders' to 'keep account of every precious hair-pin ... dilute the last drop of nail varnish for just one more application. Gouge out the last crimson goodness from your lipstick ... know that a carpet sweeper or a stiff broom is a far better present now than any orchids' and 'that the battle is to the strong – and that our strength depends on thrift'. Of course, there were also numerous pieces on women's war work – be they wives of foreign ambassadors, professional British women in the forces or American Army nurses and Red Cross workers (*British* Vogue, March 1942; March 1944; May 1943; June 1943).

But there was virtually no reporting on the war in Europe until Miller began writing for British *Vogue* in 1944. And her writing often seems, perhaps unsurprisingly, influenced by surrealism.[9] Miller's piece for the October 1944 issue, for example, includes a scene that could have been lifted from a Buñuel film. She had been at the siege of St. Malo, where she had 'believed the newspapers when they said that St. Malo had fallen on 5th August', 'captured not occupied'. But the war wasn't over there and she found herself in the midst of the B26 bombing. Lines from that piece include:

> Gunfire brought more stones down into the street. I sheltered in a kraut dugout, squatting under the ramparts. My heel ground into a dead, detached hand and I cursed the Germans for the sordid ugly destruction they had conjured on this once beautiful town. I wondered where my friends that I had known here before the war were; how many had been forced into disloyalty and degradation – how many had been shot, starved or what. I picked up the hand and hurled it across the street, and ran back the way I'd come bruising my feet and crashing in the unsteady piles of stone and slipping in blood. Christ it was awful! (Miller 1944: 51)

In her evocative, nightmare rendering of the scene, Miller's anger at the Germans is focused on their aesthetic crimes against St. Malo, along with their crimes against its people, some of whom were her personal friends.

Miller's June 1945 piece, 'Germany – The War that is Won', also relied on juxtaposition to make her description as discomfiting as possible. Miller had been one of the first people to enter Dachau concentration camp, photographing it on 30 April 1945. Hard-hitting from the first line, she wrote:

> Germany is a beautiful landscape dotted with jewel-like villages, blotched with ruined cities, and inhabited by schizophrenics. There are blossoms and vistas; every hill is crowned with a castle. The vineyards of the Moselle and the newly ploughed plains are fertile. Immaculate birches and tender willows flank the streams and the tiny towns are pastel plaster like a modern water-colour of a medieval memory. Little girls in white dresses and garlands promenade after their first communion. The children have stilts and marbles and tops and hoops, and they play with dolls. Mothers sew and sweep and bake, and farmers plough and harrow; all just like real people. But they aren't; they are the enemy. This is Germany and it is spring.

Evoking travel writing that you could have found in *Vogue* at the time, Miller continued:

> My fine Baedecker tour of Germany includes many such places as Buchenwald which were not mentioned in my 1913 edition, and if there is a later one I doubt if

> they were mentioned there, either, because no one in Germany has ever heard of a concentration camp, and I guess they didn't want any tourist business either. Visitors took one-way tickets only, in any case, and if they lived long enough they had plenty of time to learn the places of interest, both historic and modern, by personal and practical experimentation.

She went on to recount the horrors of the concentration camps, and slave labour, as well as her incredulity at the 'slimy invitations to dine in German underground homes'. 'How dare they?', she wrote.

> Who do they think we'd been braving flesh and eyesight against, all these years in England? Who did they think were my friends and compatriots but the blitzed citizens of London and the ill-treated French prisoners of war? Who did they think were my flesh and blood but the American pilots and infantrymen? What kind of idiocy and stupidity blinds them to my feelings? What kind of detachment are they able to find, from what kind of escape zones in the unventilated alleys of their brains are they able to conjure up the idea that they are liberated instead of conquered people?[10]

Miller's disdain for repression and her emphasis on 'eyesight' both point to important themes in surrealism.

Lee Miller employed a similarly eerie juxtaposition in her quirkily titled 'Hitlerania', published in *Vogue* in July 1945. It began with a vivid description of Hitler's mountain retreat going up in smoke and ended with a portrayal of the interior of his mistress, Eva Braun's, Munich villa. This is the article that included the famous photo of Miller in Hitler's Munich bathtub taken by her friend and colleague, *Life* photographer, Dave Scherman. In the piece, Miller described how portraits of 'Hitler tenderly autographed to Eva and her sister Gretl, who lived with her, were in plain view... Part of the china was modern peasant and part was white porcelain dotted with pale blue flowers. The furniture and decorations were strictly department store like everything in the Nazi regime: impersonal and in good, average, slightly artistic taste... Eva's bed was upholstered in self-striped ice blue satin. The linen was initialled E.B.'[11]

Drawing the reader further in, Miller wrote: 'I took a nap on her bed and tried the telephones which were marked Berlin, Berchtesgarden, Wachenfeld, the name of Hitler's house on the mountain above Berchetesgarden'. She later explained that: 'Her bathroom was supernormal, except for two medicine chests, both of which were crammed with drugs and patent preparations, enough for a ward of hypochondriacs.' But, in the move we have now come to expect, Miller shattered this 'supernormal' setting at the end:

> I wonder what collector will capture the large brass globe of the world which opened out to hold liqueur glasses, which was on Eva's living room table. The continents were

> in hammered relief and it sagged open on its hinges, empty except for the little prongs which had once held the glasses and bottles for toasting... 'Morgen Die Ganze Welt' ... 'Tomorrow the Whole World'.

Her strange combination of the sort of detailed descriptive writing you could expect to find in an article on domestic interiors with the staggering reminder of Hitler's plan of world domination, is a fine example of the sort of juxtaposition Miller employed. These unsettled pairings are what make her wartime photojournalism so arresting.

Miller's Post-war Photography for *Vogue*

Perhaps not surprisingly, Miller's fashion photography for British *Vogue* in the post-war period is elegant, lively and appropriate. But it is not arresting; it generally lacks the directness, as well as wit, that mark her Second World War work. Yet, how *would* one follow work like that with fashion photography that could rival it? Tony Penrose claims that in the early 1940s, 'the bold, realistic images in the pages of *Life* magazine were providing photographers with a strong stimulus to break away from the posed studio style shot'. Thanks to the Rolleiflex and the 35 mm Leica, 'fashion photography took to the streets, Lee and Toni Frissell setting the pace'. 'Backgrounds both mundane and profound appear suddenly in the pages of *Vogue* in Spring 1941 as legitimate settings for clothes... By now Lee knew her way around London well enough to pick good places for her shots' (Penrose 2002: 113).

However, although Lee Miller, along with Cecil Beaton, was one of the first photographers to use natural settings and movement in the fashion pages of British *Vogue*, this was not really a breakthrough by 1941 in terms of the history of fashion photography. Actually, at least in American and French *Vogue*, by the mid 1930s, 'natural' settings, such as beaches, dance halls, monuments, shop windows, automobiles, restaurants, yachts, trains, and even underwater scenes, appeared on the fashion pages.[12] And, according to the historian of photography, Martin Harrison, the first fashion photograph 'on the move and on the street' was taken by Harrison Jean Moral in 1932, but the most famous one is Martin Munkacsi's 1933 shot of Lucille Brokaw, running – both for *Harper's Bazaar* (Harrison 1991: 11). Harrison explains that Toni Frissell's 'action snapshot style' had to be accepted at *Vogue* from 1934 because of the success of Munkacsi's photographs for *Harper's*. Yet, like Penrose, he acknowledges that the Rolleiflex was only really allowed to dominate work at *Vogue* from 1942. This fact he explains by the death of Condé Nast, who did not like the photographic style the new camera produced (Harrison, 1991: 42).

It is very likely that the realities of life in Britain during and after the war were the overwhelming reason why British *Vogue*'s fashion photographers left the studio and chose outdoor and other 'natural' settings. *Vogue*'s London studio had been bombed, and we know that Miller was happy to develop her photographs anywhere that she could find what she called the 'holy three' of water, electricity and gas (Conversation between the author and Tony Penrose, Lee Miller Archives, 22 November 2002).

Her post-war fashion photography for British *Vogue*, utilising outdoor settings, in fact often resembles Norman Parkinson's, Erwin Blumenfeld's or Irving Penn's work of the same period.[13] Like Parkinson, Miller frequently took her fashion photographs around her homes, either in London or at Farley Farm or the nearby village in East Sussex. Interestingly, however, Lee Miller has not been included in some of the big photographic books, like the *Vogue Book of Fashion Photography.* And in *On the Edge: 100 years of Vogue*, Miller only appears as a Second World War field photographer. This is probably primarily due to the dominance of American and French *Vogue* over British *Vogue*, but it also tells us something about how others have viewed her post-war work as clearly not her best. Her son now says she had post-natal depression after he was born in 1947, as well as post-traumatic stress syndrome, both of which seem like reasonable diagnoses (Penrose, as quoted by Anonymous, 18 August 2003, WWD.com). Of course, looking at the contact sheets, one can find more interesting, imaginative, and even what might be called more surrealist, photographs taken by Miller for *Vogue* assignments that did not make it into the magazine. Yet, the 'Unseen *Vogue*' exhibition at the Design Museum in 2002 shows us that this is not unique to Miller.

Miller wrote her penultimate article for the July 1953 issue of British *Vogue*. (The last was in the early 1970s and concerned surrealist cinema.) It was a piece, illustrated by her photographs, entitled 'Working Guests'. It is an extremely witty article and the photos alone deserve serious attention. They include Alfred Barr, director of the Museum of Modern Art in New York, feeding the pigs at Farley Farm, the Victoria and Albert's keeper of sculpture, H.D. Molesworth, re-covering Farley Farm's living room chairs (fig. 2.3), Henry Moore 'hugging his sculpture' on the lawn, as well as Renato Guttuso wearing a chef's hat. In *Vogue*, Miller explained that: 'The visitors' book is flanked by a photo album of grim significance: in it are no "happy hols" snaps of leisured groups wearing sun glasses and sniffing Pimm's Cup. It could easily be taken for a set of stills from a Soviet's workers' propaganda film. Everyone busy doing a job: Joy Through Work' (Miller 1953: 55 and Penrose 2002: 191–3).

However, according to Tony Penrose, 'The process of writing had become so traumatic that the turmoil it caused threatened to engulf Roland [Penrose]. He wrote secretly to Audrey Withers – "I implore you, please do not ask Lee to write again. The suffering it causes her and those around her is unbearable"'. Miller

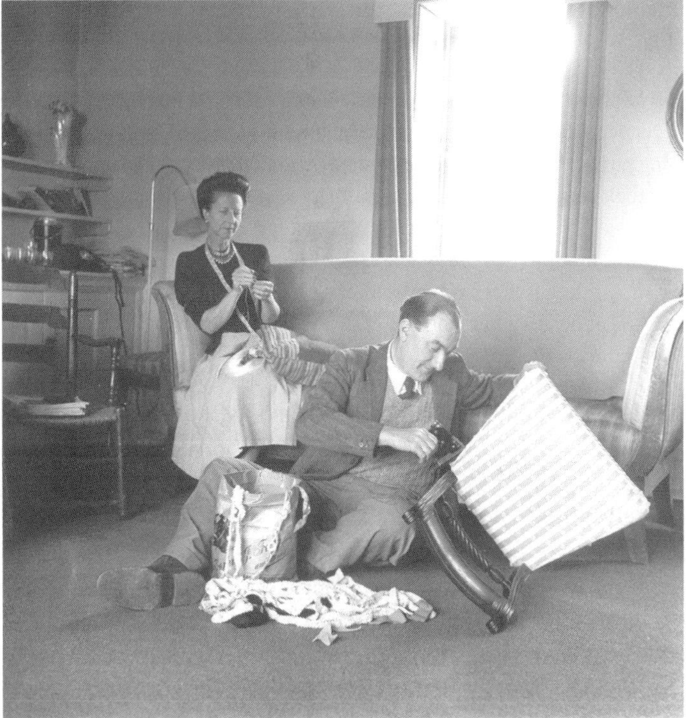

Figure 2.3 H.D. Molesworth, the Victoria and Albert Museum's Keeper of Sculpture, and his wife, Eve Molesworth, re-covering the living room chairs at Miller's house, Farley Farm House, Chiddingly, 26 August 1950, published in Miller's article, 'Working Guests' for British *Vogue*, July 1953. (© Lee Miller Archives, courtesy of the Hulton Getty Picture Collection)

had always had trouble with deadlines, often not meeting them, and Withers found her work so 'distinctive' that it had to be 'accommodated' in *Vogue*, rather than merely included. Miller herself quit writing and turned her creative energies to cooking and entertaining (Penrose 2002: 193–5). At about this time, Miller stopped responding to requests for her photographs and negatives. Her answer to enquiries was along the lines of: 'Oh, I did take a few pictures – but that was a long time ago'. According to Tony Penrose, she was so persuasive that 'everyone was convinced that she had done little or no work of significance' (2002: 209).

The Rest of Miller's Post-war Life

The other story that Miller's son as biographer tells about her life in the mid-1950s is that she was very depressed, suffering from mental illness, having 'found herself unable to get any pleasure from sex' after giving birth to him, as well as 'rapidly losing her looks'. He writes:

> By 1955 Lee was in the grip of a vicious downward spiral that nearly killed her… Her face no longer had its fineness – wrinkles and folds were proliferating and her eyes were becoming puffy. Her hair was getting thinner and lifeless. The fat was piling on, making her body look coarse and bulky. To make matters worse, the woman who had once been described as a 'snappy dresser' was fast becoming a slob. She would turn up at smart dinner parties in scruffy or unsuitable clothes – calf-high stockings under a knee length skirt, or an ill-fitting jacket worn over slacks. But of all the vicissitudes of age, it was the deterioration of her face that wounded Lee the most, and drove her to a painful face-lift and ill-fitting wigs (Penrose 2002: 194).

What can we make of this information, especially when reported by Miller's son? Are post-traumatic stress syndrome and depression not reason enough for adopting a slatternly appearance? How often did she 'turn up at smart dinner parties' inappropriately attired? On the following page we learn that at this time Roland Penrose was 'in love with an acrobat from the flying trapeze, Diane Deriaz' and that Miller had been very upset when Victor Gollancz commissioned him, rather than her, to write a book on her friend Picasso (Penrose 2002: 195).

Tony Penrose then writes that it was 'food that saved her life', explaining that Miller became a serious gourmet (fig. 2.4). But he never returns to the intertwined issues of appearance, identity and fashionability. Snapshots and other photographs, however, from the 1960s and 1970s reveal Miller fashionably and often elegantly attired, be the occasion formal or informal. There are existing photographs of her travelling and on holidays and special occasions, depicting her trips to Venice, Amsterdam, and Arles, Christmas at home, Glyndebourne, the knighting of Roland Penrose in 1966, and Man Ray's retrospective at the ICA in 1975. In many of these photos Miller is sporting a manicure and pedicure. Other examples of Miller's continuing interest in dress and fashionability include the gingerbreadman dress she gave to her good friend Bettina McNulty's young daughter, Claudia, one Christmas and her present to her daughter-in-law, Suzanna, when she was pregnant with her first child (McNulty, interview with the author; Penrose 2002: 210). According to Tony Penrose, it was a great joy to his mother taking her daughter-in-law shopping for maternity clothes. Miller had proclaimed: 'I'm not buying anything for the baby… Everyone else will do that as it's your first. Instead we're going to get you fitted out so you can feel good and look great' (Penrose 2002: 210). These varying takes on what matters in Lee Miller's life, what is emphasised and what is disregarded – ranging from her agency, her status as an artist and her appearance – lead to one of the primary points of this chapter. In many cases, if not most, aren't the confines of traditional biographical writing too limited?

Figure 2.4 Lee Miller in the old kitchen, Farley Farm House, Chiddingly, East Sussex, England, as photographed for American *House and Garden* magazine, June 1973 by Ernst Beadle. (© the Artist's Estate, courtesy of the Lee Miller Archives)

Lee Miller, Post-war Modernity and the Limits of Biography

Carolyn Steedman has written that women's biography as a form is so successful because it promises to offer us proof that 'the inchoate experience of living and feeling can be marshalled into a chronology' (Steedman 1992: 163). But, when we look at the life of Lee Miller, model, muse, surrealist, photographer, gourmet and hostess – a quintessential 'modern woman' – especially in relation to her neglected post-Second World War photography for *Vogue* and the rest of her story after the war, perhaps we come away with something else. Perhaps Miller's life cannot be recuperated in a biography in which the 'central and unified subjects reach the conclusion of a life, and come into possession of their own story' (Steedman 1992: 163). As a woman who had such a fascinating first half of her life and such a stunning career as a photographer before the age of forty, what would we expect the rest of Miller's life to be like?

Penrose and more recently David Hare, writing in the *Guardian Weekend* magazine, have blamed what Hare calls 'Miller's postwar eclipse' on 'bitterness and alcoholic despair that made her such a difficult companion in later years' (Hare 2002: 24). But what might we see if we put Lee Miller in historical context? Curiously, although biographers and other scholars have generally placed Miller's life narrative within the greater historical accounts of the surrealist movement, interwar Paris, the Depression in America, and the Second World War, such contextualisation ceases when they reach the 1950s, 1960s and 1970s. Perhaps this is partially the result of the larger problems with post-war British historiography.[14] However, the later 1950s and early 1960s are broadly thought of in terms of a return to domesticity and the growth in consumer culture – a time when the separation of the public and private spheres and its consequences for gender roles were revitalised after the severe disruptions of the war. So, if we reinsert Miller's experiences and choices after the Second World War into this historical account, what might we learn?

For one thing, domestic life was not easy; rationing continued in Britain until 1953. Tony Penrose relates the amusing stories of Miller's attempts to make her own butter and slaughter her own pigs for bacon in 1948 in what she seems to have called her 'self sufficiency' programme (2002: 187). They are indeed comical tales. But they are also part of a particular historical moment, one in which all sorts of goods and services were still very hard to come by in Britain. Meat, bacon, cheese, eggs, butter, margarine, sugar and sweets were rationed until the Korean war ended in 1953, but coal rationing continued even after that (see, for example, Clarke 1996: 243). Carolyn Steedman, who was born in 1948, has written in *Landscape for a Good Woman* that: 'The war was so palpable a presence in the first five years of my life that I still find it hard to believe that I did not live through it. There were bomb sites everywhere, prefabs on waste land, most things still on points' (1987: 27). Domestic life, even for privileged Brits, was not straightforward in the immediate post-war period; it was often a time-consuming and frustrating affair.

In addition, it is now, of course, a cliché to say that in 1950s and 1960s Britain and America 'homemaking' was constructed by various sources, including women's magazines and radio programmes, as 'the new art' (P.L. Garbutt 1954, as quoted by Jeremiah 2000: 166). 'The Happy Home', a guide published by the Good Housekeeping Institute in London in 1954, 'provided a detailed account of how to manage a home, from choosing goods and appliances, planning work, nursing the family, entertaining and modernising so that with ease and charm the housewife would create a happy and cheerful home life' (Jeremiah 2000: 166).

Certainly Lee Miller was not your ordinary British housewife. We know she had a staff and often chose to live away from any form of family life at the London flat, rather than the countryside home. We also know that her writing and photographic work for *Vogue* carried on until 1953. But it seems to me that very few married women, with a child, could resist all of these clear and persistent messages about a woman's true worth being measured by her domestic abilities. However, rather than seeing Miller's turn to the domestic realm as merely a sign of her 'depression and self-abnegation', as Jane Livingstone does, isn't it possible to view Miller's gourmet cooking and rather eccentric entertaining as different outlets for her creativity and wit? (Livingstone 1989: 98)

In a way Miller's turn to these domestic tasks in the English countryside perfectly fits the 1950s and pre-feminist 1960s narrative of a woman's role being in the home after the bizarre and terrifying circumstances of the Second World War in Britain. Similarly, in an interview with me, Miller's best friend in the 1960s and 1970s, Bettina McNulty, contributing editor to *House and Garden*, explained both that 'she was not the person with the job' and that 'there wasn't any real famous job for her' (McNulty, interview with the author). McNulty also emphasised that this was not an uncommon arrangement for marriages in this period. Another anonymous friend of Miller's and Penrose's told me that she believes that at some point Miller, who believed Roland was 'an angel', decided that there was to be only one career in their household and it was to be Roland's (Anonymous, interview with the author). So, these statements remind us that this so-called 'barren' period in Miller's life occurs in 1950s–1970s Britain, in the midst of the upper-middle-class art world, in the life of an American woman in her last two decades of life.[15] Is it really surprising that after being involved in surrealism in interwar Paris and then being a front-line war correspondent in the Second World War, Miller either did not know how to continue to be a creative person on a payroll or did not choose to be? There is much evidence that she tremendously enjoyed her gourmet cooking and quirky entertaining at Farley Farm after the war, as well as the foreign travel that often motivated the next culinary experiment. McNulty, her accomplice in much of this in the 1960s and 1970s, told me: 'We had more fun than our guests did. Most hosts don't have fun; they do it, but they don't have fun' (McNulty, interview with the author).

So, seen in a different light, Miller's turn to the domestic does not fit that staid and simplistic narrative of 1950s and 1960s life as being one of stultification and domestication for bourgeois women. Miller's creative cooking and entertaining problematise the public/private divide, for example. Taking a long view of surrealist games, parties, and orgies as sites of fun, creativity, community-building and politics allows us to place Miller's choices in a context that suggests she may have seen herself as some sort of surrealistic hostess. Miller and Penrose had clearly considered themselves to be at the centre of modern art, and especially surrealism, in Britain since 1939 when they began living together in Hampstead. To view Miller's cooking and entertaining as merely the result of 'depression and self-abnegation' is to refuse the creativity and meaningfulness of such acts, as well as their potential importance to the creation and continuance of a genuine community of artists. According to their son, Lee Miller and Roland Penrose both loved entertaining; 'Art was vital and had to be lived and shared, otherwise it became academic, sterile and as good as dead. They both enjoyed creating the kind of atmosphere in which new ideas and projects could be spawned' (Penrose 2002: 190).

An insight into Miller's witty entertaining style, coupled with her dedication to modern art is offered by a party she threw in Alexandria, Egypt in 1937, shortly after she was painted by Picasso on a holiday in the South of France. Word had spread amongst the Egyptian elite that Miller had had her portrait painted by a famous artist. Miller had hung her portrait featuring 'two smiling eyes and a green mouth . . . on the same side of the face' by Picasso on the wall in the entryhall and positioned her sister-in-law to eavesdrop on the guests' responses. As Miller had anticipated, once the drinks were flowing, many guests began announcing that they could have done better than this artist with their eyes shut, etc. According to Tony Penrose, Miller then 'flung open the doors to another room where paints, paper and brushes were all laid out. "OK!" she challenged, "Let's see how you make out." The party was a memorable success with all the guests ruining their evening clothes by daubing away with abandon' (Penrose 2002: 76–7).

Bettina McNulty related other pranks to me from the 1960s and 1970s, including one where they dressed up McNulty's daughter, Claudia, to look just like the little Victorian girl who Valentine Penrose had described as appearing in her dream the day before. Then during Valentine's subsequent afternoon nap they had Claudia walk quietly through her room pushing a hoop (McNulty, interview with the author).

Cooking elaborate meals and playing pranks on members of the international art world, along with enlisting them in all the chores associated with running a farm, in your home filled with paintings, drawings and sculptures by the greatest modernists of the twentieth century, can be seen as community-building, as well as individually enriching. The home can be understood here, not as private and secluded, but as vibrant and open – abuzz with people, food, games, drink, art and ideas. Looked at this way, Miller's cooking and hostessing were a natural progression from both her previous interwar role as muse and her post-war fashion photography, which also broke down the public and private by bringing her work into her homes and their environs. Interestingly, although this role has generally been downplayed in writings on Miller, her husband, Roland Penrose, included a short chapter entitled 'Lee The Hostess' in his *Scrapbook* (1981: 186).

Conclusion

As I have argued elsewhere, along with Frank Mort and Chris Waters, 'The British experience of modernity after 1945 was never a linear history of progressive advance. Perhaps the most striking feature of so many of the modernising projects pioneered during this period is that they were continually compromised and contested. British modernity was always a balancing act between innovation and tradition' (Conekin *et al.* 1999: 19–20). And if the breakdown of separate gendered spheres is considered as a sign of modernity, then Lee Miller's life narrative offers us an important reminder of how complicated such change is. A woman who worked as a model in the inter-war period in New York and Paris and a US Army war correspondent during the Second World War might *choose* to turn to gourmet cooking and entertaining, as her form of self-expression for the last two decades of her life. And if a man in similar social and economic circumstances had made such a choice, would subsequent biographers dub it an act of 'self abnegation' or the result of 'bitterness and alcoholic despair' (Livingstone 1989: 98; Hare 2002: 24)? I wonder.

Another key paradox we see through Lee Miller's biographical story is that it was *Vogue*, arguably fashion's pre-eminent magazine, which offered Miller work on both sides of the camera and both sides of the Atlantic. As we have seen, Miller's first paid work was as a model for *Vogue*, then she became a fashion photographer, often working for them, and later she was British *Vogue*'s Second World War correspondent. Yet, it was probably her affiliation with *Vogue*, rather than a magazine like *Life* in America or *Picture Post* in Britain, that added to the trivialisation of Miller's photographic career and the ease with which she seems to have been excluded for decades from stories of the development of the art of photography or even photojournalism. Furthermore, it is apparent that after the war, *Vogue* had difficulty fitting Miller's unique vision and voice into its pages. It is very likely that all sorts of 'difficult' women were hard to accommodate in the post-war period. Because of her arresting and important wartime photojournalism, Miller clearly had an established reputation in post-war London. And, yet, she complained to her close friend and physician, Carl H. Goldman, 'I get so depressed.' To which Goldman sternly replied: 'There is nothing wrong with you, and we cannot keep the world permanently at war just to provide you with excitement' (Miller and Goldman, as quoted by Penrose 2002: 188). Today we might have a better understanding that a woman who had photographed Dachau might find returning to shooting designer dresses a strange, if not demoralising and dispiriting, thing to do.

But, the larger point I am making here has to do with the problem of biography as a form. In contrast to autobiographical writing, biographical writing is surprisingly undertheorised.[16] According to Catherine N. Parke, 'biography has proved remarkably "immune" from deconstruction' (J. Batchelor 1995: 2, as quoted by Parke 2002: 31). Why is it that we feel compelled both as writers and readers to tie up the threads, to weave it all together – to make a life a coherent whole? An astute reader will have realised that I have just made this move. I have suggested that the *real* way to read Miller's biographical story, especially after the war and the end of her photographic career, is to put her in a different historical context – that we should attempt to understand her through the peculiarities of British post-war modernity. To do so, I have claimed, calls for a re-examination of the notion of the public and private spheres and their relationship to gender in this period. I could, of course, also suggest we read this part of Miller's story in terms of the childhood sexual abuse she had suffered, or via a narrative of her as a drunk and abhorrent mother of a young child. Or I could explain her life story from the opposite direction as another sort of mother – one which some feminists theorists have argued the culture does not know what to do with – the laughing mother. Susan Rubin Suleiman has asserted that, as Freud said, 'humour is not resigned; it is rebellious'. She contends that if we could imagine a woman artist also as a laughing, playing mother, then we might be able to 'change the way we in the West think about the constitution of human subjectivity' or at the very least find a 'recipe' for changing the way things are (Suleiman 1990: 163–80). But I did not choose to take my reading of Miller's life story after the war in these directions.

And, in the end, I think we must acknowledge that biographical writing as a story where 'the central and unified subjects reach the conclusion of a life and come into possession of their own story' is a naïve notion and not actually what we should be attempting as twenty-first-century scholars (fig. 2.5). Lives are

Figure 2.5 Lee Miller at Farley Farm House, in her home office 'built especially to house Lee Penrose's vast collection of cookbooks ... "How will we do the pork, the turkey, the ham?" is often answered with a game – a sort of kitchen roulette in which you grab some cookbooks and make the first dish for which you have all the ingredients on hand', wrote Bettina McNulty in American *House and Garden* in 1973, four years before Miller's death (McNulty 1973). Notice the gastronomic dictionary at her feet. Photograph by Ernst Beadle. (© the Artist's Estate, courtesy of the Lee Miller Archives)

complicated and messy and far more interesting because they are. Why, then, should we make the stories of our subjects less so? Surely, the unevenness of a life, like the unevenness of modernity in post-war Britain, is really the point.

Acknowledgements

I would like to acknowledge my research fellowship from the London College of Fashion, and various people who offered advice on the chapter, especially Deborah Cohen, Laura Downs, Christopher Reed, Carolyn Steedman and Adam Tooze. I would like to thank Bettina McNulty for sharing her memories of Lee Miller with me, as well as Tony Penrose and his team at the Lee Miller Archives, Carole Callow and Arabella Hayes, for sharing their expertise and assisting me with my research.

Notes

1. The definitive biography to date is *The Lives of Lee Miller* by her son, Anthony Penrose (2002).
2. On new readings of the post-war period in Britain, see Conekin et al. 1999.
3. On the 'modern woman', as opposed to the 'new woman', see Mary Louise Roberts 2002, especially p. 249.
4. This childhood sexual assault may have something to do with Miller's son's recent description of his mother's relationship with her father as possibly 'inappropriate' (Anonymous 2003).
5. Even though we know that Miller took surrealism's commitment to free love seriously and almost always had lovers in addition to Man Ray, which clearly distressed him, this is generally how she has been discussed in this period (Penrose 2002: 38–42).
6. See, for example, Richard Martin 1988: 18–19.
7. Anthony Penrose is clearly impressed with her wartime articles and says that 'her ability as a writer was now poised, fully primed and ready to go', but he doesn't actually analyse the texts, separate from the photographs (Penrose 2002: 116). The scholar who has written on some of Miller's wartime articles is Jane Gallagher (1998).
8. 'Make Do and Mend' was a government slogan during the Second World War in Britain.
9. Some feminist scholars of surrealism deny that Lee Miller was a surrealist. One claims that she was merely a model and muse for male surrealists and

primarily a victim (ie. Caws 1991: 11), while Whitney Chadwick and Sandra Phillips argue that Miller was a perpetrator of what they perceive to be Man Ray's 'misogyny and his cold, fetishistic objectification of beautiful women in *Vogue* and *Harper's Bazaar*' (Chadwick 1999: 315 and Sandra Phillips in Foster et al. 1989). But, at least two other feminist scholars view Miller as a surrealist. See Amy Lyford (1994: 230–41) and Penelope Rosemont (1998: xxix–lvii) in her introduction, 'All My Names Know Your Leap: Surrealist Women and Their Challenge'. There are many other ways of reading Miller's work – as a photographer, model, actress and possibly maker of objects – as surrealist, especially in the late 1920s and early 1930s, but the word limit does not allow me to explore this here.

10. It is, however, worrying that Miller did not mention Jews at all in this piece. Is it possible that she did not yet know the details of who had been killed in the camps?
11. Interestingly, this article was published in the same month's issue of American *Vogue,* under the title 'Germans are Like That', pp. 102–5, passim.
12. See photos by Toni Frissell, George Hoyningen-Huene, Edward Stiechen, Erwin Blumenfeld, Roger Schall, Andre Kertesz, Remie Lohse, and more, as reproduced from American and French *Vogue*, in '1930s', *Vogue Book of Fashion Photography* (1979), pp. 46–69 and for the 1940s and 1950s, on pp. 80, 81, 85–6, 88, 89, 92, 93, 96, 97, 101–3.
13. For an accessible way to make these comparisons, see their work reproduced in *Vogue Book of Fashion Photography* (1979), pp. 80, 81, 85–6, 88, 89, 92, 93, 96, 97, 101–3.
14. I have written on these problems with Frank Mort and Chris Waters in Conekin et al. 1999. In brief, the argument there is that post-war British historiography had been dominated by narrowly defined topics, especially formal politics and policy-making, as well as conservative methodologies. I take up the issue similarly, but somewhat differently, in the introduction to my book *The Autobiography of a Nation: The 1951 Festival of Britain*, especially pp. 5–7.
15. In an initial telephone conversation with Tony Penrose in September 2002, he discouraged me from attempting to work on Lee Miller's life as a hostess in the mid-1950s and 1960s, describing it as a 'barren period'.
16. On autobiographical writing, see, for example, C.K. Steedman 1992; K.J. Weintraub 1975 and L.O. Mink 1981. On biographical writing, see C.N. Parke 2002. I would like to thank Carolyn Steedman for this insight. It seems from Parke that the last time biography as a form was seriously interrogated was by individuals such as Lynton Strachey and Virginia Woolf in interwar Britian. Parke explains that Woolf was very worried that our understandings of other people were just 'emanations of ourselves' and that this left her dubious about how anyone could ever write an accurate biography (2002: 28).

References

Primary Sources

Interviews

Anonymous, telephone interview with the author, London, August 2002.
McNulty, Bettina, interview with the author, London, 13 August 2002.

Articles and Photographs

Anonymous (1944) 'Doing things By Halves', British *Vogue*, August: 76.
Miller, L., Photographs and Contact Sheets, the Lee Miller Archive, Farley Farm House, Chiddingly, East Sussex, England.
—— (1944) 'St. Malo', British *Vogue*, October.
—— (1945a) 'Germany – The War that is Won', British *Vogue*, June.
—— (1945b) 'Hitlerania', British *Vogue*, July: 36–7, 74.
—— (1945c) 'The Pattern of Liberation', British *Vogue*, January: 80.
—— (1953) 'Working Guests', British *Vogue*, July: 54–7, 90, 92.

Secondary Sources

Amaya, M. (1975) 'My Man Ray', *Art in America*, May–June: 55.
Anonymous (2003) 'Snapshots in Time: Lee Miller', Hamilton, Bermuda, report on an exhibition at the Bermuda National Gallery and Ace Gallery, August to September 2003, from 18 August 2003, WWD.com.
Burke, C. (2001) 'Framing a life: Lee Miller', in *Roland Penrose, Lee Miller: The Surrealist and the Photographer*. Edinburgh: Scottish National Gallery of Modern Art, exhibition catalogue.
Calvocoressi, R. (2002) *Lee Miller: Portraits from a Life*. London: Thames & Hudson.
Caws, M.A. (1991) 'Seeing the Surrealist Woman: We are a Problem', introduction to M.A. Caws, R. Kuenzli and G. Raaberg (eds) *Surrealism and Women*. Cambridge, MA: MIT Press.
Chadwick, W. (1999) 'Fetishizing Fashion/Fetishizing Culture: Man Ray's Noire et blanche', in Naomi Sawelson-Gorse (ed.) *Women in Dada: Essays on Sex, Gender, and Identity*. Cambridge, MA: MIT Press: 294–329.
—— (2002) 'Claude Cahun and Lee Miller, Problematizing the Surrealist Territories of Gender and Ethnicity', in T. Lester (ed.) *Gender, Nonconformity, Race and Sexuality: Charting the Connections*. Madison: University of Wisconsin Press: 141–59.

Clarke, P. (1996) *Hope and Glory: Britain 1900–1970*. London: Penguin.

Conekin, B.E. (2003) *The Autobiography of a Nation: The 1951 Festival of Britain.* Manchester: Manchester University Press.

—— F. Mort and C. Waters (eds) (1999) 'Introduction', in *Moments of Modernity: Reconstructing Britain 1945–1964*. London: Rivers Oram Press.

Ernst, Max. (1934) *Une Semaine de bonte, ou les sept elements capitaux*. Paris: Jeanne Bucher.

Foster, S.C. et al. (eds*)* (1989) *Perpetual Motif: The Art of Man Ray.* New York: Abbeville Press.

Gallagher, J. (1998) 'Vision, Violence and *Vogue*: War and Correspondence in Lee Miller's Photography', in *The World Wars: Through the Female Gaze*. Carbondale, IL: Southern Illinois University Press: 68–96.

Hall, C. (1985) *The Forties in Vogue*. London: Octopus Books.

Hare, D. (2002) 'The Real Surrealist', *Guardian Weekend*, 26 October 26: 14–24.

Harrison, M. (1991) *Appearances: Fashion Photography Since 1945*. London: Jonathan Cape.

Jeremiah, D. (2000) *Architecture and Design for the Family in Britain, 1900–70.* Manchester: Manchester University Press.

Keenan, B. (1977) *The Women We Wanted to Look Like*. London: Macmillan.

Kerr, J. and K. Ware (1994) 'Women Photographers in Europe 1919–1939', *History of Photography:* 18 (3) Autumn: 219.

Livingstone, J. (1989) *Lee Miller: Photographer.* London: Thames & Hudson.

Lyford, A. (1994) 'Lee Miller's Photographic Impersonations, 1930–1945', *History of Photography*, 18 (3) Autumn: 230–41.

McEuan, M.A. (2000) *Seeing America: Women Photographers Between the Wars*. Lexington: University of Kentucky Press.

McNulty, B. (1973) 'Lee Penrose', American *House and Garden*, June.

Martin, R. (1988) *Fashion and Surrealism*. London: Thames & Hudson.

Mink, L.O. (1981) 'Everyman His or Her Own Annalist', *Critical Inquiry*, 4: 777–83.

Palmquist, P.E. (1994) 'Resources for Second World War Women Photographers', *History of Photography*, 18 (3) Autumn: 247–55.

Parke, C.N. (2002) *Biography: Writing Lives*. London: Routledge.

Penrose, A. (ed.) (1992) *Lee Miller's War.* Boston: Bullfinch Press.

—— (2002 [1985]), *The Lives of Lee Miller*. London: Thames & Hudson.

Penrose, R. (1981) *Scrap Book*. London: Thames & Hudson.

Roberts, M.L. (2002) *Disruptive Acts: The New Woman in Fin-de-Siècle France*. Chicago: University of Chicago Press.

Rosemont, P. (ed.) (1998) *Surrealist Women: An International Anthology*. Austin: University of Texas Press.

Steedman, C.K. (1987) *Landscape for a Good Woman: A Story of Two Lives*. New Brunswick: Rutgers University Press.

—— (1992) *Past Tenses, Essays on Writing, Autobiography and History*. London: Rivers Oram Press.

Suleiman, S.R. (1990) *Subversive Intent: Gender, Politics and the Avant-Garde*. Cambridge, MA: Harvard University Press.

Vogue Book of Fashion Photography (1979) introduction by Alexander Liberman, text by Polly Devlin, design by Bea Feitler, and creative research by Diana Edkins. London: Thames & Hudson.

Weintraub, K.J. (1975) 'Autobiography and Historical Consciousness', *Critical Inquiry*, 1: 821–48

Woolf, V. (1980) Letter to V. Sackville-West (3 December 1939) in N. Nicholson and J. Trautmann (eds) *Leave the Letters till We're Dead: The Letters of Virginia Woolf, Vol. VI, 1936–1941*. London: Hogarth Press.

Response

Carol Tulloch

A key issue for Becky Conekin is how to write a biography of an individual, particularly with resources which consist of thousands of photographs taken by and of Lee Miller, a few letters and the biographies that exist. How can one achieve a sense of Miller's modernity, and attain a cohesive sense of who she was through the material that remains? A particular problem for Conekin is 'biography as a form' and its potential to not fully communicate the complications and messiness of life, as 'The uneveness of a life, like the uneveness of modernity in Britain in the post-war period is really the point' (Conekin 2002).

Conekin is not alone in coming to terms with the idea of biographical truth. Lisa Chaney appreciates that to construct a biographical text that positions the subject as 'exemplifying personal cohesion is attractive and restorative' (1998: xix). It is pointless to deny the idiosyncrasies that make an individual. To knit all aspects of a life together is the closest one can get to approaching a kind of truth. Chaney suggests biographers use the source that represents the most cohesive sense of the subject under study, which in Chaney's case was the food writing of Elizabeth David. For Conekin it appears to be the large portfolio of photographs taken by and of Miller, and her journalistic writing that has been under-researched.

Catherine N. Parke has realised that to undertake a biography is to face a 'complex challenge', yet it entails an 'appeal to the imagination … an essential part of experience'. This is built on the basic requirements of 'getting the facts right, finding an appropriate form of presenting them, and understanding the significance of any person's life' (Parke 1996: 30–4). To respond to Conekin's dilemma in attempting to write a biography of Miller and an account of her relationship with fashion and modernity which acknowledge inconsistencies, perhaps a closer scrutiny of the significance of fashion to Miller on different personal planes (as a professional photojournalist, as a woman, as a wife and mother) could be entertained. For example, the consideration of the relevance of clothes and self-image in the last phase of her life, and in the private space of her home, would help to provide a more rounded version of Miller. Here was a woman who, since the 1920s, had been both immersed in the liberal and hedonistic culture of the century and made a sharp social and cultural critique of it through her lens and writing. Yet by the 1950s this aspect of her life was fading. In addition, Miller was no longer sexually active and was losing her looks. Inspite of this, Miller maintained a space 'between the ordinary and the extraordinary' (Landy 1993: 162), where she performed her take on modernity through extraordinary food creations and 'eccentric entertaining' (Conekin 2002).

This aspect of Miller's life was in step with the modern approach to cooking that emerged in Britain in the 1950s. A leading exponent of this was Elizabeth David. Her first book, *Mediterranean Food*, was published in the 1950s. David wanted to expand the repertoire of cooking in England and suggested to cooks that they look to south-western France and the Mediterranean. Throughout the next decade she wrote recipes for *Queen*, the *Spectator* and *The Sunday Times*. David was not an advocate of the virtues of the good housewife that were so prevalent during the 1950s. She wanted the English to move into new territories in their home cooking and to discover that food could be exciting and the act of cooking invigorating. For David, cooking was an art that was integral to one's whole being, and dress was part of this engagement with different tastes, and different styles of cooking. For example, whilst in Cairo during the Second World War a friend, Leigh Fermor, commented on the circle in which David mixed. They would visit Arab restaurants and eat dinners of kebabs, rice and egg fruit on the roofs of the restaurants. To compliment this 'oriental touch', Fermor observed, 'She [Elizabeth David] wore caftans of rather nice material, with many buttons down the front. But then it didn't look affected to dress up, we all did' (Chaney 1998: 183). Chaney does not claim to write the definitive work on David, as she feels there can be no such thing as all biographies are 'faced with the shifts and alterations of perception from time'. Instead Chaney offers a biography which she defines as 'a candid and responsible study' (Chaney 1998: xx).

My research on the African-American jazz artist Billie Holiday has some bearing on the issues Conekin is trying to unravel in her study of Miller (Tulloch 2001). The work is not so much a biography, but a piece which challenges the hagiographic texts published on Billie Holiday, which have left us with the myth of an iconic twentieth-century figure with a great voice, who became a victim of drugs. I wanted to look at her anew through her dress within the context of what Paul Gilroy calls the distinctive counterculture of modernity – black music (Gilroy 1993: 36).

What also intrigued me about Billie Holiday was the creation of herself out of Eleanora Harris (her birth name), and the need to balance the components of her self-construction – the pervasive 'dark' strains of drugs and racism, and the self-defining agencies of dandyism that turned her styled-body into the essence of America's jazz artist 'Billy Holiday'. Of course her engagement with modernity placed her as an outsider due to boundaries such as race, and the traditional place of women as homemakers in American society, a position she fought throughout her adult life in order to create the life *she* desired. This I think applies equally to

Miller, particularly during the 1950s. Although her life was based in the private sphere, Miller was still able to maintain an independent spirit and go against the grain of what was expected of a homemaker. She brought her practice of modernity into the home and onto the dinner table, as *she* desired it to be expressed. Perhaps a way forward for Conekin to attain a biography of Miller that goes beyond 'biography as form' would be to incorporate Miller's own style of dress to this aspect of her life.

References

Chaney L. (1998) *Elizabeth David*. Oxford: Pan Books.

Conekin, B. (2002) 'Modernity, Fashion and the Feminine: The Paradoxes of Lee Miller and the Limits of Biography'. Unpublished paper.

Gilroy, P. (1993) *The Black Atlantic: Modernity and Double Consciousness*. London: Verso.

Landy, R.J. (1993) *Persona and Performance: The Meaning of Role in Drama, Therapy and Everyday Life*. London: Jessica Kingsley Publishers.

Parke, C. (1996) *Biography: Writing Lives*. Boston: Twayne Publishers.

Tulloch, C. (2001) 'All of Me: Billie Holiday'. Unpublished paper.

–3–

People Dress so Badly Nowadays: Fashion and Late Modernity

Andrew Hill

I would like to take as my point of departure some basic observations. First, our historical moment is supposedly one of unprecedented individualism. The individual is purportedly free to make decisions about how they live with a freedom and range of choice not witnessed previously. Concomitantly, questions of individual identity and a reflexivity about these questions have come to be foregrounded in a way not seen in earlier eras.

Second, consumption is conceived as integral to individual identity, again, to an extent not witnessed before. Consumption, then, has come to stand as one of the most significant means through which this sense of contemporary individualism is developed and articulated. Fashion has typically been analysed in terms of its relationship to identity. Fashion has repeatedly been identified as bearing a close relationship to the identity of the wearer. So, as a significant form of individual consumption, and, through the supposed closeness of the relationship between the identity of the wearer and what is worn, what people wear should present a vivid representation of the contemporary individualism of our moment.

We should, then, be living in an age in which the way in which people dress stands as a testament to the individualism celebrated in our era. You can imagine the possibilities this would open up – with individuals using what they wear as a means of exploring and articulating the intricacies and complexities of their identities. We should, then, be living in an era of remarkable sartorial expressiveness, richness and heterogeneity.

Something is wrong though. This doesn't seem to have happened. I was living in London, one of the 'fashion capitals' of the globe – a place where, if anywhere, the relationship between the individualism of the era and clothing should be quite apparent. As I made my way through the city I tried to assess what had happened, and what this might say about clothing and people.

Figure 3.1 The London Underground, November 2003.

I ride the Northern Line from zone three down into the centre, and back again in the evenings. I look at what people are wearing. It is dominated by the same plain, dark colours, cuts and shapes. The clothing can be divided into two basic categories. Many are dressed in what can loosely be labeled as casual wear – that melange of indistinct styles in relation to which it has been said 'Everybody looks like everybody else'(Lipovtesky 1994: 123). Others are dressed in office wear of the type seen everywhere in London and beyond. There is little or nothing that stands out as distinct. The thought occurs to me that you could swap people's clothes around and it would not make much difference to many people – they would look virtually the same.

On the Northern Line, moving in and out of the centre of London, it is hard then to detect the individualism of our era being celebrated in what people wear. And, when I turn to look at the people themselves, to see the wearer, and to try to understand their relationship to their clothing, they look as tired and worn as their clothing does. Their faces and bodies don't seem so redolent of this individualism either.

Figure 3.2 Oxford Street, London, November 2003.

I took a walk along Oxford Street, one of the principal shopping routes in the capital. It was midweek, end of the afternoon, in November. I walked from Centrepoint down to Marble Arch. The pavements were hectic. The crowds of people moved past. Again, the people were dressed in highly similar clothes, with the same preponderance of plain, dark colours, and the same mixture of unremarkable casual wear, and, it seems, almost regulation office wear. They were indistinguishable by their clothing. Few stood out. In fact, thinking now as I write this, I cannot remember a single person in terms of what they were wearing.

'Indistinguishable by their clothing' – this, I realise, is a key phrase. If what people wear is supposed to display the individuality foregrounded in our era, then people should be distinguishable from their clothing. But most people aren't. Imagine piles of clothing made up of what people wear today, and imagine trying to identify people from these piles. It would be very hard. What signs would there be that this pile belonged to a certain person, rather than any other? What would become evident is the lack of attention paid to distinguishing one's clothes from those of other people.

Something else emerged on my trips on the tube and along Oxford Street. It was the role played by the setting in which clothes are worn – how this might shape what people wear and their relationship to their clothing.

The Underground is not a pleasant environment. In the crowded tunnels and tubes, you are pressed up against strangers, with the only other predominant form of stimulation being adverts reminding you what your life lacks. It is the type of environment that pummels one with the demands of endurance and boredom. And people's clothing reflects this. It is not the type of environment that encourages people to dress in a more distinctive or individually spectacular way. The very cities we inhabit refuse to support the type of individualism we are told we should be living out. They work against it. They act against the type of dressing the claims of this individualism should deliver.

Things are at their worst in the rush hour. Being packed, twice a day, onto platforms and trains doesn't prioritise a sense of dressing to display one's self. It militates against display and encourages practicality and contingency. What one wears becomes more about managing and surviving in this environment than individual expression. But it also militates against the other side of this relationship. It disrupts the chance to actually look at and understand what others are wearing.

I think back to the fêted figure of the *flâneur*, invoked as an archetypal observer of urban life, and singularly sensitive to the richness of urban experiences and the people he sees as he wanders the nineteenth-century metropolis – 'botanizing on the asphalt' (Benjamin 1973: 36). I imagine him rammed onto the Underground in the early evening now and wonder how his botanising would proceed under these conditions.

As I walked along Oxford Street I passed by clothes shops – Zara, H&M, Byrite, Selfridges, Next ... piled high with the same things. They are offering something new and the same to everyone. Some of the shops have images of models in the windows, wearing their clothes. You can stop and look at these images, and up there, by themselves, out of time, the clothing and their wearers' look quite distinct.

On the street itself, the people hurried past. The pavements are crowded and there is little time to observe what they are wearing. And, people don't seem too concerned about showing what they are wearing to others anyhow. London isn't designed to do this. It is wet, the streets are dirty, the pavements are too small, the traffic is too close, the other people move you along as they proceed to where they're going. As with the tube, here, the context in which people are wearing their clothes does little to facilitate the relations of display and observation that would be required to understand the connections between what people wear and their identities. The gap between the way in which images in the shop windows operate and the people moving past on the street seems vast.

There is the issue of the weather. The cold and the wet of the November evening seem to limit the desire of the passers-by to put their clothing on display – they scurry past, hunched against the elements, covering themselves up – and they reduce one's desire spend more time observing what is being worn. This may seem a marginal issue, but historically climate has been identified as critical to determining the characters of nations and their people (Barrell 1990). In this weather, who would want to stop and observe for longer? Again there is the contrast between Oxford Street and the images in the shop windows. In the images the weather conditions are always appropriate for whatever is being photographed.

Something is not quite right then. Something doesn't add up. Dress doesn't seem to be functioning as it should. The display of individuality that should be evident hasn't happened. It seems very far away.

I am struck by the sense that what people wear reveals a fault line in the claims made about individuality and the contemporary historical moment. Yes, consumption might be very important to people's identities, but if we look at what people consume to wear there seems to be little sense of this manifesting the promises of individuality and identity associated with our era.

It wasn't only that people were wearing the same thing though. There was something else going on as well. My journeys through London suggested another, perhaps more complex, development – one that couldn't simply be seen. I had come to feel that something had happened to the degree of meaning attached to what people wore. This meaning, the significance of what people wore, had become worn down – the signifying power of clothing had been eroded.

How can this erosion of clothing's signifying power be understood?

Lipovsteky in *The Empire of Fashion* identifies a similar development, suggesting that in the late twentieth century 'clothing no longer arouses the interest or passion it used to elicit' (1994: 120). A critical manifestation of this is, as Lipovetsky indicates, the increased predominance of casual wear – the type of clothing so evident in my jouneys across London. Casual wear is casual precisely because it is perceived as holding little meaning beyond being practical, comfortable, and relaxed.

In turn, the very rise of casual wear can be seen, in part, as deriving from the attitude that it doesn't really matter if people want to dress in a casual way, as what people wear doesn't hold much significance anyhow. People can dress however they want, the rules about dressing are relaxed, because what people wear carries little meaning.

Even the workplace has become susceptible to the desire for casual dressing – with the spread of policies like 'dress-down Fridays' and 'five-day casual'. 'Even' because the workplace and work identities have come to assume an almost sacred significance for many in our era. Work is fundamental to people's sense of who they are and where their lives are going. People are obsessed with what they do at work. In the workplace they find meaning, but increasingly, what they wear there seems to renounce meaning for comfort and informality.

This process of casualisation relates to much more than what people wear. We can see it as a process changing social relations across Western societies. Older hierarchies, rituals, and formalities have been marginalised as people have turned from them to embrace a casual, laissez-faire attitude to sociality that eclipses (and even derides) these older models. With these changes though, the clearly structured and tightly organised patterns of meaning associated with the older models – meanings that were fundamental to the ordering of societies – have diminished. Durkheim identified this version of loss of meaning as an *anomie* afflicting modern societies – a state of normlessness which produces a sense of meaninglessness, directionless and pointlessness (1997: 304–8). If anything goes, does anything really matter? And it is this process that we can identify at work in what people wear nowadays. If people can wear whatever they want, if they can wear whatever they feel comfortable in, then it matters very little what people wear, doesn't it? It doesn't mean anything very much at all. Without norms, without hierarchies, without some central point of reference, there can be little in the way of a system of values or meaning at work in what people wear. And so the meaning of clothing flattens out, it empties, it fades.

Partly, we should also understand this loss of signifying power in terms of Weber's notion of 'entzauberung der welt' – the disenchantment of the world, which he identifies with the development of modernity (Weber 1948: 139). The emphasis placed upon rationality and science in modernity robs the world of its sense of wonder, mystery, strangeness and inexplicability. Everything can be explained away; meaning is not mysterious – it is clear and rational and follows laws. So, the meaning of clothing can be reduced to this type of analysis as well. Garments come to possess little power. They can be said to mean scarcely more than they physically are – physical objects, an arrangement of material – that is all. They lose their symbolic power. Who would want to touch the robes of a monarch now? (Although, which monarch would want to have people touching their robes?)

I was down in Archway. A clown was waiting outside the Co-op. I'd seen posters advertising Zippo's Circus on Hampstead Heath. He was wearing oversized shoes, a green and yellow checked suit, a bright ginger wig and a green bowler hat. He looked absolutely remarkable. He stood out. I've remembered him. Isn't this what is possible? Isn't this a demonstration of how people could dress if they were going to display their individuality?

Sumptuary laws have existed in different forms in diverse societies. Statutes in the Tokugawa period in Japan (1603–1867) set out the fibres that could be worn by each class. In England in 1372 laws were introduced to order 'the outrageous and excessive apparel of divers people against their state and degree' (quoted in Barnard 2002: 78). In France Henry IV passed decrees against the bourgeoisie wearing silk.

No comparable legislation exists today. The very absence of such laws is revealing. Clothing is no longer associated with the type of social hierarchies it once was. And, clothing has lost its signifying power – there's no need for legislation to govern what people wear as it's not important enough to warrant it. It doesn't really matter, or matter in the way that it did, what they wear.

The fact that such laws today seem so strange is indicative of the distance we have come from previous perceptions of the significance of clothing. But imagining the existence of such laws produces some intriguing lines of thought. We can picture such laws transplanted onto contemporary Britain and the discourses, disputes, and challenges this would generate – and the new significance clothing would have.

Money though has, in our moment, become its own sumptuary law of course. Money, rather than formal status or hierarchies, sets the parameters for what people can consume – what clothes they can afford to wear. As is evident with so many other social processes, money, rather than any other set of values and meanings, has come to dominate life. Money comes to replace other sources of meaning. Money is all that matters.

It is to Simmel that we can turn for a conception of 'the blasé attitude' (1964: 413). He locates the development of this attitude as bound up with the centrality of metropolitan experience to modernity. The blasé attitude presents the individual with a means of coping with the incredible diversity of experiences confronting them in the modern metropolis. Under the blasé attitude newness and difference lose their capacity to surprise and provoke interest – they lose their significance then, and the strength of their meaning. The new and the different become not remarkable and interesting, but commonplace, more of the same, and not worthy of attention.

Clothing finds its power to signify eroded by the blasé attitude. We have seen people dressed in many different ways. We may be familiar with the history of fashion. We have seen how the twentieth century is littered with examples of garments and styles that have provoked shock and outrage. We have absorbed this, and now: who cares? We have seen it all before and so what? What did it matter?

It occurred to me that maybe I had been so infected with the blasé attitude that as I made my way through London I could no longer see the richness and distinctiveness of what people wore, and, could not detect what was signified. Perhaps this malaise of the modern metropolis had gone to work on me – and all I was writing was a symptom of this.

I thought about going out to Bluewater, the giant satellite shopping complex just beyond the M25 in Kent. I thought that this would present another good archetype of the locations in which people buy and wear clothes. But I don't have a car, and without one the place is apparently inaccessible. So I had to opt for somewhere that could be reached more easily. I took the 210 bus up to Brent Cross, the first shopping centre to be opened in Britain, in 1976. Bluewater's little old mother.

It was a Sunday morning and the place was full. This was the first shopping centre I had ever come to, and I remembered how when I was a child it seemed on entering it that I was entering a space station. Looking back on this now I think most of all about how this association illustrates the sense of placelessness I experienced there. A space station inhabits no location on earth; it is not rooted in a fixed place. And shopping centres stand as exemplars of the type of 'non-places' which Marc Augé (1995) identifies as endemic in our era. Inside them you could be in almost any other shopping centre in Britain or even the world, and the experience would not be very different. I looked at what the people were wearing, and it seemed to fit with and confirm this sense of placelessness. People would be dressed like this in Cité Europe, in a mall in Los Angeles or Tokyo. In shopping centres across the world our clothes would all look about the same. How then did what the people wear here function as an index of their individuality? Perhaps it was the case that people across the world all felt like distinct individuals in the same way? Maybe, they had the same sense of their own individuality?

Maybe – and the world felt very flat, empty and boring.

Jameson's (1991) famous conception of postmodernity seemed readily applicable to this state of affairs. Clothing has repeatedly been understood as functioning as a system of signs. But what concerned me in Brent Cross was what these signs actually signified – what they referred to, what they were supposed to mean.

My sense of this was similar to Jameson's: nothing much. We have come to inhabit a world filled with 'culture', with its signs proliferating – but where do they lead? What was there to understand about the clothing worn in Brent Cross? Did it have anything to do with the identity of the people there? And, if so, what identities did they have that could be traced in trainers, jeans, and sweatshirts? Perhaps though what people were wearing was indicative of the type of individuals they had become – adrift in a world of consumption, without direction, context and meaning. Perhaps clothing did reveal everything after all.

I am in Waterlow Park, looking at the birds in the bird hospice. There is a golden pheasant who looks quite startling in his plummage, especially his hooded crest. I can't help but draw the contrast between his plummage and the clothes I see humans wearing in the city around me. Nature has given something more spectacular than culture now offers up at this point in history.

Sennett in *The Fall of Public Man* (1993) plots the historic relationship between conceptions of individual identities as displayed in public and what people wear. He draws a telling historical contrast. In mid-eighteenth-century urban society, with its taste for costume and masquerade, people did not dress to represent the truth of who they were. Clothing was not understood as linked to the truth of the self. What people wore was marked by a sense of decoration, artifice, spectacle and display that fitted with the public culture of the era.

As Sennett goes on to discuss, by the 1840s things were very different. The emphasis in dressing was now upon neutrality, on not standing out, on passing unnoticed. The conception of the self, identity and appearances had shifted. What people wore was taken as indicative of the type of person they were. One had to be very careful not to reveal too much, not too give oneself away, not to leave oneself open. This was an era of 'personality created by appearances', where 'appearances ... are guides to the authentic self of the wearer' (Sennett 1993: 153). We are, I think, still living with a version of this idea – that what people wear can tell us something significant about them, that it can reveal their selves to us. And this fear lies behind the pervasive anxieties about what people wear. We may live in an era dominated by casual wear, but many people are still deeply concerned about what they wear, even if it is so often a form of casual wear. This offers an intriguing perspective on the state of the contemporary individual – dressing in a way that signifies very little, but at the same time anxious about what they are wearing.

There is an advert running at the time that I am writing this. It is for Clark's shoes. Various people are going about their everyday tasks – walking along the street, shopping in the supermarket, working in an office. They are moving in a stylised way though, which looks vaguely ridiculous. The tagline is 'Remember – life's one long catwalk'. The advert is, I think, supposed to be ironic. But, it's not simply a joke. If it was it wouldn't make any sense. It plays upon that sense of anxiety about how we dress and our relationship to what we wear that I have just alluded to. We are concerned about looking good and we are afraid about how to do this. But when you look at what people actually wear you wonder why they are concerned at all. The gap between our ideas about how we look and what this says about us, and what most people wear and what clothing can now signify is vast, and this gap is at once tragic and pathetic.

What are we left with then?

It is a strange situation. On the one hand there is the sense that what people wear should represent the individualism celebrated in our era. What people wear should stand as testament to the role consumption is supposed to play in this time of individuality. If we look to what people wear as an index of their individuality in the sense of their difference and distinctiveness as individuals, it appears inadequate.

Then, there is the sense that clothing has lost its power to convey meaning. So, the ability to represent or display one's individuality through what one wears is diminished. Thus, even if people do want to attempt to convey their individuality through what they wear, their capacity to do this is checked.

Clothing, then, in its state of homogeneity and with its lack of ability to signify is perhaps deeply revealing about the contemporary world and the state of the individual.

You will be an individual – distinct, unique, and only yourself – but you will be just like everyone else; you cannot be anything else.

This is the promise of individualism wrecked on the shores of late modernity.

This is individuality as a mirage in the desert of our historical moment.

References

Augé, M. (1995) *Non-places: Introduction to an Anthropology of Super Modernity.* London: Verso.

Barnard, M. (2002) *Fashion as Communication.* London: Routledge.

Barrell, J. (1990) 'Sir Joshua Reynolds and the Englishness of English Art', in H. Bhabha (ed) *Nation and Narration.* London: Routledge.

Benjamin, W. (1973) *Charles Baudelaire: A Lyric Poet in the Era of High Capitalism.* London: New Left Books.

Durkheim, E. (1997) *The Division of Labour in Society.* New York: Free Press.

Jameson, F. (1991) *Postmodernity: The Cultural Logic of Late Capitalism.* London: Verso.

Lipovetsky, G. (1994) *The Empire of Fashion: Dressing Modern Democracy.* Princeton: Princeton University Press.

Sennett, R. (1993) *The Fall of Public Man.* London: Faber and Faber.

Simmel, G. (1964) 'The Metropolis and Mental Life', in K. Wolff (ed.) *The Sociology of Georg Simmel.* New York: Free Press.

Weber, M. (1948) 'Science as a Vocation', in H. Gerth and C. Wright Mills (eds) *From Max Weber: Essays in Sociology.* London: Routledge and Kegan Paul.

Response

Adam Briggs

My response to Andrew Hill's paper is ambivalent – yes and no. Yes, I can appreciate the sense of ennui which results from the apparent flatness of contemporary fashion. No, in that I feel there are three rhetorical straw men in the assumptions which underlie the argument.

First, does the argument regarding identity in late modernity really emphasise individuality to the extent suggested? I would suggest that it does not. Rather than the age of the individual this is often seen as the era of the 'Minimal Self' (Hall 1993) and 'The Time of the Tribes' (Maffesoli 1996).

As I understand them many contemporary arguments regarding identity concern the collapse of social class as a grand narrative of identity providing an umbrella under which differing aspects of our sense of self are stitched together into equivalence between members of a certain class and differences between classes. This is not the same as a radical individualism. It is not the end of collective identity, but, rather, a profusion of the collectivities we look to for the answer to the question 'who am I'? In other words, we have seen a shift from class to the 'familiar mantra' of gender, ethnicity, sexuality, nationality, occupation etc., all of which, it is true, will be articulated together in shifting combinations, and no one of which has a fixed essential nature. Nevertheless, each is based on a sense of social collectivity and can, and clearly does, significantly impact on style choices.

Second, consumption is understood as being integral to identity, with fashion as an exemplar of this. This I entirely agree with. Fashion, particularly within 'fashion studies', is generally analysed in relation to identity and consumption. I would argue that this is problematic, not so much with regard to what is included in this analysis, but with regard to what is omitted – the question of production. While fashion is very much about identity, this is not the entire story, and the understanding, which emerges from the analysis of fashion consumption in these terms, is partial due to the neglect of issues of production and the way in which these are *articulated* with consumption and issues of identity.

Third, we all dress the same: this I find misleading as despite the relative uniformity of modern fashion we do *not* all dress the same. Contemporary fashion is far more heterogeneous than suggested, as two examples illustrate. We no longer have singular seasonal colour trends – the last I can identify being the ubiquity of brown in autumn/winter 1996/97. Subsequently it has been suggested, season after season, that black will become the new black, but this clearly has not occurred. Similarly, take the hemline pluralism which has been with us since the mid 1990s. The new skirt is any length you care to choose – as long as it is in the shops. Despite arguing this I can share a sense of boredom with modern fashion, but I attribute this to the bricolage of fashion history, which currently passes for directionality. We have seen all the new looks before.

This relative heterogeneity does not mean that anything goes. There are norms, and these, admittedly temporally unstable norms, are supplied by fashion as a discourse (those ideas that specify that which is considered to be desirable and appropriate at any point in time). Moreover, radical choice is also constrained by fashion as a 'System of Provision' (Fine and Leopold 1993) determined by production management issues in the manufacture and distribution of the clothing object. Would I be able to dress as Zippo the clown without having to shop in a theatrical costume supplier?

This leads to the suggestion of the diminished signifying power of fashion. This is an argument that has also been explored by Colin Campbell (1997) in his critique of the 'Consumption as Communication Thesis', where he uses what he sees as fashion's diminished signifying power as his central example. I have always felt that this is a brilliant essay which singularly fails in its intent, in that, rather than undermining the idea as clothes as a means of signification, it in fact adds considerable nuance and sophistication to this argument. Campbell suggests that the heterogeneity of contemporary fashion renders it a Tower of Babel with a multitude of clamouring languages being spoken but not being understood by those not speaking the same shared language. The implication of this is that the meaning of individual clothing 'acts' will only be readable in a way recognisable to those wearing a specific ensemble by observers who share the same subcultural capital as the wearer and that this will be heavily context dependent.

Interesting methodological points arise from this. A casual observer in the public realm will not be privy to the context in which these clothes are eventually embedded. Where are the people on the tube going to? Where will the shoppers of Brent Cross and Oxford Street wear the clothes that they are shopping for and who will see them doing so? Maybe the *flâneur*, in order to understand fashion, needs to be less of a disinterested observer wandering at random and more of a peeping tom gazing through quite specific half-drawn curtains. In this sense all fashion is becoming more like traditional menswear in that it is all in the detail. The difference between Armani main line and Emporio may not be readily observable to those outside the specific consumption community that values Armani but can be both seen at a glance and be highly significant to those within it.

So why the sense of sameness? Why the perception of fashion's undercoded weak signification? To answer these questions we need to consider the production of both fashion's objects and its meanings, and, to explore the relationship between these. As already suggested, this sense of sameness is understandable when we study the specific systems of provision by which clothes come to be in our wardrobes. In terms of the object it is necessary to understand that, despite flexible specialisation in clothing manufacture and despite short order and in season sourcing, the design specification of a manufacturer's range still has to be relatively stable in order to be financially viable; market segments of one person are still not economically feasible.

In terms of fashion's meanings, the minimalism and tribalism of our modern subjectivities lead to an active quest for identity. This quest is readily enabled by the lifestyle connotations so carefully constructed in brand identities, the production of which is now as important as the production of the clothes themselves. Brands provide a palate of off the peg identities which we can don and cast off at will. In this way, *if we see fashion branding as a demand management technique functioning in such a way as to produce high aggregate demand*, fashionbrands emerge as a limit to truly radical pluralism in clothing, but also as a highly significatory practice. In this respect it is worth noting that the signification of fashion can be intended for the self and not others; wearing near identical garments from Zara, John Lewis or Browns may speak to the wearers' sense of self in a highly invested manner, but this is unlikely to be observable to the casual observer.

So, as Andrew Hill argues, maybe it all does come down to money, and, in order to understand this, we are going to have to extend our gaze beyond consumption to see how it connects to production. It is important to stress, however, that this should not preclude attention to consumption, and that this is not economic determinism, as I would argue that fashion is a space where industry articulates issues of identity and signification for the purposes of competitive advantage to such a degree that culture and economy become mutually constitutive to the extent of being analytically inseparable.

References

Campbell, C. (1997) 'When the Meaning is not a Message: A Critique of the Consumption as Communication Thesis', in M. Nava et al. (eds) *Buy this Book: Studies in Advertising and Consumption.* London: Routledge.

Fine, B. and E. Leopold (1993) *The World of Consumption.* London: Routledge.

Hall, S. (1993) 'Minimal Selves', in A. Gray and J. McGuigan (eds) *Studying Culture.* London: Edward Arnold.

Maffesoli, M. (1996) *The Time of the Tribes.* London: Sage.

Part II
Performing Bodies

–4–

Court Masques: Tableaux of Modernity in the Early Seventeenth Century?

Andrea Stuart

> Let's have the giddy world turn'd the heeles upward
> And sing a rare blacke Sanctus, on his head,
> Of all things out of order
>
> Ben Jonson, *Time Vindicated*

In this chapter I will explore the court masque, a form of spectacular entertainment that has been somewhat neglected by cultural historians. My aim is to examine the evolution, political significance and above all the aesthetics of this theatrical form which was so significant to the court life of the early modern period. I will argue that, during the Stuart dynasties, the court masque simultaneously managed to be both escapist, ephemeral entertainment and the site for a significant discourse – that explored the challenge of modernity to the notion of the divine right of kings. As much as the Shakespearean theatre, these court entertainments showcased the social concerns of the era, exploring and exorcising subversive social elements.

It is in the detail of these visual extravaganzas that we can see played out the social, sexual, racial and national anxieties of the age. In particular, it is the costumes produced for these masques that most clearly manifest the tension between tradition and modernity, as well as providing a barometer of the era's shifting fashion movements. It is no wonder, then, that the masques became essential to the life of the Renaissance court where 'their allegories gave a higher meaning to the realities of politics and power, and their idealised fictions created heroic roles for the leaders of society' (Orgel 1991: 34).

The masque was, according to Jane Ashelford, one of the most popular of English court entertainments. It had originated in Italy and was first mentioned in England in 1512: 'The kyng with then others were disguised, after the manner in Italie, called a Maske, a thyng not seen afore in Englande' (Ashelford 1988: 122). Masques continued as a stable – if rather stagnant – feature of court life for the next 100 years, until the early decades of the seventeenth century when the form was revitalised by the creative partnership of Inigo Jones and Ben Jonson. Under their guidance 'a deep truth about the monarchy was realized and embodied in action, and the monarchs were revealed in roles that expressed the strongest Renaissance beliefs about the nature of kingship, the obligations and pre-requisites of royalty' (Orgel, 1991: 34).

Historical Context

The backdrop to these aesthetic developments was a swiftly changing society. New ideas about citizenship, constitutional monarchy and the rights of free men were burgeoning: in the years to come they would lead to 'the English revolution' and fuel its counterpart in France. The sixteenth and seventeenth centuries witnessed a great flowering of intellectual thought and scientific development epitomised by the works of thinkers as diverse as Bacon and Descartes, Copernicus and Harvey. Their intense questioning of the givens of the previous centuries provided the bridge and the impetus that moved the medieval towards the modern. They were the product of a society that was concerned as much with witches as with wars, with tradition as much as with transformation. They wrestled with old customs and the New World, with pirates and the plague. They dared to wonder whether sovereignty was decreed by divine right, and how the subject could become a citizen. Questions never before asked needed to be answered; certainties previously assumed where irrevocably shaken. As Descartes and Bacon would have concurred, the entire work of the understanding would have to be commenced afresh.

This new mood of enquiry, this new sense of possibility, are there, implicitly explored, in the dazzling displays that were court masques. These usually took place in the banqueting house at Whitehall, which burnt down on 12 January 1619. It was replaced by a building that has been described as the most substantial architectural project of the early Stuart period. Designed by Inigo Jones, it was eventually completed in 1622. One hundred and ten feet by fifty-five feet, the ballroom was shaped like a double cube and magnificently decorated, with a stage at the lower or northern end of the hall. Since Jones was both the architect of the hall and the orchestrator of the court's masques, it seems likely that his designs were conceived with theatrical staging in mind. Certainly he was adroit at exploiting his newly designed hall as a theatrical space; after it was built his staging and costume design grew more and more elaborate, exploiting the banqueting hall's new layout and enhanced grandeur.

Masques were traditionally performed during the festive season (from Christmas to Twelfth Night). Responsibility for the production of a court masque fell to the master of revels, who in turn delegated tasks to an army of carpenters, painters, embroiderers, tailors, haberdashers and feathermakers, who worked night and day – often for months – to produce their spectaculars.

The result of their labours was an extravaganza of music, dance and performance that often lasted for several hours. Its form was shaped largely by the court context in which it appeared. Since the ladies and gentlemen appearing in the masque had at all times to be mindful of their social status as well as observant of the niceties of court behaviour, certain actions were unacceptable. They could dance, because that was permitted to those of their station, but they could not 'act' – that is, perform speaking parts. These had to be undertaken by professional players. As a result of these protocol challenges, the masque eventually evolved into a two-part performance, divided into a masque and an anti-masque. The latter, which opened the proceedings, was performed by professionals who declaimed from a written script, usually presenting a world of disorder or vice, everything that the ideal world of the courtly masques was to overcome and supercede. Then, when the moment of transformation arrived, 'the dancers in their splendid costumes descended from the stage and moved the heroic fiction into the court itself' (Orgel 1991: 64). The ideal world then merged into that of the real, and, under the gaze of the king, the extravaganza turned into a great ball.

Without Inigo Jones, the splendour of these courtly displays would have been inconceivable. He was England's Renaissance man – an engineer, architect, artist, designer of sets and costumes, antiquary and connoisseur. Though the details of his early life are obscure, he is known to have travelled widely through the Continent: France, Germany and especially Italy. In these early years Jones was primarily a painter, but these sojourns had a profound impact on him; his encounters on the Continent enlarged his sense of the possible, while the architecture and royal spectacles he viewed would influence his future work. On his return to his homeland all the knowledge of modern arts and design that he had acquired was transmitted to the Stuart court; and from the death of Elizabeth through to the civil wars he was the dominant aesthetic force in court life.

Despite his vast achievements in numerous media it was arguably his masques that were Jones's most continuous form of creative expression. Most of these were made in partnership with the writer Ben Jonson. 'If', as the historian Graham Parry writes, 'Inigo Jones set the visual tone for the Stuart Court, Ben Jonson expressed the contemporary morality' (1981: 165). Jonson modelled himself on the likes of Horace, and his plays, poems and epigrams largely eschewed the themes of courtly love that preoccupied writers of the time, in preference to observing and commenting on the society in which he lived. But the pair had profoundly different visions of what the masque meant. Jones modestly declared that 'these shows are nothing else but pictures with light and motion' (Orgel and Strong 1973: 36). But, ever the moralist, Jonson wrote in 1631 that 'all representations, especially those of this nature in court, public spectacles, either have been or ought to be the mirrors of man's life' (Orgel and Strong 1973: 1–2). The energy and commitment they devoted to creating masques suggests that, of the two, Jonson expressed more accurately the depth of emotion and meaning they attached to the masque, and their ambition to make it something more profound than mere spectacle. In an age that believed devoutly in art's ability to persuade and transform, the masque's portraits were more than flattery, but positive images for the ruling caste to live up to. Thus, the court masque as a genre, according to Stephen Orgel, 'is the opposite of satire; it educates by praising, by creating heroic roles for the leaders of society to fill' (1991: 40).

The Evolution of the Masque

The masque was a florid, concoction of pageantry, pantomime and propaganda, but its content, structures and costumes clearly demonstrate the political and cultural concerns of the day. This was evident even in the very first masque that Jones was involved with, *The Masque of Blackness.* This was first performed on Twelfth Night 1605, commissioned by Anne, the Danish consort of James I, who was the key champion of court masques in the Stuart period. Queen Anne wished that she and her ladies could appear as blackamoors, a popular disguise in this decade. This desire was developed by Jonson into a fiction in which the ladies were cast as Ethiopians living by the river Niger, which flows into the Western Ocean. In his story the dark ladies have had a vision which tells them to seek out a land whose name ends in *-tania,* where their complexion shall be 'bleached' and their beauty made ideal. It is explained to them that the prophesy refers to Albion or Britannia, and beyond the reach of the sun that 'leaves that Clymat of the sky/ To comfort of a greater light/ Who formes all beauty with his sight' (Parry 1981: 145).

During these years the colonial race had begun in earnest. Attracted by the financial rewards to be found in the Caribbean, Americas and Orient, British settlers and government were at the forefront of this 'race'. The justification for this is expressed within *The Masque of Blackness*, as it is within other masques of the time. England, as personified by the king, has a special destiny: to civilise the world. 'This best isle' which 'refines All things on which his radiance shines' is England in relation to the colonised New World, as well as the king in relation to his subjects. The king is the 'sunne' who shines virtue and good fortune on his people; his 'scientall light' is the light of knowledge that is cast over his dominion, a mysterious regenerative power that makes a king a supernatural force (Parry 1981: 104). *The Masque of Blackness* therefore explores topical political concerns while simultaneously containing and defusing their radical potential. The conclusion is a conservative message about the nature of kingship, its civilising influence, benevolence and omniscience. This message was driven home by the web of allegory, symbol and myth that were the substance of masques.

The setting of the *Masque* was particularly startling:

> The Masquers were placed in a great conaue shell, like mother of pearle, curiously made to moue on those waters, and rise with the billow; the top thereof was stuck with a cheu'ron of lights, which, indented to the proportion of the shell, strooke a glorious beame vpon them, as they were seated one aboue another: so that they were all seen, but in an extauragant order... These thus presented, the Scene behind, seemed a vast sea (and vunited with this that flowed forth) from the termination or horizon of which (being the leuell of the State, which was placed in the vpper end of the hall) was drawne by the lines of Prospectiue, the whole worke shooting downewards, from the eye; which decorum made it more conspicuous, and caught the eye a farre off with a wandring beauty. To which was addled an obscure and cloudy nightpiece, that made the whole set of. (Parry 1981: 151)

The Masque of Blackness cost something in the region of £3,000, an exorbitant sum in that day. Jones's designs for the stage were utterly new in England. He employed complicated machinery, wonderful lighting effects, and illusionistic settings that he designed according to the rules of perspective. Despite his innovations, which were so much a product of the great engineering and aesthetic advances of the age, the production provoked ambivalent responses. Nicolg Molin, writing to the Doge and Venetian senate, said, 'the masque ... was very beautiful and sumptuous' (Orgel and Strong 1973: 204). But much of the local response was hostile, particularly in relation to the daring of the costumes. These included ladies dressed as 'Daughters of Niger' (fig. 4.1) who wore 'Barbaresque mantells to the leg' revealing diaphanous blue and green patterned robes, with moorish helmets perched on their heads and metallic sandals on their feet. Instead of masks, their faces, arms and legs were painted black.

The final masque of Charles I's reign also simmered with political tension, although its focus was rather closer to home than that of *The Masque of Blackness*. *Salmacida Spolia* was, argued the historian Alison Plowden, author of *Henrietta*

Figure 4.1 *Daughter of Niger*, by Inigo Jones, from *The Masque of Blackness*, 6 January 1605. (The Devonshire Collection, Chatsworth. Reproduced by permission of the Duke of Devonshire and the Chatsworth Settlement Trustees. Photograph: Photographic Survey, Courtauld Institute of Art)

Maria (2001) 'unmistakably political in content' (Plowden 2001: 174). In the last months of 1639, when the masque was being developed, Charles I was under siege both externally and internally. His impotence abroad had been amply demonstrated that September. Rather than honour his undertakings to his Spanish allies, currently being besieged by the Dutch in the Channel, he had decided to offer his support to the highest bidder. Eventually the Dutch lost patience with his game-playing and attacked the Spaniards – leaving the English king appearing both inept and dishonourable.

Domestic political affairs were even more difficult. A deputation of the Scottish parliament had declared that it would resist all attempts to be governed 'by orders and directions from the Council in England' (Plowden 2001: 173). In England, Charles I's intractable problems with his own parliament dragged on. He continued to assert his right to demand funds without being questioned, while the Commons resisted and countered with their own grievances.

It is unsurprising that the opening act of *Salmacida Spolia*, which was performed three times in February 1640, features a terrible tempest, 'as if darkness, confusion and deformity had possesst the world'. Discord, an envious Fury wreathed with serpents, enters the stage and summons other malignant spirits in an attempt to spread chaos in a tranquil realm' (Plowden 2001: 174). These anti-masquers, played by professional actors, are then symbolically chased away by the arrival of 'Secret Wisdom', the king, who – under the name of Philogenes or Lover of his People – tames the threatening storm as he ascends the throne of honour. At the end of the masque the king and queen were serenaded by a chorus from the collected masquers: 'All that are harsh, all that are rude/Are by your harmony subdu'd/Yet so into obedience wrought/As if not forc'd to it, but taught' (Plowden 2001: 175). It was as if Charles hoped that through the sheer power of spectacle and magisterial display he could bring healing to his delinquent subjects.

Costuming

Scholars in the field of theatrical costuming in the early seventeenth century are confronted with substantial challenges. Since the earliest 'surviving dress' of the period only dates from the 1640s, visual evidence for this study is provided by the portraiture of the period and the series of sketches Inigo Jones made for his costumes, very few of which are in colour.

If the plot line of the masques revealed genuine cultural, social and political concerns, the costumes designed by Inigo Jones were equally revealing. As is so often the case in periods of social dislocation, these concerns coalesced around gender differences and representation. 'Dress', according to the cultural historian Jean Howard, 'as a highly regulated semiotic system, became a primary site where the struggle over the mutability of the social order was conducted' (Ferris 1993: 23).

Jones's insistence on designing the costumes as well as the choreography and the sets demonstrated his desire to control every aspect of the visual spectacle as well as the extent of his aesthetic vision. Since the court was the centre of fashion and luxury, and thus even in normal circumstances notoriously extravagant, Jones's first challenge was to create costumes that would substantially trump any of the extraordinary styles that were daily on display.

His influences for these designs were wide. He drew on costume books such as Cesare Vecellio's *Habiti Antichi e Moderni* to give accuracy to foreign or antique dress, and he took care to stress the symbolic appropriateness of costume to character. Jones's use of his sources was quite innovative, however, as we can see in his costume for *The Masque of Blackness*. Whereas Vecellio's representation of an Ethiopian young lady has her wearing a loose striped dress over which there is a looped mantle, Jones uses the mantle but embellishes the underskirt by introducing a rectangular cutaway taken from the costume of an Ethiopian soldier. He also replaces the rather dull hairstyle (tight curls) depicted in Vecellio, borrowing in its stead a headdress that Vecellio had used on a Thessalonian bride.

Since performances usually took place at night, an important consideration for costume design was what would look best in candlelight. Francis Bacon, in his 1594 essay 'Of Masques and Triumphs', gave advice on the choice of colours and trimmings: 'The colours that shew best by candlelight, are white, carnation and a kind of sea-water-greene; and oes, or spangs, as they are of no great cost, so they are of most glory. As for rich embroidery, it is lost, and not discerned' (quoted in Ashelford 1988: 136). This advice still held for theatricals staged during the time of Charles I. Henrietta Maria, who was a moderate spender most of the year, was always extremely extravagant when spending on theatricals, commissioning thousands of yards of satins, gauzes and tinsels. (Some costumes cost as much as £300, the annual turnover of three good-sized manors.) Tinsel, a silk material interwoven with silver or gold, was much used because it was cheaper than cloth of gold. Other sparkling or highly ornamented surfaces were also very popular, such as tassels, silver or gold lace, shiny sequins and beads.

Masque costumes were closely associated with the developments in contemporary dress. The first four decades of the seventeenth century represented a major revolution in the history of fashion, as one would expect of a period of intense social transformation. During these years the artificial gothicism of the late Elizabethan period gave way to the elegant lines of cavalier clothing. Inigo Jones's designs often elaborated on an existing silhouette: for example, his designs for *Tethys' Festival*, a masque staged in January 1610 in the banqueting house, were based on the farthingale, tilted up at the back, allowing the hands to rest on the front of the wheel. Jones's acute antennae picked up the fashions that young people were wearing at court, such as the long loose dresses and looped mantles evident in the *Lords' Masque*, staged in February of 1613 to celebrate the

Figure 4.2 *A Star*, by Inigo Jones, from *The Lords' Masque*, 14 February 1613. Pen and ink and watercolour heightened with gold and silver. (The Devonshire Collection, Chatsworth. Reproduced by permission of the Duke of Devonshire and the Chatsworth Settlement Trustees. Photograph: Photographic Survey, Courtauld Institute of Art)

occasion of the marriage Princess Elizabeth to Frederick, Elector Palatine. In the same production the male masquer's costume 'A Star' (fig. 4.2) has, despite the orange flames erupting from the masquer's head, almost an identical silhouette to the male fashion presented that year in Larkin's portrait of Richard Sackville, third Earl of Dorset. Both feature a large ruff, a tight sloping doublet, narrow sleeves, voluminous trunk hose and garters tied below the knee with stockings visible above (fig. 4.3). At other times Jones anticipated fashion, as in Blackness, where the mantles predicted the coming trend.

But Jones's costumes for these masques were more than the product of aesthetic concerns; they also reflected social concerns. Female immodesty and misbehaviour, for example, were a constant source of worry. As early as 1587, social commentators like William Harrison in *His Description of England* complained bitterly about the decline of modesty and decorum in dress. In 1618 Joseph Hall asked his readers to imagine what their ancestors would think of contemporary women: 'Here is nothing to be seen but a verdingale, yellow ruffe, and a periwig ... a poudered frizle, a painted hide ... breast displayed ... Is this ... flesh and blood ... the shape of woman?' (Ribeiro 1986: 75).

The déshabillé gowns that were fashionable by the 1630s – gowns that were looser and unboned, displaying rounded breasts and bare arms – also caused

Figure 4.3 Richard Sackville, 3rd Earl of Dorset, 1613, by William Larkin (d. 1819). (Kenwood House (Suffolk Collection) © English Heritage Photo Library)

concern. Dudley Carleton, writing to Ralph Winwood about the *Masque of Blackness*, declared

> Their Apparell was rich, but too light and Curtizan-like for such great ones. Instead of Vizzards, their Faces, and Arms up to the Elbows were painted black, which was Disguise sufficient, for they were hard to be known; but it became them nothing so well as their red and white, and you cannot imagine a more ugly Sigt, then a troop of lean cheek'd Moors. (Orgel and Strong 1973: 96).

Cross-dressing, whether on stage or in the street, emerged as another source of concern. By 1620 the new visibility of the cross-dressing woman on the streets and in entertainment had provoked James I to order the priests of London to inveigh against the practice of female transvestitism from the pulpit. In the same year a political tract, *Hic Mulier*, was published cautioning women to 'Remember how your maker made a coat for the man, and a coat for woman ... as the man's coat is for his labour, the women's for her modestie' (Ferris 1993: 23–4). The man who dressed in women's clothes was disturbing because he implied emasculation, evoking the shameful prospect of taking on the women's role in sex. The cross-dressed woman was a monstrous figure, however, popularly associated with sexual profligacy and masculine power.

The intense social and personal unease caused by cross-dressing was explored, and perhaps partly exorcised, in public theatre. Shakespeare's cross-dressing heroines Viola in *Twelfth Night*, Portia in *The Merchant of Venice* and Rosalind in *As You Like It* were joined by productions like Dekker and Middleton's *Roaring Girl*. Inigo Jones also played with these potentially subversive representations in his court masques. In Henrietta Maria's first performance at court, in Racan's *Artenice*, a number of the ladies were disguised – shockingly – as men with beards. This French pastoral drama was innovative in its recreation of time and weather changes: its opening scene was of a village, over which the moon rose through high clouds. The scene then changed into a wood, where there was a storm with thunder and lightning that blotted out the moon. Then the sky cleared and the moon reappeared. When the play was completed a masque was presented in which the pastoral setting was transformed into a mountain on which the masquers were seated. They descended and danced in a theatrical representation of Somerset House.

Though *Artenice* had been performed seven years earlier at the French court, the queen's participation, actually speaking and playing a part, scandalised a substantial portion of British public opinion. Her actions, however seemingly innocuous, jolted a nerve of anxiety that ran through this swiftly changing society. This anxiety was expressed in William Prynne's *Histrio-Mastix, The Player's Scourge*, a publication that ran to over 1,000 pages. In it Prynne railed against all the theatrical innovations – licentious dress, transvestitism, women players- that reflected, for many, the growing degeneracy of English society. He demanded to know how 'any Christian woman' could be 'so more than whoreishly impudent as to act, to speake publiquelie on a Stage (perchaunce in man's apparel and cut haire) in the presence of sundrie men and women'. He lashed out at 'swaggering lasses in strange meretricious lust-inciting apparel' dancing on the stage before swarms of lustful spectators all for the 'fomentation of lechery'. Thundering that 'our play houses resounding always with ... voluptuous melody, profane, lascivious laughter, and immoderate apparell, pricking men on to flagitious lubricity', he asserted that women actors were 'notorious whores'. As for the boys in the plays, it was an abomination that they 'put on women's apparell' since it incited 'unnatural sodomitical uncleanness'. In addition to denouncing all actors, male and female, he also criticised 'effeminate mixed dancing, dicing ... lascivious pictures and lascivious effeminate music and excessive laughter'. His conclusion might even be seen as a call to revolution: 'O let such presidents of impudency, of impiety, be never heard of or suffred among Christians' (Bowles 1975: 135).

An 'Utter-Barrister of Lincoln's Inne', Prynne was the author of a number of pamphlets regarded as offensive to the monarchy but this one was the last straw. Though he would later deny that he was making any reference to the queen, in 1633 he was sent to the Tower and the following year he was fined £5,000, imprisoned for life and stripped of his academic and legal degrees. He was made to stand in the pillory and have both his ears cropped, one at Westminister, the other at Cheapside, while his book was burned under his nose. The extremity of this penalty was a mark, according to historian Roy Strong, of how important the theatre was to the Stuarts.

> In a profound way the theatrical medium was Charles's truest realm. No other English monarch has ever been so intensely concerned with his own iconography, and in the masques and court plays of the 1630s we may observe the royal imagination fashioning, through the art of Inigo Jones as well as Van Dyck and Rubens, a kingdom and a self. (Orgel and Strong 1973: 51)

Conclusion

In this chapter I have speculated about the nature of the court masque and whether this theatrical form in any way reveals the dawning of modernity. My conclusion is essentially an ambivalent one. While some of the plays' themes, the theatrical innovations, costume design and staging (including the appearance of aristocratic women on stage), might provide some sort of harbinger for the future, the overarching message of the masques was ultimately retrogressive; an assertion of traditional beliefs that were already beginning to seem anachronistic.

Sex and gender, kings and colonies: the racial, sexual, social and political anxieties of the Stuart age were hardly unique to that time, but their artistic expression played a particular part in the downfall of the monarchy. Charles I *believed* in art and spectacle: he invested extravagantly in it, infuriating his people and hastening the dawn of the puritan age. Steven Greenblatt has described Charles' almost frantic funding of art and architecture as an 'aesthetic mania' (Greenblatt, 1984: 141). Power is not, after all, simply about the ability to raise taxes and lead armies. It demands and allows the imposition of of a fiction about the inevitability and virtue of the ruler's power over the subject, and that fiction is communicated to a great extent through the arts. Charles' arts – not least his masques – failed to impose his fiction.

Looking back in retrospect, the message of the masques appears almost pathetically over-triumphalist, a desperate last assertion of a disappearing age. The display and defusement, of the changing social order that would destroy monarchical power in both the short and the much longer term provides a fascinating insight into the arrogance and unease of the times.

References

Ashelford, J. (1988) *Dress in the Age of Elizabeth I*. London: Batsford.

Babcock, B.A. (ed.) (1978) *The Reversible World: Symbolic Inversion in Art and Society.* : Ithaca: Cornell University Press.

Blake, R. (1999) *Anthony Van Dyke: A Life 1599–1641*. London: Constable.

Bowles, J. (1975) *Charles the First*. London: Purnell Book Services.

Entwhistle, J. and E. Wilson (eds) (2001) *Body Dressing*. Oxford: Berg.

Ferris, L. (ed.) (1993) *Crossing the Stage: Controversies in Cross dressing*. London: Routledge.

Greenblatt, S. (1984) *Renaissance Self-Fashioning: From More to Shakespeare*. Chicago: University of Chicago Press.

Harris, J., S. Orgel, and R. Strong (1973) *The King's Arcadia – Inigo Jones and the Stuart Court: Quatercentenary exhibition catalogue*. London: Arts Council of Great Britain.

Hartnell, N. (1971) *The Royal Courts of Fashion*. London: Cassell.

Oman, C. (1936) *Henrietta Maria*. London: Hodder & Stoughton.

Orgel, S. (1991) *The Illusion of Power: Political Theatre in the English Renaissance*. Berkeley: University of California Press.

—— and R. Strong (1973) *Inigo Jones: The Theatre of the Stuart Court*. Berkeley: University of California Press.

Parry, G. (1981) *The Golden Age Restor'd: The Culture of the Stuart Court, 1603–42*. Manchester: Manchester University Press.

Plowden, A. (2001) *Henrietta Maria: Charles I's Indomitable Queen*. London: Sutton Publishing.

Ribeiro, A. (1986) *Dress and Morality.* London: Batsford.

Response

Susan North

Was the Stuart court masque a manifestation of modernity in the Renaissance world? Did the costumes designed and created for these spectacles influence contemporary fashions and herald revolutionary styles of non-theatrical dress? The issue of modernity and fashion is often difficult to define when dealing with historical dress. It can mean the appearance of contemporary practices in the past, for example, the origins of industrialisation in tailoring and dressmaking. Modernity can also define that which separates characteristics of contemporary society from those of the past, for example, the eclipse of the aristocracy as leaders of fashion by the elites of popular culture such as football heroes and pop stars. Moreover, the definition of what exactly is meant by 'fashion' in the past, needs to be made clear.

In her excellent book on Italian dress, *Dressing Renaissance Florence*, Carole Collier Frick makes a comment particular to the period of her study but significant to the whole of dress history and contemporary fashion: 'Clothing exist(s) in three distinct realms, which all refer to one another, that is: the clothes themselves, writing about the clothes, and the manufactured image of the clothes' (2002: 147). The actual garments themselves belong to the field of material culture, which relies on the observation of physical characteristics of surviving garments. From such concrete evidence are determined the relationships these objects had with their wearers, makers, observers and the society in general in which they were worn. Any new developments in these empirical qualities of dress occur at a very slow pace; indeed, so subtle are the differences between a pair of nineteenth-century trousers and a contemporary pair that it requires special training to distinguish the two. Yet even at this literally material level, 'the clothes themselves' and the technologies by which they are produced can be associated with modernity. The mechanisation of spinning cotton in the 1770s revolutionised the textile industries, while the introduction of the sewing machine some eighty years later allowed a democratisation of fashion that was to come into fruition in the twentieth century, two developments that are associated with modernity.

Most cultural historians make connections between fashion and modernity in the other two realms that Frick speaks of, writing about dress and images of it. In the former area, developments in advertising and merchandising since the late eighteenth century have revolutionised fashion and the way it is presented and sold to the consumer. In the latter realm, images of dress in the form of photography and moving images have altered fundamentally how we view clothing and how we view ourselves in relation to it. The issue is often confused because aspects of modernity do not always appear in these three perspectives on dress at the same time; for example, the industrialisation of textile manufacture began long before the advent of photography.

The question of modernity and the Stuart masque relies on the first of the definitions mentioned above: seeking foundations of contemporary style or practice in Stuart society, in particular the popular form of private theatre, the masque. From a political perspective, its main purpose was to reinforce the concept of divine right of kings against those of a nascent democracy, a conflict in which the latter would ultimately prevail. Authors on the subject Roy Strong and Stephen Orgel demonstrate that all Stuart masques were an expression of the benevolence of royal power, a fascinating sentiment but not one indicative of modernity. There is certainly a concept of utopia embodied in these performances, but one based on status quo, on a romanticised belief in traditional practices, rather than a revolutionary vision that overthrows all preconceived social tenets. The context of the Stuart masque has been revisited by historians in the collection of essays, titled *The Politics of the Stuart Court Masque*, edited by David Bevington and Peter Holbrook, 1998. They argue that the masques delineate the underlying political tensions of the Stuart court and highlight the complex relationships between the king, members of his family, particularly Queen Anne and Prince Henry, and his courtiers. This revisionist view adds new meaning to the subject, but none of the authors makes reference to modernity, nor do their arguments contradict in any way the absolutist theme of the masque.

While these spectacles were visually splendid, their iconography was based on a romantic ideal of pagan antiquity. Populated with gods and goddesses, sylvans and nymphs dressed in fanciful concoctions simulating 'classical dress', neither the inspiration nor the symbolism could be conceived of as in any way forward looking or progressive. Revisiting antiquity is not always retrogressive; the intellectual foundation of the French Revolution was based on the proto-democratic model of the Roman Republic and those promoting insurgency consciously used the iconography of the antique world as visual propaganda for a Brave New World in late-eighteenth-century France. The resulting fashions inspired by this association caused an abrupt transformation in dress. However, this cannot be argued for the Stuart masque which was supremely exclusive – put on by the members of court strictly for their own amusement. It had very limited influence on early-seventeenth-century society as a whole.

In terms of the history of theatre and entertainment, an argument can be made for the modernity of the masque itself as a form of performance. Certainly the active participation of Queen Anne may count for some advance for women and the stage, although it had no immediate influence and women did not begin to participate fully as actors until the Restoration. The political agenda she put forward through masques such as the *Masque of Queens* and *The Vision of the Twelve Goddesses* might be seen as establishing a new transgressive role for women, but it was only for those privileged to be at court, whose actions have always been treated with greater leniency than those of women in the rest of society and then only within very restrictive confines. More important perhaps than the private and ephemeral performances themselves are the portraits of women in masque costume, which illustrate David Bevington and Peter Holbrook's point about the masque being 'a literary form so devoted to the art of self-fashioning and role playing' (1998: 5). It can be argued that the quasi-classical costumes designed for the court masque and recorded in contemporary portraits were a catalyst for the later seventeenth-century conventions for female portraiture. In her recent book, *Anthony Van Dyck and the Representation of Dress in Seventeenth-Century Portraiture*, Emilie Gordenker argues that the clothing seen in Van Dyck's portraits was far more imaginary and contrived than previously thought. Rather than illustrating fashionable dress, he was portraying a costume constructed between the desires of the subject and aesthetic ambitions of the artist, providing a direct link between the masque portraits of Marcus Gheeraedts and the allegorical nature of Peter Lely's female portraiture. But in such works the garments themselves are not indicative of modernity, but rather a tool by which a radical construction of feminine identity is achieved.

Masque costume had little influence on contemporary fashion (ie: what one wore when *not* having one's portrait painted). The first two decades of seventeenth century dress were really a continuation of the elaborately decorated, stiff and highly constructed fashions of the Elizabethan period. Queen Anne was in fact very conservative in her retention of the farthingale for court dress, long after it had been abandoned in France. The contrastingly soft clothes and smooth silks that begin to make their appearance in the late 1620s were contemporary French fashions, introduced to Britain by the young French princess Henrietta Maria when she married Charles I in 1624. The evidence for modernity in seventeenth-century fashion may lie elsewhere: in the forms of the clothes themselves, their origins, methods of production. In terms of actual garments it rests primarily with the ensemble of coat, waistcoat and breeches worn with shirt adopted for male dress in the 1660s which evolved into the modern suit. In her book *Sex and Suits*, Anne Hollander argues that suits 'express classical modernity, in material design, in politics and in sexuality' (1994: 113). If we accept mass consumerism as a sign of modernity, then the formation of the East India Company and their introduction of exotic textiles and garments to British tastes rank as early beginnings. Authors such as Maxine Berg, Lorna Weatherill and Margaret Spufford have demonstrated that working- and middle-class consumerism, particularly for clothing, can be pushed back a hundred years from the eighteenth century. And the production of ready-to-wear clothing, another mark of modernity, begins in the seventeenth century, as ably established by Beverly Lemire in *Dress, Culture and Commerce*. All of these developments occur in Britain after the Civil War, suggesting that radical political reform was essential before these elements of modernity in dress could emerge. The world represented by the Stuart masque had to be swept away first, making the masque a catalyst for the establishment of modernity (in the sense of representing the old regime in need of destruction) rather than a sign of modernity itself.

References

Berg M. and H. Clifford (eds) (1999) *Consumers and Luxury: Consumer Culture in Europe, 1650–1850*. Manchester: Manchester University Press.

Bevington, D. and P. Holbrook (eds) (1998) *The Politics of the Stuart Court Masque*. Cambridge: Cambridge University Press.

Frick, C.C. (2002) *Dressing Renaissance Florence*. Baltimore: Johns Hopkins University Press.

Gordenker, E.E.S. (2002) *Anthony van Dyck and the Representation of Dress in Seventeenth-Century Portraiture*. Turnhout, Belgium: Brepols.

Hollander, A. (1994) *Sex and Suits*. New York: Knopf.

Lemire, B. (1997) *Dress, Culture and Commerce: The English Clothing Trade before the Factory 1660–1800*. London: Macmillan.

Orgel, S. (1975) *The Illusion of Power: Political Theatre in the English Renaissance*. Berkeley: University of California Press.

Spufford, M. (1984) *The Great Reclothing of Rural England: Petty Chapmen and their Wares in the Seventeenth Century*. London: Hambledon Press.

Strong, R.C. (1984) *Art and Power: Renaissance Festivals 1450–1650*. Bury St. Edmonds: Boydell Press.

Weatherill, L. (1988) *Consumer Behaviour and Material Culture in Britain 1660–1760*. London: Routledge.

–5–

Ambiguous Role Models: Fashion, Modernity and the Victorian Actress

Christopher Breward

In August 1903 the *Globe* newspaper recorded the passing of the old Gaiety Theatre in the Strand; its demolition was a consequence of the rebuilding developments at the Aldwych which were currently rationalising traffic circulation and creating new architectural vistas in the vicinity. The *Globe* reporter noted that

> the Gaiety entered into its final stage of existence yesterday afternoon when Messrs Home & Co., submitted for auction the stage on which so many historic triumphs have been achieved: the gilt erections of the prosceniums, the floors, panelled doors … tons of lead and even the bricks. Only a week ago dresses and other effects used by members of the Gaiety companies were sold under similar conditions, and attracted the bids of a large number of costumiers and others. (Gordon 1903: 213)

The old Gaiety had enjoyed a certain notoriety since the appointment of impresario John Hollingshead as manager in 1868. Under his leadership the theatre attracted attention for providing mildly erotic dance and burlesque revues to a select audience of men-about-town. From 1886 the appeal of its productions was broadened out by innovations introduced under the management of George Edwardes, whose most significant contribution to the business was his reorganisation of the plots and pace of typical Gaiety performances. These were transformed into the hybrid genre of musical comedy, which, while retaining the sexual undertones of the established repertoire, favoured modish contemporary settings and topical storylines that drew in a mixed audience that now included young women, suburban couples and tourists. This new constituency was enticed by the consumerist fantasies of the lavish productions and the attention paid to the comfort of the clientele. When the Gaiety reopened in October 1903, in new premises designed by Ernest Runtz, its unrestrained fittings proclaimed this shift in priorities. Finished in grey Portland stone with strips of green marble, its cupola supported a golden female figure blowing on the trumpet of Variety. She was a version of the famous siren who had always adorned the interior act drop of the theatre in her 'diaphanous clothing … with a girdle round her waist, in the buckle of which shone a real jewel, and in her hand above her head she held a lamp which actually shone and burned, for there was an electric light behind it' (McQueen Pope 1949: 384). But her sphere of influence now extended out from the rather risqué zone of the theatre interior into the bracing exterior world of mass publicity.

I wish to argue in this chapter that the transformation of the Gaiety was echoed by the passing of a largely homosocial and thus compromised conception of fashionable pleasure in the city, for a more inclusive understanding of glamorous leisure which embraced modish dress as a signifier of progress towards a slick and democratic modernity, one in which women figured as a new and proactive audience. In this shift the figure of the actress (symbolised by the trumpet-toting statue of 'Variety') played an important role in creating and promoting appropriately revised forms of sartorial display which substituted a popular rhetoric of 'stylishness' or glamour for the old emphasis on sexual titilation, in much the same way that the pristine Portland stone and green marble of the new Gaiety Theatre erased the memory of faded gilt and tobacco-stained velvet which had characterised its predecessor. Through focusing on the sartorial identities of four actresses whose careers spanned this transitional period, I hope to be able to show how the manipulation of theatrical costume was implicated in a process that presaged twentieth-century conceptions of fashion built around notions of celebrity, spectacle and the beguiling promises of commodity culture.

The theatrical memoirist William McQueen Pope reflected on the old regime of Hollingshead when he characterised the theatre district of the Strand in the 1870s and 1880s as an exclusively masculine domain, where women featured either as helpmeets or passive objects of display. 'The Strand' he stated 'was essentially a man's street ... it was no shopping centre, and such ladies as you might meet there were either escorted by their men folk from lunch at Gatti's, or taking their children to buy toys at the Lowther Arcade... Or if the ladies did not fall into any of these categories, then they were shop assistants out on business ... or most likely of all actresses or music hall performers' (McQueen Pope 1947: 116). Member of Parliament Justin McCarthy paid extravagant homage to the conspicuous, yet strangely unreal, presence of these latter working women when he noted in 1893 that 'the longer one lives in London, the more the Strand comes to be a phantom haunted thoroughfare'. Amongst such spectres he placed the ballet dancer 'with her gauzy petticoats, and her pink legs, and her powdered and rouged face, and her smiles and her suppleness and her general splendour of attire', 'the circus-riding woman in the velvet bodice and the short skirt and the pretty buskins, who stands upright on the horse's back ... with pretty pantings of fatigue and bewitching little shudders of exhaustion ... a vision of youth, beauty and spangles – a plump phantom if ever there could be such a thing of delight' (McCarthy 1893: 55–7).

The plump figure of burlesque actress Kitty Lord demonstrates in a very physical manner the ways in which McQueen Pope and McCarthy's descriptions of a kind of proto-glamour both ceded to and informed the emergence of less controversial yet similarly spectacular models of theatrical fashionability by the first decade of the twentieth century. Little is known about Miss Lord, other than that she played at the major London music halls between 1894 and 1915 and that she worked with household names including Maurice Chevalier and Gladys Cooper. She also appeared in Paris and Naples, where she was described on the bill as 'an American Star', an 'Eccentric Englishwoman' and 'an International Eccentric Star'[1] (eccentricity in this context referred to the solo singing and dancing turn whose dress and posture formed an important focus of the act). At the Ambassadeurs Theatre in Paris, she was included in a twenty-four-scene pageant of fashionable life set in flowered courtyards, the post office, the dressmaker's and the palm house, whose content appealed both to the consumerist aspirations of the women in the audience and the scopophilic concerns of the men. Between the picturesque tableaux, 'les flip flap girls' presented pose plastiques versions of historical and artistic subjects, and the programme for the whole shebang carried prominent advertisements for hat makers, perfumiers, shoes, and women's underwear.

Studio portraits of around 1900 show Kitty Lord wearing the trademark stage costumes that now survive in the Museum of London (fig. 5.1). In these provocative promotional images her spangled tunics fit tightly and are worn over a corset which thrusts her heavy figure into the desired 'S' bend. They ride high and close over the tops of her smoothly padded stockings and her open sleeves similarly draw attention to the exposed skin of her upper arms. In several portraits Miss Lord sports a wide-brimmed and ostrich-feathered hat over loosely dressed hair. Her neck and fingers display ostentatious jewellery and she supports herself regally with a tall cane. The overall effect is opulent, combining the poise of the acrobat with the over-emphatic posturing of the principal boy. These are costumes designed to dazzle and excite, they hint at excess and transgress contemporary ideas of decency and in this they mark out Kitty Lord as a transitional figure. Her style relates to the theatrical genres associated with the old Gaiety, drawn from those traditions of burlesque and pantomime which had been established there since the 1860s; yet her emphatic form of physical address, the confident circulation of her image and her studied artificiality anticipate the concerns of the twentieth-century fashion and entertainment industries.

This deft manipluation of the natural and the artificial had also become a defining concern of those moderns who set the parameters of sartorial and sexual debate in the fin de siècle. One is reminded, for example, of Max Beerbohm's celebrated essay on cosmetics of 1896 (Beerbohm 1896: 97–124). The journalist James Douglas echoed this obsession in 1909 when he referred to the dancers at the Alhambra as

Figure 5.1 Kitty Lord, c. 1900. (Museum of London)

syllables in a visible song... They are the gestures of an artificial femininity. The civilised woman is always artificial, but here her artificiality is multiplied. A woman is natural only when she is alone. She wears the armour of artifice in public, and the aim of the ballet is to generalise her artificiality. It submerges her in a long undulation of fluid femininity... The rouged lips, the painted cheeks, the pencilled eyebrows, the bistred eyes, the blackened eyelashes, the pearl powder, the gaudy skirts, the stretched texture of tights ... the jumble of mimic and real life – all this upsets your centre of levity and plunges you into a brief insanity... You lose sense of your values. You are in topsy-turvy land where beauty is business and business is beauty. (1909: 50–2)

The business of beauty found its ultimate champion in the guise of musical comedy, which had emerged at the Gaiety during the 1890s as the genre which made explicit the escapist potential of London's fashionable scene as a fitting and coherent subject for popular theatre. It ironed out those transgressive contradictions of burlesque, music hall and pantomime which so fascinated commentators like Douglas, drawing on the promotional strengths of each to create a new kind of performance premised on the idea of glamour and stardom. Besides its contemporary settings, its highly controlled delivery, and its tone of light frivolity borrowed from French revues, the most dramatic departure in musical comedy was in its attitude towards costume. As one subsequent memoirist put it 'Tights were banned and Bruton Street frocks and Savile Row coats ... were substituted for the costumes which the wardrobe mistresses or Covent Garden costumiers had run up for earlier Vaudeville players' (Short 1946: 43). George Edwardes staged an early example of the type at the Prince of Wales theatre in October 1892. The production *In Town* was set in theatreland and its reviewer in *The Players* devoted a great deal of print to the description of the wardrobe :

> Some very, very smart frocks are worn by the 'chorus ladies of the Ambiguity Theatre' in the first act, Miss Maud Hobson being well to the fore in the way of style and presence. Her dress ... is quite of the smartest I have seen for some time. The skirt, which is made in a demi-train, lined underneath (and seen only when the wearer moved) with pale pink silk, was composed of a beautiful shade of dove coloured silk – over this was worn a bodice of the richest purple velvet, designed in a new and very quaint manner, the fronts being cut very long so as to form kind of tabs ... Miss Hobson wears with this dress a large spoon shaped bonnet with a black velvet bow... The eyes of many of the female portion of the audience grew large with envy as they watched this creation and its tall and graceful wearer move about the stage. (Mander and Mitchenson 1969: 13)

The review did not stop at a description of stage dress, but went on to note the mantle of a member of the audience 'made of turquoise poult de soie, and lined all through with the same material in a most delicate peach colour'. Such synergy was clearly novel, underlining the claim of another reviewer that the play 'embodies the very essence of the times in which we live' (Mander and Mitchenson 1969: 13). A concern with the fadishness and ephemerality of contemporary fashion arguably left these new comedies vulnerable to accusations of superficiality, but this was perhaps preferable to the older charges of vulgarity which had been levied at burlesque. Indeed, in many ways the frothy subject matter of the plays helped to bracket them with other innovative departures in illustration, commercial advertising and journalism, where a gossipy tone and a wry understanding of contemporary 'trends' signified a sophisticated 'continental' sensibility. The reviewer of *The Gaiety Girl*, which succeeded *In Town* at the Prince of Wales in 1894, grudgingly acknowledged the import of these shared influences:

> This type of musical farce is not an elevating or intellectual art form, but it is at least an improvement on the solemn and stodgy Gaiety burlesque of the old school which it seems to be supplanting. In selecting Mr Dudley Hardy to design the handsome memento which was distributed in the theatre, the management showed a nice sense of appropriateness. Along with French methods of draughtsmanship, the tone of the French comic papers is gradually permeating a large section of English journalism; and A Gaiety Girl is, on the stage, an unmistakable symptom of the same tendency. 'Spiciness' is the distinguishing trait of this class of work. (Archer 1895: 59–60)

That such 'spiciness' might now be evoked through the directed use of contemporary rather than the burlesque costume associated with figures like Kitty Lord, was both a reflection of the growing acceptance of the outré theatrical lifestyles increasingly displayed without fear of censure in the promenades and restaurants of a revitalised West End or the pages of popular magazines, and evidence that the well-oiled machinery of a professionalised and commercially astute entertainment industry could translate such manners onto the stage with easy confidence. When the Gaiety Theatre produced its first musical comedy, *The Shop Girl*, in 1894, the critical reaction focused particularly on its well-regulated glossiness, its manufactured sense of modernity. Commenting on the character of the leading actress the correspondent for *The Theatre* stated that 'one is tempted to forget she is anything more than a lay figure, intended for the exhibition of magnificent costumes. In this respect, however, she merely fulfils the law of her being' (Mander and Mitchenson 1969: 17). An extended description of the production in the *Sketch* further revealed the promotional mechanisms which lay behind the froth:

> The first sensation connected with the performance was one of surprise at the costume. Nineteenth-century dress had succeeded for once the absence of dress peculiar to the century of Gaiety burlesques. On the prompt side the 'stage beauties' were collecting for their entry in such costume as they might wear in the street. What would an old time Gaiety Girl think of such a condition of things, I wonder? With the termination of the first act, the old Gaiety traditions asserted themselves... Soon shapely women, in the traditional Gaiety attire, which was probably originated for summer wear only, came from their dressing rooms... There was a combined sparkle of eyes and diamonds, a frou-frou of scant but delicate drapery, as someone came off singing or went on smiling... From the front, several of the dresses, or suggestions of dresses, looked somewhat daring, but on the stage they appeared quiet enough. There was such a business-like air about the proceedings ... that a Sunday School meeting ... could not have been more free from offence. (Mander and Mitchenson 1969: 18–19)

Historian Peter Bailey (1996: 39–40) locates the musical comedy within those broader regimes of late Victorian modernity which included the routines of the office and the factory production line, the military drills of imperialism and the speculative systems of the financial markets.[2] And whilst it is certainly possible to read the fashionable stage confection as another regulatory device, controlling unruly desires and encouraging unthinking consumption amongst the broadest possible audience, it is necessary to recognise the psychological compensations which the form offered. As Bailey suggests

> within a generation.. London women came to use the greater range of cheap consumer goods in ways that not only followed the promptings of popular fashion and femininity but realised a more independent sense of self. Although a blithely manipulative mode, musical comedy may have stimulated such new imaginative gains for women in a more overtly sexualised identity that was no longer merely hostage to the designs of men. (1996: 55)

The trajectory of sexualised stage presentation that ran from burlesque to *The Shop Girl* lay behind such stimulation and is framed by those changes which saw the Strand mutate from a shady refuge of pornographers, hacks and stage-door johnnies to a brightly shimmering thoroughfare of hotel lobbies, catering companies, theatrical extravaganzas and advertising hoardings. Entirely symbolic of this shift was the figure of the actress herself, about whose body consumers could now weave all manner of aspirational dreams without reproach. As the Italian journalist Mario Borsa noted in 1908: 'The cult of the actor and the actress is a new development – of the nature of Carlyle's "hero-worship". The actor looms large in the public eye; London lies at his feet. His portrait is everywhere – at the photographer's, the bookseller's, on posters, picture postcards, and even on table services and other articles of china' (1908: 7).

Borsa was an astute observer of the London theatrical scene as it evolved in the first decade of the twentieth century. He recognised that the prosperity of the stage, evidenced through a 44 per cent increase in audience figures, an 18 per cent rise in the total number of theatres, and a 45 per cent expansion in the music hall sector over the previous ten years, was testament to a public insatiability for an easily accessible glamour which was peculiarly English in nature. As he stated

> the British public goes to the theatre in search, not of intellectual enjoyment, but of a placid and comprehensive gratification of all the senses. On the stage it expects to behold palatial edifices, gorgeous dresses, spectacular effects; in the auditorium propriety, elegance and comfort. The characteristic English taste for a judicious combination of utility and beauty nowhere reveals itself to greater advantage than at the theatre. (Borsa 1908: 279)

The turn-of-the-century actress perfectly incorporated these properties by virtue of such factors as an emergent star system, which regulated her public image according to prevalent desires; a concurrent cult of the celebrity, which placed her at the centre of popular interest; and the existence of a well-networked garment and retail industry, which bracketed the thespian identity with a sartorial renaissance. In the concluding section of this chapter, a study of three very different actresses, all associated with the Edwardian theatres of the Strand, demonstrates the powerful influence these factors wielded in progressing a style that was closely identified with the culture of London's West End and anticipated the promotional drive of twentieth-century fashion culture.

The chorus of one of the hit songs of George Edwardes's production of *In Town* illustrated well the manner by which this new generation of actresses were fitted up to represent an approximation of popular aspirations for the high life, proclaiming:

> We are the fair Ambiguity Girls
> Worshipped by bankers and brokers and earls
> Gorgeous in genuine diamonds and pearls
> Daintiest mantle and hat!
> Though we are terribly modest and coy
> Nice little lunches we rather enjoy
> Chicken and quails with a glass of 'the Boy'
> Surely there's nothing in that!
> We are so beautiful dancing in tights,
> Mashers adore us for hundreds of nights
> Sending us bracelets and little invites
> Waiting outside on the mat! (Davis 1991: 161)

The actress Constance Collier was the embodiment of this type (fig. 5.2). She graduated from the chorus of the Gaiety Theatre to the giddy heights of classical theatre and was acutely aware both of the ambiguous status enjoyed by the actress promoted solely as an icon of fashionability, and of the highly constructed and transient nature of her professional image. Her career had been launched on the basis of little else. In her autobiography she constantly returned to the idea of the theatre as a chimerical space of transformation in which spectacular scenes of excess could be conjured out of nothing and might also rapidly disappear at the whim of the management. Significantly, her memoirs open with a description of a pantomime transformation scene witnessed during her Bradford childhood:

> It was a blaze of glittering glory. The background went up revealing a gigantic silver oyster shell, out of which stepped the fairy queen... Lovely girls in tights the colour of pickled cabbage posed on water lilies, or moved across the stage; magnificent flowers ... blossomed everywhere; gauzes went up and down and everything moved like a kaleidoscope. Suddenly there he was – My Harlequin! Tip, tap – the oyster shell became

Figure 5.2 Constance Collier, by Bassano, 1897. (National Portrait Gallery)

> a tree . . . A whirl, a twist – down came the sausage shop, sausages and all, and the clown with a poker. The transformation scene was ended in all its glory. (Collier 1929: 3–4)

The fragile contingency of thespian glamour implied by this recollection haunted Collier, whose continuing prosperity was guaranteed by her beauty rather than any contrived pretentions towards serious acting. At the Gaiety between 1893 and 1895 she enjoyed all of the trappings of celebrity which George Edwardes engineered to keep his charges in the public eye. Her wardrobe was provided gratis by 'two famous dressmakers, one in London and one in Paris'. For special occasions the couturier Reville lent mantles and hats, and her throat was dressed by 'a famous jeweller'. All such finery was recorded three times a week by the society photographer Downey, and Collier's image was subsequently used to advertise, in her own words: 'all sorts of ware, and face creams and soaps' (Collier 1929: 60–1). The flimsy foundations of such magnificence were, however, everywhere in evidence and Collier made sympathetic reference to the 'lovely photographs of bygone stars' which decorated her agent's office 'with [their] enormous hips, in tights and swans-down-trimmed boots. Very faded, fly-blown pictures they were'

(Collier 1929: 20). The faded actress was also a permanent feature of the day-to-day life of the theatre and Collier remarked how:

> It is amazing how short is the successful life of the girl who goes just for the glamour and excitement of the stage; how soon for her the outer darkness – the most ghastly life in the world... Gradually her few trumpery possessions go – no more flowers, no more champagne, no more parties... I knew some of those girls who, when their beauty began to fade hid their shabbiness beneath fur coats and jewels; they put all their wealth in the shop window of life and, behind their seeming prosperity, were often very hungry... I knew one of them very well in the old days. I met her once in the Strand. It was summer, and she was wearing a beautiful fur coat which was fastened up rather tight... I asked her if she wasn't very hot... Tears came into her eyes. She opened the coat and showed me a very thin, threadbare little dress. (Collier 1929: 69)

Whilst blatant melodrama clearly played well to Collier's voyeuristic fans, the precarious realities of a profession which had always shared some common ground with the world of prostitution lent a chilling veracity to such morality tales. Collier herself was able to fall back on a repertoire of skills which protected her from sexual compromise or destitution. Though even these hinted at an uncomfortably close engagement with the corrupting world of the demi-monde and an abandonment to Sevengali-like manipulation, both signs of the tendency to compromise which adhered to the figure of the actress in the popular imagination. In her 'resting' periods she modelled for artists including Solomon J. Solomon, Byam Shaw and Charles Conder, and Edwardes had trained her in 'dancing, singing, elocution and fencing, as he did to all his girls who showed promise' (McQueen Pope 1949: 346). Such accomplishments undoubtedly served Collier well in her transition from popular pin-up to celebrated player of the famous tragic roles. Yet her reminiscences betray a continuing faith in the greater currency of the former mode of presentation, which in Collier's day still defined a calling premised on a passive abandonment to regimented display rather than on individual interpretation or notions of personal empowerment:

> Oh how I suffered from the admiration of my friends! I was taken up by all sorts of people, treated as if I were an authority on the difficulties of speech, told that my poses were purely Greek, asked all sorts of questions as to whether I had taken them from Flaxman or the Tanagras; if I had studied in South Kensington or the [British] Museum... I didn't dare say I hadn't the remotest idea... All that I had managed to achieve came naturally. (Collier 1929: 110)

Whilst Collier's self-conscious naivety was a little disingenuous (for this was the period during which dancers such as Isadora Duncan and Loie Fuller were also trading precisely on the idea of a practice of performance that was 'primitive' and intuitive), her attitude is strongly suggestive of prevailing expectations that the actress's public persona was necessarily manufactured and inauthentic. In its very artificiality lay its eroticised fascination and its safely contained sense of spectacular otherness. Against this ideal of mass-produced glamour, and as powerful in its projection of a distinctive mode of theatrical fashionability, was positioned the cultish and perhaps more self-determined figure of the character actress. The pointed lyrics of *The Shop Girl* trumpeted her rising popularity in forthright terms:

> I'm a lady not unknown to fame
> Critics call me by my Christian name
> And you see my photograph on show
> Just wherever you may care to go!
> I've been taken in my dinner gown
> Looking modestly and shyly down
> Or kicking high with petticoats that fly
> The smartest girl in town. (Davis 1991: 162)

Smartness was certainly an apt description for Marie Tempest, who from 1895 had performed the lead roles in Edwardes' comic operas (fig. 5.3). Lauded in 1914 as 'one of the best dressed women in London' her fashionable image was also dependent upon the concept of artificiality, but in Tempest's case this was not in any way imposed by a patriarchal management. An expert in the art of self-promotion, she drew inspiration from the urbane environment in which she worked, and she laboured hard to project a coherent representation of her tastes and prejudices to an appreciative audience. According to one critic 'this of course means that she thoroughly understands her own personality, a highly important thing for an actress' (Dark 1914: 12). In the case of her stage costumes, this attitude meant that she avoided the services of theatrical costumiers, preferring to commission fashionable dressmakers such as Jay's in London and Doucet, Worth and Felix in Paris (Bolitho 1936: 89). The resulting garments, whether made for stage or civilian life, were always distinctive, sometimes problematically so. Tempest recounted several instances when her everyday clothing drew attention from passers-by. Her biographer recorded two anecdotes centred on altercations in Regent Street. In the first

> she was wearing a green velvet dress covered with black lace... The skirt hung over a water-fall, a bird cage contraption then worn, fixed to the bodice. Marie Tempest suddenly felt discomforted and turned to find herself confronted by a man, holding her water-fall in his hand. 'I think that this is yours Miss Tempest' he said. 'Not at all, you have made a mistake' she answered, and walked on. (Bolitho 1936: 92)

Figure 5.3 Marie Tempest, by Bassano, 1887. (National Portrait Gallery)

On the second occasion a prostitute accosted her whilst window shopping and ordered her off her 'beat' on pain of a thrashing with her umbrella. Such stories pitted 'her own fierce individualism ... with her inherent respectability' (Bolitho 1936: 91) and revealed the tensions which lay at the heart of the actress's social predicament. In Tempest's case these were resolved through her skilful understanding of the transgressive power of masquerade and its usefulness as an active career stratagem.

Individualism in dress coupled with a regard for propriety was thus a promotional idea pioneered by Tempest. As she recalled, over the period of her career 'fashion in clothes changed and within the Morris rooms of the day languid ladies reclined, draped in Liberty's robes. They wore slabs of uncut stone in their brooches and their wrists were noisy with slave bangles. I did not wear them' (Bolitho 1936: 90–1). Rather than follow the trend for aesthetic or bohemian dressing that was taken up by so many others in the theatrical community of the 1890s, she favoured a sharper sophistication engineered to play well with her suburban and provincial followers, dressing 'with precision rather than artistic abandon' (Bolitho 1936: 103). The underlying premise of her personal style segued into the sentimental morality, reactionary political outlook and belief in 'keeping up appearances' beloved of her rising lower-middle-class audience, anticipating the concept of conservative modernity that would go on to define popular taste after World War I. Her biographer noted that 'her feelings about clothes are deep and serious. Self respect, courage, duty to others: these are the terms she will use in explaining why she cares so seriously about what she wears' (Bolitho 1936: 103). These were qualities she was able to explore more fully in the designing or acquiring of her stage costumes after her resignation from Edwardes's company to star as Nell Gwynn in *English Nell* which played at the Prince of Wales Theatre in 1900. Nell had become a popular icon of English femininity in the jingoistic years around the turn of the century and Tempest's 'celebrated cart wheel hat of white chiffon, lined with yellow and trimmed with large black and orange plumes' (Bolitho 1936: 150) which she wore in the final act, cemented her own place in the nation's affections.

Tempest's independence as an actress was underlined by her insistence on the personal control of her wardrobe. The early fashion and lifestyle journalist Mrs Aria interviewed her for a 1906 book on the history of costume and uncovered forthright opinions regarding appropriate design:

> To the designer, it seems to me, the actress is merely a note of colour in his general scheme. Only that, and nothing more! I would urge that exactly the same kind of costume cannot possibly be becoming alike to tall majestic women and a little insignificant nay retrousse person like me! ... I always think that a woman ought to have a large share in the designing and arranging of stage dresses, for she can understand what is becoming far better than a man. (Aria 1906: 257–8)

Her own efforts in this direction clearly made the desired impact, for James Douglas writing three years later in 1909 described an electrifying stage presence as visually and sartorially compelling as any succeeding version of stardom produced in the golden age of Hollywood :

> Marie Tempest is the last cry in the comedy of feminine artifice. Eve would stare and gasp at her frocks... Marie Tempest is ineffably artificial and divinely meretricious, from the jaunty hat on her saucy head to the red gold wavelets of her hair; from the naughty ruff round her naughty ears to the tempestuous hang of her tempestuous skirt. She belongs to her clothes... [Marie Tempest] adds a new terror to simplicity... Her polished brightness is inhuman for she has improved nature out of existence... She is an absolute amalgamation of the body and the soul, a miraculous union of all the senses, everything in working order, from the first hair to the last eyelash, a continual effervescing triumph of calculated harmony and sharp design and flawless symmetry. Marie Tempest is a blend of Longchamp and the Rue de la Paix, of Trouville and Monte Carlo, of Dieppe and Dinard. (Douglas 1909: 127)

The Marie Tempest 'look' evidently set a challenge to the insipid prettiness often associated with the Gaiety and its protégés, not least in its consumerist echoes and commercial possibilities. Critics agreed that 'her influence on fashion was astonishing… Her pannier dress, which startled the first night audience of *At the Barn* [1912] appeared a few weeks after in the enclosure at Ascot… She made yellow fashionable… When she wore fur, London wore fur. She was a prophetess in dress and it was a role that pleased her greatly' (Bolitho 1936: 150). However, though 'the shrine of her devotion [had] always been the shopping street' Tempest's interests stopped short at engaging directly with the marketing of fashionable products for profitable ends. Material links with London's fashion and retail sector were initiated instead by her competitor Mary Moore, whose association with various couturiers capitalised fully on the potential for publicity inherent in popular theatre and high fashion (fig. 5.4). Her productions of the late 1890s brought to fruition the expectations which had been raised in the opening chorus of *The Gaiety Girl*, first produced in 1893:

Here come the ladies who dazzle Society
Leaders of etiquette, pinks of propriety,
Creme de la creme of the latest variety
End of the Century girls!
Strictest observers of social formalities
Wearers of modern modistes specialities
Only residing in tip top localities
Flocking where fashion unfurls. (Davis 1991: 159)

Moore's elegant 'drawing room' plays were perhaps easier settings for sartorial experimentation and dissemination, providing a discrete space for display that would have been more difficult to achieve within the operatic scale of the productions associated with Marie Tempest. Her audiences at Wyndham's Theatre which she managed with her husband, Sir Charles, were also wealthier than those who flocked to the Gaiety, offering a remunerative target to those collaborators who wished to market their elite products directly via the stage. Moore's, costumes therefore aimed at a level of magnificence appropriate to Society as opposed to suburban events. She remembered that

> one of my first successful gowns – which was hugely copied – was a black watered silk with sequinned bodice, and soft billowy sleeves of white chiffon and lace. Large sleeves were then all the fashion. I wore this in *The Case of Rebellious Susan* [1894] and it was so becoming I had the gown copied for private wear. One Sunday, when spending an evening at the Metropole Hotel, Brighton, I donned this dress for the first time, only to discover on entering the dining room that there were three other facsimiles of it there already. (Wyndham 1925: 243)

PHILCO SERIES 3375 F
MISS MARY MOORE.
DOVER STREET STUDIOS
IN "THE LIARS"

Figure 5.4 Mary Moore, c.1898. (Theatre Museum)

Moore paid close attention to the dressing of all the productions she was involved with, developing sound business partnerships with various couture houses who shared her belief that the stage provided 'the finest medium for dressmakers to advertise their wares' (Wyndham 1925: 242). Parisian designers including Beer, Deuillet and Lacroix contributed to plays including *The Liars* (1898), *Lady Epping's Lawsuit* (1907) and *The Mollusc* (1908). In the case of the last-named production she even went to the lengths of reupholstering the interior of the Criterion Theatre to match the Nattier blue chiffon velvet of her gown

(Wyndham 1925: 245). Besides providing stage costumes, French companies would also discount items that Moore promised to wear at prestigious events such as appearances at Ascot. The actress recalled that 'for these occasions I generally had two or three dresses sent over from Worth's Paris house, which – as they had my pattern over there – arrived ready to put on, without all the trouble of fitting. How delightful it was to receive such lovely gowns at a special prix d'artiste. In those days one could afford to dress well!' (Wyndham 1925: 247).

Moore generally deferred to Paris as the home of sartorial innovation, but she also famously turned to the risqué London couturier Lucile for the dressing of *The Physician* in 1897. Moore recounted a particular coat 'of black charmeuse, covered with sequins and lined with ermine which showed when she moved' adding that 'I used to go and look at it growing under Madame Lucile's direction, and my only criticism each time was "more sequins", as I wanted the material completely covered, as I had seen it on the French stage' (Wyndham 1925: 242). The relationship between patron and client was clearly uneasy, as in her own reminiscences Lucile complained that

> I had made Mary Moore a dress of coffee coloured lace, embroidered with sequins. It seemed to me to suit her perfectly, but it had long sleeves, which I had not known she particularly disliked. She refused to wear it, said that I was trying to make her look old . . . Fortunately for me Sir Charles Wyndham took my side . . . and she wore it for the first night. She had one of the greatest triumphs of her career, and generously wrote and told me so, completely taking back her previous objections. (Duff Gordon 1932: 48)

Despite such setbacks, Lucile continued to provide dresses for Moore and for other celebrity actresses such as Lily Elsie, Gertie Millar and Irene Vanbrugh (Vanbrugh 1948: 50; Etherington Smith and Pilcher 1986: 55–87, Kaplan and Stowell 1994). Her signature style with its fluid line and floating textures successfully blurred the boundaries between stage and civilian dress, embracing that sense of theatricality which inflected the cultural life of the capital between the turn of the century and 1914. In her own typically immodest words Lucile 'had a message for the women I dressed. I was the first dressmaker to bring joy and romance into clothes, I was a pioneer. I loosed upon a startled London, a London of flannel underclothes . . . a cascade of chiffons, of draperies as lovely as those of Ancient Greece' (Duff Gordon 1932: 65).

This chapter, though supporting Lucile's assessment of London's renewed propensity to accept permissive and pleasurable entertainment as a central component of the city's appeal and cultural clout, locates the underlying causes of that shift in a wider network of influences than the self-promotional efforts of one designer. It was a change which emanated from the 'residual zone' of the theatre – a site, as historian Tracy Davis reminds us, which carries long associations with 'the greater informality of the evening', an informality which 'deliberately confused the mixture of official and unofficial public spaces and behaviours' (Davis 1991: 140–3). Such creative confusion as that promoted by late Victorian and Edwardian theatre offered real imaginative compensations to its audience, especially its new female audience. Borsa correctly identified the hunger of this crowd for novelty and freedom of expression:

> the shopgirls, milliners, dressmakers, typists, stenographers, cashiers … telegraph and telephone girls … who avail themselves of the liberty allowed them by custom, and the coldness of the English masculine temperament, to wander alone at night from one end of London to the other, spending all their money in gadding about, on sixpenny novels, on magazines, and above all on the theatre. (1908: 5)

For them the sequins which adorned Lucile's gowns and had also embellished Kitty Lord's bodices, glittered more brightly than anything produced in Paris or worn by the 'Upper Ten', illuminating the question raised by the chorus of *The New Aladdin* staged at The Gaiety in 1906 and lighting the way for the emergence of a truly modern metropolitan style:

> What's the matter with London?
> That's what we want to know:
> It once was a city you'd hardly call pretty,
> Not very long ago.
> What's the matter with London?
> Everyone's making a fuss,
> For we have just realised
> London's idealised,
> London and all of us. (McQueen Pope 1949: 405)

Constance Collier, Marie Tempest and Mary Moore were members of a generation of English actresses who refined a theatrical rhetoric of excess and artificiality formerly reserved for a small coterie of 'stage door johnnies' (and epitomised by the stage costume of Kitty Lord), bringing it to the attention of this mass, and by 1900, largely feminised audience. Utilising Stallybrass and White's influential conception of the 'low other' as a progressive force, I would thus argue that the actresses' vibrant mode of sartorial communication is thereby revealed as a formation commonly 'despised and denied at the level of political organisation and social being whilst it is instrumentally constitutive of the shared imaginary repertoires of the dominant culture' (Stallybrass and White 1986: 45). Such a reading certainly helps to explain the gradual incorporation of burlesque elements into the theatrical mainstream during the 1890s. It also supports a decoding of the opposite flow, whereby the very looseness and seeming 'irrationality' of Kitty

Lord and the old Gaiety's dramatic construction allowed it to scatter its wit across a wide field of contemporary fashions, informing the appearance and mores of its newly expanded audience in unprecedented ways. Therein lies the modernity of the twentieth-century fashion system.

Notes

1. Costumes, photographic portraits and ephemera relating to Kitty Lord are held at the Museum of London.
2. See also Rappaport 2000.

References

Archer, W. (1895) *The Theatrical World of 1894*. London: Walter Scott.

Aria. (1906) *Costume: Fanciful, Historical and Theatrical*. London: Macmillan.

Bailey, P. (1996) 'Naughty but Nice: Musical Comedy and the Rhetoric of the Girl 1892–1914', in M. Booth and J. Kaplan (eds) *The Edwardian Theatre: Essays in Performance and the Stage*. Cambridge: Cambridge University Press.

Beerbohm, M. (1896) *The Works of Max Beerbohm*. London: John Lane.

Bolitho, H. (1936) *Marie Tempest*. London: Cobden Sanderson.

Borsa, M. (1908) *The English Stage of Today*. London: John Lane.

Collier, C. (1929) *Harlequinade: The Story of my Life*. London: John Lane.

Dark, S. (1914) *The Marie Tempest Birthday Book*. London: Stanley Paul.

Davis, T. (1991) *Actresses as Working Women: Their Social Identity in Victorian Culture*. London: Routledge.

Douglas, J. (1909) *Adventures in London*. London: Cassell.

Duff Gordon, Lady (1932) *Discretions and Indiscretions*. London: Jarrolds.

Etherington Smith, M. and J. Pilcher (1986), *The It Girls*. London: Hamish Hamilton.

Gordon, C. (1903) *Old Time Aldwych, The Kingsway and Neighbourhood*. London: T. Fisher Unwin.

Kaplan, J. and S. Stowell (1994) *Theatre and Fashion: Oscar Wilde to the Suffragettes*. Cambridge: Cambridge University Press.

Light, A. (1991) *Forever England: Femininity, Literature and Conservatism Between the Wars*. London: Routledge.

Mander, R. and J. Mitchenson (1969) *Musical Comedy: A Story in Pictures*. London: Peter Davies.

McCarthy, J. (1893) *Charing Cross to St Paul's*. London: Seeley & Co.
McQueen Pope, W. (1947) *Carriages at Eleven: The Story of the Edwardian Theatre*. London: Hutchinson.
—— (1949) *Gaiety: Theatre of Enchantment*. London: W.H. Allen.
Rappaport, E. (2000) *Shopping for Pleasure: Women and the Making of London's West End*. Princeton: Princeton University Press.
Short, E. (1946) *Fifty Years of Vaudeville*. London: Eyre & Spottiswoode.
Stallybrass, P. and A. White (1986) *The Politics and Poetics of Transgression*. London: Methuen.
Vanbrugh, I. (1948) *To Tell My Story*. London: Hutchinson.
Wyndham, Lady (1925) *Charles Wyndham and Mary Moore*. London: Private Printing.

Response

Lynda Nead

I want to start by thanking Chris for his paper. The richness and diversity of his archival sources – drawn from theatrical memoirs; fashion journals; histories of London and so on – make it a particularly vivid piece of cultural history which bears important insights for historians of modernity as well as historians of dress.

The points and questions which I want to raise have been partly stimulated by Chris's reading of those sources and also by the general premise of the symposium at which this response was originally presented: 'to test the definitions of modernity and to examine the role, importance and meaning of fashion in relations to these definitions'. In this sense, the central issue is one of the *relationship* between fashion and modernity and how their histories might mutually elaborate each other.

My points are made under three large, general headings, although I shall attempt to elaborate with specific instances. The headings are (1) 'London, Modernity and the Strand'; (2) 'Stage to Street – Fashion and Dissemination'; and (3) 'Class and Gender'.

London, Modernity and the Strand

The geographical setting for Chris's paper is the Strand, in central London.

Chris describes the Strand as a site of flux: 'a point of transit between places, roles and attitudes'. The point I want to raise here is about the specificity of the Strand within London's modernity at the turn of the century. Certainly, I would agree that the Strand has a long and complex history within the metropolis and that it carried its past reputation with it into the twentieth century. Topographically, it also had a particular role as the main route across London from west to east; it linked Whitehall and Westminster with the economic and political fortress of the City of London. In between, it hosted wealthy housing; retailing; publishing; theatres; and slums. To this extent, then, the Strand was particular and distinctive. But its heterogeneity and ambiguity and its focus on the business of pleasure were qualities which the Strand shared with other sites and locations within the metropolis in this period (for instance, Piccadilly or Queensway). Chris describes the Strand as a 'residual zone'. Now I'm not quite certain what is meant by this term, but if it is to do with the peculiar nature of the Strand's past within its present, then I would say that this was the distinctive quality of London's modernity generally.

My point is, then, that urban historians need to work with a nuanced definition of modernity. The working definition offered by the symposium was 'the development of consumer culture in the wake of industrialisation'. As far as it goes, this is a useful working definition. But really to unpick the relationship of fashion and modernity in London at the end of the nineteenth century, it is helpful to be more precise. London's modernity was unlike that of Paris, or Berlin or New York. London was a huge, imperial metropolis, with a complex and unwieldy local government. The fashioning of modernity came in fits and starts and for most writers on London in the early twentieth century, Dickens still provided the paradigmatic image of the city. Heritage was part of the emerging metropolitan modernity both in the Strand and in London generally. The story of the Strand needs to be written, then, within this model of London's modernity as an ongoing and diverse process. We also need to be aware in writing these micro-histories of specific places and spaces of what they are made to represent within bigger histories. Are they, indeed, representative? Are they typical of some larger process, or do they deviate from broader patterns and modes of representation?

Stage to Street – Fashion and Dissemination

Chris's paper examines the relationship between fashion and modernity as it was played out in the late-Victorian and Edwardian theatres of the Strand. He traces the evolution of popular theatre in this period from the burlesque pantomime of the 1870s (embodied in the figure and costumes of Kitty Lord) through to its refashioning in the 1890s as musical comedy (figured in the very different images of Lydia Thompson and eventually of Marie Tempest). Although this is described as a linear development, we must assume that both of these genres would have been produced on British stages during this period and that they represent (to use Raymond Williams's terms) residual and emergent forms, rather than a sequence of one form replacing the other entirely.

Chris sketches the economic and social background to this historical development, referring to the theatrical managers and entrepreneurs who were keenly tuned to the public demand for novelty and spectacle. Women played a central role in this history; on stage their dress and appearance and mode of presentation were key to the public attraction of the theatre in this period. Critically, the shift in female presentation was from a form of fantastic pantomimic costume, quite divorced from the possibilities of everyday public life, to a style of modern fashionable dressing which had strong connections to current definitions of elite modishness. In this way, theatrical style was able to cross the boundary from stage to street and to play a formative role in the fashioning of modern femininity. The actresses in musical comedy were figures of glamour and stardom, icons of fashionability, and in their stories we see the emergence of our modern conception of celebrity. And yet, I am skeptical whether this process could have occurred if it was only happening on the stage. How were these new images of fashionable, cosmopolitan femininity disseminated and popularised?

I would suggest that another history has to be woven into Chris's history of fashion and leisure, and that is the history of photography and the growth of the modern press. By 1900, daily and Sunday newspapers were routinely using photography to illustrate their stories; circulations were growing and the *Daily Mirror* hit the magic figure of one million readers. On the pages of the tabloid newspapers fashion was displayed and celebrity created. Here, I would suggest, the styles of the stage went beyond the limited numbers of the auditorium and hit the street. Photography provides the transitional medium between the stage and the later medium of the cinema through which fashion and celebrity were apotheosised.

Class and Gender

Reading Chris's paper, at times it seemed to me that the Strand was actually a blank canvas, on to which various writers could project their particular, preferred version of the metropolis. On the one hand, it was regarded by one theatrical memoirist as 'a man's street', providing what Chris describes as an 'untamed pleasure zone', but the sources make it equally clear that women moved through this space for a wide range of leisure and work purposes. How did female fashionability mutate across different class identities? Chris gives the fantastic example of a gown designed for a Mary Moore production at Wyndham's Theatre. Moore became attached to the dress and decided to wear it for private occasions, but her stage look spread quickly and on its first outing three women were already wearing copies. Here is indisputable evidence of Chris's case that the stage provided the prototypes for new forms of cosmopolitan fashionability, but what about the other classes of women who may have been in the audiences and who were certainly amongst the crowds of the Strand?

At the end of his paper, Chris quotes a source from 1908 which describes the female audience for turn-of-the-century theatre; it includes: 'showgirls, milliners, dressmakers, typists, stenographers, cashiers ... telegraph and telephone girls ...' This is not simply a list of female types, it is a catalogue of the most up-to-date jobs for women. It is in these women, I would argue, rather than in the elite leisured classes, that one recognises a new turn in London's modernity. The telephonists and stenographers go out together in London, have money to spend on plays and magazines, and move fashionability into a new mass market.

References

Mort, F. and L. Nead (eds) (1999) 'Sexual Geographies', Special issue of *New Formations*, 37, Spring.

Nead, L. (2000) *Victorian Babylon: People, Streets and Images in Nineteenth-Century London*, London and New Haven: Yale University Press.

Williams, R. (1977) *Marxism and Literature*. Oxford: Oxford University Press.

–6–

Multiple, Movement, Model, Mode: The Mannequin Parade 1900–1929

Caroline Evans

Mannequin parades

In the first three decades of the twentieth century the fashion model – or mannequin – was a cipher for many of the commercial, cultural and national tensions in early-twentieth-century modernity: between creativity and business, between French and American cultural and commercial identities, and between elite consumption and mass production. The mannequin embodied all these contradictions, and more. An ambiguous figure who simultaneously evoked both awe and disapproval, she disconcerted contemporary critics by parading fashionable dress for money rather than for its own sake. Taking her name from the nineteenth-century lay figure that she came to replace in the dressmaker's salon, her status hovered uneasily between that of a subject and an object, animate and inanimate, live woman and dummy. Her representation oscillated between these poles, even within the same publication, where she might be represented on one page as an elegant and glamorous figure (fig. 6.1) and on another as a static, dressmaker's dummy, the foil to the couturier's artistry (fig. 6.2). If, as Jennifer Craik argues, the fashion model is 'the technological body of the Western consumer' (1994: 76), hers is a body freighted with contradiction. For although the fashion show was a pivotal part of fashion marketing and consumption, the image of the mannequin was also – as this chapter will seek to show – a symbolic representation of the processes of modern industrial production.

Charles Frederick Worth is generally credited with the innovation of showing his designs on live women, or mannequins, from the 1850s, both to individual clients and to trade buyers in his Paris salon. However, it was to be another fifty years before this custom mutated into the fashion show proper, or mannequin parade as it was termed. The very first mannequin parades may have occurred in the late 1890s in London, but little is known about them as they are scarcely documented.[1] Above all, they were pioneered by the English dressmaker Lucile from about 1897. By the time she opened in New York (1910) and Paris (1911) the practice had preceded her and, despite her claims to innovation, during the

Figure 6.1 The Paris mannequin as a glamorous and fashionable figure, 1910, from Roger-Milès 1910. (Musée de la Mode de la Ville de Paris)

first decade of the new century, mannequin parades became a regular feature not only of Lucile's London salon but, equally, of both American stores and French fashion houses.

In the US, mannequin parades were staged from 1903 in the department stores of Philadelphia, New York and other large American cities where they were generally accompanied by music and lighting effects, and sometimes staged on a specially constructed ramp or stage (Leach 1993). In Europe, they developed in tandem; in 1903 the French magazine *Femina* featured a photograph of mannequins modelling to clients in the salon of 'un grand couturier Parisien' which, judging from the décor, could be either Doucet or, more likely, Worth. As the decade progressed, mannequin parades became an institution in the high-ceiling first-floor salons of the rue de la Paix couture houses. The mannequins tended to walk sedately and the silence would occasionally be broken by either the mannequin or the *vendeuse* saying the name of the gown; there was no applause. In both continents, mannequin parades rapidly became, as they remain today, one of the most significant marketing and promotional tools of the business.

Figure 6.2 The couturier Redfern fitting a gown on a mannequin, 1910, from Roger-Milès 1910. This and the previous illustration are from the same publication, and the differing treatments of the mannequin show how equivocal and sometimes contradictory her representation could be in the early twentieth century. (Musée de la Mode de la Ville de Paris)

Their origins lay in new forms of light theatre that developed in Paris and London in the 1890s. These were plays whose meagre plots – some even set in couture houses – were thinly disguised vehicles for the display of luxury fashion (Kaplan and Stowell 1994; Sanderson 1984). *Era* noted in 1912 that 'it is behind the footlights that the new fashions make their début on both sides of the Channel' (*Era*, 1912). French couturiers such as Paquin depended on the publicity generated by these popular plays in which they had dressed the leading actresses. Just like the contemporary fashion show, with its dramatic showpieces that never actually go into production, in the late nineteenth century dressmakers' extravagant designs for the stage generated the publicity and prestige necessary for the real business of the house, the sale of less extreme everyday fashions to individual clients and trade buyers. For couturiers already designing for the theatre, such as Lucile and Paquin, it was but a short step to staging their own parades; indeed, Lucile had designed for the London stage in the 1890s before initiating her own shows and, twenty years later, returned to her theatrical origins by designing for the Zeigfeld Follies in New York. However, the mannequin parade did not put an end to the fashion play. Paquin continued to dress actresses for the stage at the same time as pioneering new ways of showing fashion in her salon. Even after the inauguration of mannequin parades, new fashions continued to be launched from the stage until well into the 1920s, the couture houses budgeting for them under their advertising budgets (Wilson 1925: 56).

Multiple

Although the fashion show developed out of late-nineteenth-century theatre in both France and Britain, and had a close relation to review in the US, its development is almost exactly paralleled, in time, with the rise of the cinema as a form of popular entertainment in a period in which the interaction of new technology and culture, in the form of the phonograph, cinematograph and telephone, had profound consequences for the perception of space and time (Kern 1983). The visual effect of the early mannequin parade replicated not only the effects of cinema but also those of its nineteenth-century precursors, from early-nineteenth-century optical toys to the chronophotography from the 1880s of Edweard Muybridge in the US and Etienne Marey in France. Muybridge's series of images of women dressing, undressing or arranging their costume (fig. 6.3), and Marey's 'man in black' with his arms and legs outlined in white strips, are the forerunners of the freeze-frame image of the mannequin on parade, as much as they are of the film still. Frame by frame, the film is a sequence of identical bodies, like the fashion show, although there are few pictures of the earliest fashion shows that began to be staged around the turn of the century in Paris, London and the big American cities. With the advent of cinema, the image of the mannequin on parade begins to converge stereoscopically with the human figure in the film still, even more so when, for instance, the early pioneer George Méliès used ballet girls from the Châtelet and acrobats from the Folies Bergères in his 1902 film *Voyage dans la Lune*, due to the reluctance of 'serious' theatre actors to appear in the new medium. Méliès's actresses relate, in turn, to the emerging figure of the chorus girl on stage, a single figure who lost her individuality when placed in a line of identically dressed and dancing girls, whose military formation created the same visual effect of identical bodies multiplied to infinity of both the freeze-frame film still and the earliest optical toys from the nineteenth century.

The new visual technologies (film and its precursors) did two things: they showed bodies in movement, and when slowed down they replicated a single body into many bodies so they looked mass-produced. Fashion comes out of visual culture and ways of seeing; and, as ways of seeing become mechanised, people begin to

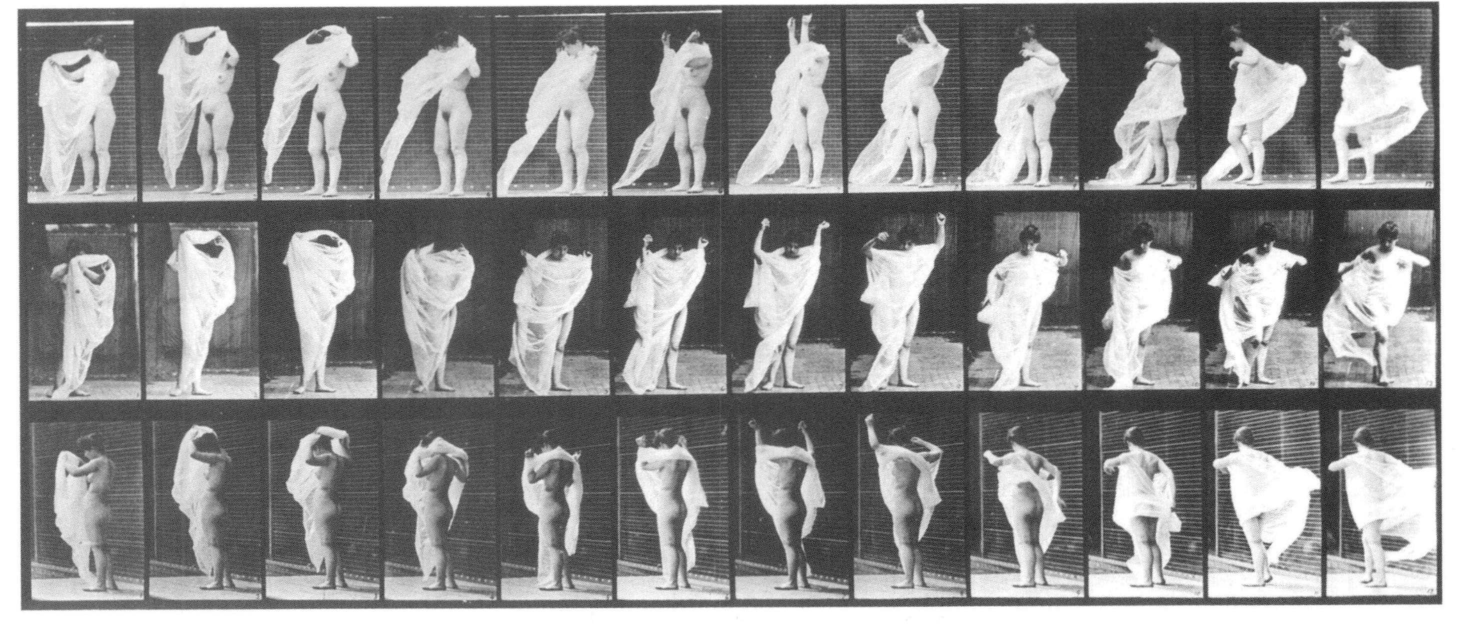

Figure 6.3 *Woman Dressing*, by Eadward Muybridge, first published in *Animal Locomotion*, 1887. (From the Collections of the University of Pennsylvania Archives)

'see' or look differently, as Jonathan Crary (1990) has argued in relation to optical toys in the nineteenth century. Fashion harnessed these new technologies and ways of seeing commercially, and the audience accepted them. It is the cinematic 'freeze frame' effect of the early-twentieth-century fashion show, rather than the show's historical origins in nineteenth-century theatre, that reveals the modernity of the mannequin whose image is everywhere doubled. Indeed, from the 1860s, Worth's mannequins were known as *sosies*, or doubles, before they became known as 'mannequins'. As the practice became widespread at the beginning of the twentieth century, a number of conventions in couture houses had the effect of making mannequins look identical. Until about 1907 all mannequins wore a uniform black satin sheath from neck to wrists under every gown they modelled, to distinguish them from the client to whom they were nevertheless frequently compared, her double in terms of chic, although her inverse in terms of status and position. The mannequin was liable to be put on a diet by the couturier (Henriot 1913: 113; Roubade 1928: 27). Her body was replicated in the commercial and social spaces of the city: she mirrored the inanimate dummies of the shop window, with whom she was often paired, and she herself was frequently duplicated in the mirrors of the salon where she worked (fig. 6.4). Once beyond the confines of

Figure 6.4 House mannequin photographed with dual reflection in the mirror. From Roger-Milès 1910. (Musée de la Mode de la Ville de Paris)

Figure 6.5 Paul Poiret and his mannequins in their touring uniforms, Denmark, 1925. (Musée de la Mode de la Ville de Paris)

the salon, she would be identically dressed with other mannequins for outings to the Paris races, or promotional tours of foreign countries. Figure 6.5 shows Paul Poiret's mannequins in their touring uniform in 1925. For his first tour in 1911 he dressed his mannequins in a travelling uniform of blue serge and beige plaid with oilcloth hats embroidered with a 'P'. According to Poiret, the effect was 'extremely chic' (1931: 117).

The mannequin models the 'model dress', that is, the original or prototype, but she herself is endlessly duplicated through the salon techniques of mirroring, uniforming, costuming and lighting. Her image thus incarnates the contradiction at the heart of couture. In her presentation as a 'multiple' or 'double' rather than original, she can be seen as a walking emblem of the dilemma of the pre-war couture house that Nancy Troy has identified in her discussion of the 'problem' of the original as opposed to the multiple. Troy's (2003) book investigates the way that early-twentieth-century French couture was plagued by the same ambivalent concerns about the status of the original and the copy as the world of art in relation to Poiret.

The mannequin revealed the visual patterns of the new technologies of seeing, and made them formal; in so doing, she revealed these visual patterns to be also commercial patterns. In the second half of the nineteenth century the Parisian couture house had become increasingly bureaucratised along Taylorist lines, even before the Taylor system was published in France, setting in place types of bureaucratic organisation that were to persist well into the twentieth century. By the 1910s, Taylorism as a principle was well established in France, partly through its enthusiastic promotion by the pneumatic tyre manufacturer Edouvard Michelin, and journalists often cited it in their descriptions of the couture house (for example, *Illustration,* November 1910; Roubade 1928). Behind the scenes, there was strict division of labour that not only facilitated production but also, more importantly, militated against staff piracy. Few employees moved between rooms and luncheon was provided in three to five separate sittings on the premises, so that staff could return to work within the half hour and had no need to leave the premises. Apart from the privileged *premières*, *vendeuses* and the *couturiers* themselves, only the mannequins were permitted to move between their *cabine* backstage, where they gossiped and chatted, and the salon front of house, where they modelled gowns on demand for the customers in a leisurely parade that belied the backstage frenzy and bustle of the house.

The invisible line between backstage and front of house was an important boundary symbolically, and mannequins were in a privileged position to cross it. As they did so, they embodied the contradiction between the one-off and the multiple. Strikingly individual, they nevertheless constituted a visualisation of the Taylorist style of organisation of the house, in which the movement of all the human parts was rationalised in the interests of efficiency and economy. As in the chorus line, individuality was renounced in favour of military precision. Just as the calibrated and standardised movements of the Taylorist worker make him a mere cog in the scientific management of the workplace, so the repetitive and stylised gestures of the fashion mannequin incorporated her as a living part of the machinery of the Parisian couture house, a huge, co-ordinated mansion of regulated and divided labour. For just as her body was endlessly duplicated, so too were her gestures repeated mechanically like the moving figures of early-nineteenth-century optical toys that swelled and pulsed in endless loops. Contemporary descriptions marvel at the repetitive nature of her gestures, and ponder the difficulties of modelling the same ten dresses ten times a day to ten different clients, each time as if it were the first. They worry that the mannequin is 'an object' (Alexandre 1902: 13) that the saleswoman has an 'industrial smile' (Roger-Milès 1910: 134) and the couture house is like a huge, well-oiled machine or Taylorist factory *de luxe* with the mannequin as its front-of-house emblem.

Movement

The replication of her body invokes the freeze-frame effect of early cinema and the chorus line. But against this formalised image of the mannequin as a multiple, is another one, of the mannequin in fluid motion, once the film is allowed to run. If movement is a trope of modernity from the beginning of the century, the mannequin's movements too are of note to her contemporaries. There was, from the early twentieth century, what was perceived by contemporaries as both a need and a desire to see clothing in motion. The period in which the fashion show developed was also the period in which Henri Bergson lectured at the *College de France* in 1900 on the 'Cinematographic Mechanism of Thought', Henri Lartigue photographed a car roaring out of the picture frame at top speed in the 1910 Grand Prix, and Robert Delaunay's 'simultaneous Orphism' produced an image of the Eiffel Tower that seems to shimmer and pulsate on the canvas (1913). These French examples, like the Italian futurist Giacomo Balla's paintings, are an index of how motion, with its concomitant relation to time and speed, seemed to capture the essence of contemporary life. The modernist fascination with speed and motion is a symptom of the same drive that produced the fashion show, an imperative not so much to represent modernity as to materialise it.

Anne Hollander argues that by the second decade of the century 'camera vision had become assimilated ... consistently bootlegged into visual consciousness' by fashion illustrators who copied photographs without acknowledging their sources. The camera caught 'the blur of chic – the dash, the vivid, abstract shapes, a face, body and clothes ... as a mysterious ... mobile unit'. And the increasingly haphazard visual styles of society painters such as Boldoni and of fashion illustration itself mimicked the immediacy of the camera. 'The quick impression, the captured instant, was the new test of elegance' (Hollander 1980: 330–2). The fashion industry rapidly took up the new medium of film too. As well as using chorus girls in his narrative films, Méliès made the first fashion film commercials in 1900, including two for Mystère corsets and Delion hats respectively, that were projected in the street outside his cinematographic theatre (Robinson 1993: 45). From 1910, Pathé newsreels, syndicated and shown in cinema theatres around the world to a mass audience, regularly featured Parisian 'dress parades'. Paul Poiret made his own film in 1910 of his mannequins parading. Early feature films like *Irene* (1914) testify to a contemporary fascination with the figure of the mannequin as career girl and the spectacle of the parade itself.

From the earliest parades, the movement of the mannequin was interesting to contemporaries. Lucile, who took four of her London mannequins to Paris in 1911 where they tangoed before the clients, had trained them in carriage and deportment, before teaching them to strike haughty and dramatic poses on stage. In 1913 a French journalist described the perpetual dance of the mannequin who moved as if to a tango rhythm with her haughty head held high (Henriot 1913).[2] And Poiret described the gyrations of his tall, blond mannequin Andrée as being like 'an anemone expanding in the sea under the influence of a genial current' (Poiret 1931: 146). Movement began to be central to the style of a designer, too, exemplified by the modelling style of the mannequin in the couture house. An American reporter at the Paris 'openings' – that is, seasonal fashion shows – in November 1917 noted that:

> The Paquin manikin still glances coquettishly out at the world across a high collar of fur. She is denied pockets this season ... but her pretty fingers are so employed in fastening the high collar and in drawing it even higher about her pretty chin that she really has no use for pockets. And this little habit of tucking up the collar, with all sorts of pretty gestures of the hands, is in effect a part of the Paquin silhouette. (*Harper's Bazar*, November 1917: 70–1)

Through such small, incremental gestures, house styles of modelling could evolve, and in the 1920s fashion journalists in both France and the US began to comment on modelling styles and gestures as well as on the fashions. The fashion editor Bettina Ballard first saw Chanel's 'tall Russian mannequins moving around in a bored, slouched way' in her salon in the late 1920s (Ballard 1960: 15). In 1926, the photographer Baron Adolf de Meyer described the modelling style at Drécoll: 'Drecoll strikes a distinctly new note in sports clothes, admirably presented by a breezy looking young woman who not only presents the models but exemplifies how such clothes should be worn out of doors, and how one should move and carry oneself' (*Harper's Bazar*, April 1926: 122). Echoing the infinitely repeated figure of the mannequin in the mirror of figure 6.4, in the mid 1920s the house of Drécoll had, near the first floor *grand salon* where the openings were held, 'an avenue of small mirrored fitting rooms' whose doors were mirrored on the outside, 'so that the client may walk up and down the corridor and see the effect of her new gown in motion. Peacock Alley, this' (Wilson 1925: 38). Peacock Alley – a stretch of framed images of a woman in motion like a strip of motion film – is not so far from Marey's and Muybridge's chronophotographs that broke down motion into its component parts like the subsequent film footage (see fig. 6.3). And it was adjacent to the actual space in which the mannequins paraded, showing the clients how to wear the clothes, their movement framed in a series of fractured and multiplied images like film stills.

Model

If the mannequin showed the customer the way to wear the clothes, someone had to teach the mannequin. In Paris, modelling was learnt in the couture house, according to the arcane protocols of the mannequins' *cabine* (studio) and under the directions of the *couturier*, *vendeuse* or *première*. Coco Chanel created her mannequins' style in her own distinctive image: hips forward, shoulders dropped, one hand in the skirt pocket, the other gesticulating vividly. However the French *couture* was specialised, craft-based and small-scale, as opposed to the more varied, industrialised and far larger mass market of the US. Looking back at the early twentieth century, the Vice President of the American department store Neiman-Marcus, H. Stanley Marcus, differentiated the French industry as a dressmaking one and the American as an apparel manufacturing industry (*Fortune,* November 1940: 81). In New York models were employed not only in the genteel and Frenchified atmosphere of the Fifth Avenue retail stores but also by the Seventh Avenue wholesalers, who deemed their presence equally necessary, but who had neither the infrastructure nor the will to train them. By the early 1930s, aspiring mannequins had, instead, the opportunity to learn their business in mannequin schools. In Manhattan the Mayfair School was run by Miss Gertrude Mayer, a French woman who trained the mannequins who worked in the Seventh Avenue wholesale houses to model to fast fox trots and those who worked in retail shops to slow waltzes, on the grounds that wholesale buyers could judge faster. The retail mannequins had to be tall – five feet eight or nine – but could earn as much as $65 a week, whereas wholesale mannequins were about five feet five and might get up to $40 a week.

> There's a regular ritual to modelling clothes. This is the procedure for modelling a dress: walk in with hands on hips and a coy look for the buyer. Turn around, cross arms in front so that the lines of the back can be seen, walk away. Turn again and walk forward to show the fall of the drapery. Then exit, with a nice smile over the shoulder. This smile, too, is for the buyer – and is important. Coats are more involved because the lining has to be shown. Fur pieces have to be wrapped along the shoulders, then around the hips, held out in front in the way a butler holds a big platter, and then laid on the floor. All very fast, like a scarf dance. (*Fortune*, January 1933: 12)

Alongside different modelling styles and traditions, both national and industrial, the fashion press as well as the industry developed an enduring idea that the French and the American customer had differently shaped bodies. From before the beginning of the century American magazines such as *Harper's Bazar* and American *Vogue* sought to differentiate the two. In 1910 in an article entitled 'American Women I Have Met' the eminent French writer Marcel Prévost wrote

> for us Europeans there certainly exists a physical type of American woman ... not small, dark-skinned or plump but, rather, ... a tall person, rather slender, though vigorous looking ... through hygene and sports and doubtless, too, through a sincere and well-directed effort of the race towards beauty, a real American type has been formed ...

> tall and strong, with dazzling complexions and attire, who, to our eyes, incarnate the physical type of the American woman. (*Harper's Bazar*, January 1910: 23)

The idea that there was a specifically American physique persisted well into the late 1930s, typified by Bettina Ballard's description of the 'tall, hipless American figure' of Bettina Bergery, Schiaparelli's American assistant in Paris (1960: 78). Whether based in fact or not, the idea had a knock-on effect on the choice of both shop window dummies and fashion mannequins. As the drop-waisted fashions of the 1920s ceded to a more waisted silhouette, Amos Parrish & Co, a New York 'bureau of fashion prophesy and information', announced in 1930 that American clothes could no longer be displayed on European shop mannequins due to the 'broader, flatter figures' of American women and that European manufacturers were accordingly modifying their dummies for the American market (*Fortune*, September 1930: 89–91).

It is hard to know if there were, anatomically, really such clear national distinctions, although journalists in the 1910s and 1920s did often make reference to the need to modify the cut of French clothes for American women. One American article reported with some national pride on the reverse situation, whereby French women were 'striving heroically to mold their figures on American lines' as the French couturiers 'continue to approximate as closely as possible the greyhound silhouette dear to their American clientele' (Lawson 1926: 18). More importantly, as this article demonstrates, the distinction was symbolic, and stood for the economic realities of the fashion trade between France and America: 'That fashions are influenced by social and economic forces – this is a dull statement. It grows exciting, however, when one notes that the fluctuations of Paris fashions in the past decade closely paralleled the fluctuations of the franc. It was essentially a struggle between the American woman and the *Parisienne*' (*Fortune*, August 1932: 80). The article went on to make some essentialist assertions about the difference between the two, and claimed that the American woman dominated the mode during the 1920s because the fashions of the decade were sporty and feminist, like – it was implied – the American woman. The French woman by contrast was identified as 'feminine', with a rounded, less athletic figure.

> But the franc was falling, falling, falling all those years from 1919 to 1926. The American dictatorship flourished, and Paris did not dare oust the tube dress and short skirt [identified by the author as being in tune with American ideals], which became the uniform of the decade... In 1926 the franc sank to thirty-one to the dollar, and exportations (and with them the American influence) reached their height. (*Fortune*, August 1932: 80)

Movement also signalled both the vogue for sport and the incursion of women into public life and the professions. In 1926, an American fashion journalist reported from Paris that 'the sports mode controls our sunlight mood as the dance mode directs our lamplight one' (*Harper's Bazar*, March 1926: 158). Movement was seen to be an inherent part of all fashionable activity, from morning golf to evening dancing. It was also, self-evidently, the hallmark of the fashion show. By the 1920s, the idea of the active, sporting figure was popularly taken to be an American rather than a French one. An American journalist wrote 'the kinetic silhouette, exploited with much financial success, was evolved by another [French] couturier out of our lives of movement and spirited activity, after a careful study of the American woman in her native surroundings' (Lawson 1926: 19).

Mode

It was against this backdrop that in November 1924 Jean Patou placed an announcement in a New York newspaper:

> MANNEQUINS WANTED FOR PARIS
> A Paris *couturier* desires to secure three ideal types of beautiful young American women who seriously desire careers as mannequins in our Paris *atelier*. Must be smart, slender, with well-shaped feet and ankles and refined of manner. Sail within three weeks. Attractive salary proposition, one year's contract and travelling expenses paid both ways. Selection to be made by jury at the offices of Vogue, 14th Floor, 19 West 44th Street. Apply Friday morning ten to ten thirty. (quoted in Chase 1954: 164)

Five hundred applicants duly turned up and six were chosen by a jury consisting of Patou himself, Edna Woolman Chase and Condé Nast, respectively the New York editor and the publisher of *Vogue*, the interior decorator Elsie de Wolfe and the photographer Edward Steichen. The desirable American figure appeared, as ever, to be one without hips: according to one of the successful mannequins, Patou was curiously interested in the slender ankles specified in the advertisement; after that 'he deigned to look at the hips or where the hips should have been. None were wanted' (Chase 1954: 164).

Patou then sailed for France, followed by his new mannequins a week later. He was thus in a good position to gauge the reaction of the French press before the mannequins' arrival, and to stress, in his own words, 'the exquisite desirability of both the rounded French Venus and the slender American Diana' (Chase and Chase 1954: 163). If his gesture outraged French chauvinism, it nonetheless guaranteed publicity. Eager anticipation of the first collection was not disappointed: Edna Woolman Chase described how 'Patou employed an amusing bit of showmanship.' Knowing his audience would expect distinct differences in the dresses designed for the French and American mannequins, he opened the show by sending them all out dressed identically in the thin cotton wrappers they usually wore between fittings, thus suggesting that they were all the same beneath the skin. 'In view of the advance publicity, this demonstration that the female form, whatever the difference of contour, was still composed of head, limbs and torso, and was all that a dressmaker had to work on, caused a good deal of laughter and started the show off in high humour' (Chase 1954: 166). There are no photographs of this *coup de théâtre*, or of the show that followed it, only publicity shots of Patou and his American mannequins en route for Paris (fig. 6.6). But the image of a series of identically dressed young women, 'head, limbs and torso' scantily clad, like a row of undressed shop dummies in motion, must have stood out in sharp contrast against the elegant evening wear of the audience, in the heady atmosphere of an evening party, with the smell of perfume and cigars.

As for the show itself, two accounts survive, one from an American mannequin who modelled in it, one from a spectator who witnessed it. Dinarzade, or Lillian Farley, a Texan who had first modelled for the English designer Lucile in New York in 1915, recalled:

> As I went through the door to show my first dress, I had the impression of stepping into a perfumed, silk-lined jewel casket, the atmosphere was so strongly charged. The men in their correct black tailcoats with the sleek, pomaded hair; the women in gorgeous

Figure 6.6 Jean Patou and his American mannequins en route for Paris, 1924. Compare with fig. 6.5. (Photograph Parfums Jean Patou)

> evening dresses, plastered with jewels. It was hot, so hot, and the air was stifling with the mixed odours of perfumes and cigarettes. It was nearly one o'clock when the collection was over ... twenty of us had shown five hundred models. The next afternoon was the opening for the American buyers. They came in droves. There was a totally different feeling from the party-like atmosphere which had prevailed the previous evening. These men and women were there on business. The European buyers came the next day and the salons sounded like the Tower of Babel. (quoted in Chase 1954: 166)

Lillian Farley's account of her first show for Patou is a reminder that behind the staging of a fashion show as high society entertainment, was a business imperative that was concealed from the individual clients. While the client was encouraged by the mystique of French haute couture to feel that she was the unique purchaser of a model gown, the reality was that overseas and store buyers always had priority and a number of model gowns were destined for serial reproduction. (It is possible that the early Parisian parades were for overseas buyers which would explain the absence of pictures, couture houses being reluctant to publicise the extent of their trade links.) In this sense, the marketing of couture was founded on a kind of discrete deception, if not an outright lie.

It was a lie perpetuated by the gossipy tone of Charles Creed the younger, heir to the Paris-based fashion house of the same name, when he wrote that Patou 'preferred to show his collections by night and these presentations became one of the highlights of Paris social life'. In particular, he had 'rocked Paris to the core by importing American model girls':

> Everybody who was anybody (and more people were then than are now) flocked to see not only Patou's graceful clothes but more especially his fabulous model girls. His most decorative salon was so arranged that the girls made their entrance walking down a ramp – which showed off their beautiful limbs to great advantage, making the women green with envy and the men pop-eyed with admiration.
>
> What girls they were too! There was Josephine Armstrong, known to her friends as 'Foxie' – who first married Erskin Gwynn, a great journalist and playboy (related, it was rumoured, to the Vanderbuilts), who founded and edited a magazine called *Le Boulevardier*, the gossip-paper of all the *beau-monde* in Europe. What became of him, or it, I cannot recall – but 'Foxie' is now Lady Sefton. Running her close in the glamour stakes were Dorothy Raynor, Carolyn Putnam, Edwina Pru (now Mrs Leo d'Erlanger), and the spectacular Lillian Farley, who was known as 'Divine'.[3]
>
> Paris purred over these lovelies and followed their exploits as if they had been royalty. (Creed and Grant 1961: 78)

In the late 1920s Chanel followed Patou's lead by advertising in the Paris-based *Herald* for American mannequins. As the decade progressed, Patou staged his shows 'with little tables crowded together as at a night club, butlers moving about with sandwiches and champagne, and Patou lipsticks, in Cartier cases, as favors for the ladies' (*Fortune*, August 1932: 80). Charles Creed the younger, who had seen Patou's American mannequins in Paris, later praised Patou in his autobiography, both for his 'strong affinity with America' and his 'wonderful flair for publicity' (Creed and Grant 1961: 67 and 77).

Patou's innovations undoubtedly put him at the forefront of fashionable 'Américainisme', as the magazine *Comoedia* termed the French vogue for everything *à l'Américaine* in 1928: jazz, the Charlston, cocktails, mah-jong and dominoes. Patou's own version of *Américainisme* made a dual appeal to both the individual client and the trade buyer, even though the latter might be well aware that there was an element of the emperor's new clothes in the fact of a Paris couturier selling American-style fashion back to New York garment importers, and off the backs of American mannequins imported to Paris:

> After seeing the American flapper in her proper *milieu*, one Parisian couturier went back home and caused his designers to make his whole season's line to fit her personality, even going so far as to import American flapper types to wear them. The reaction of the American buyers who sat through the initial showing of his Americanised line were amusing and enlightening, to say the least. Their attitude was a ludicrous mixture of disappointment, of consternation and of bewilderment. One heard excited comments on every side: 'But these are exactly what we've been making at home for years!' or, 'I'm not going to order here; I can get hundreds like this on Seventh Avenue, with no duty to pay!' Or again, 'Smith & Jones in the garment center has a better line of these things which I can buy at one quarter the money!'
>
> We looked at one another in surprise. Had we been asleep all these years? Here was a couturier we had all depended upon for something new that we wearily chased all over Europe, and he had quite unintentionally shown us the charm of our own ideas. Poor dear, he had with the most selfish intentions, unselfishly pointed us to our own markets. Nevertheless, so consistently and thoroughly had that couturier's prestige been exploited by American department stores that none of the buyers dared flout his collection, even though buying his models was definitely a carrying of coals to Newcastle. (Lawson 1925: 18–19)

Patou, like all Paris couturiers, was obliged to woo three different categories of American customer. First, the couture customers. Second, the uptown, Francophile stores such as Bergdorf Goodman with whom he maintained close links. In the mid 1920s Andrew Goodman, the son of Eddie Goodman of Bergdorf Goodman in New York, was apprenticed to Patou in Paris, where the Charles Creed the younger met him prior to being himself apprenticed at Bergdorf Goodman in 1929. And third, the Seventh Avenue wholesalers. Whereas the uptown stores bought what were effectively franchised models to copy, the American wholesalers might buy as much as £100,000's worth of designs from one house in a season, in order to make cheaper copies for the mass market (Etherington-Smith 1983: 80)

Patou's *Américainisme*, however, was not confined to his designs but extended to aspects the way he ran his business, departing from the protocols and traditions of couture and causing some hostility in the more *ancien regime* houses. His advertising budget was large, his salaries high, his prices relatively low. He introduced daily staff meetings and profit shares for executives, and extended the bonus system to mannequins who were traditionally only employed on short-term seasonal contracts. His principal innovation to the atelier system was the introduction of some elements of 'the piecework and assembly plan of production' (Wilson 1925: 72). The organisation of Patou's atelier, like that of Lucien Lelong's in the 1920s, was moving towards the 'scientific management of the dressmaking plant' (Wilson 1925: 73). The language of this commentator draws explicitly from Taylor.

But it was above all in his understanding of the role of the mannequin, that Patou revealed a Taylorist analysis of his workforce as his best business asset. Patou, according to one contemporary, replaced 'the trade's valuation of the mannequin as a piece of necessary furniture' with his own idea of 'her as an important factor in the sales organization'.

> He says his mannequin Lola is the best in the world. While she is a striking looking girl, in beauty she is overshadowed by golden-haired Gladys, a Scotch mannequin in Patou's establishment. But Lola sells twice as many gowns as Gladys, and Patou says she can outsell an ordinary mannequin six or seven to one. The reason is her great chic, a seemingly spiritual quality whose value in actual francs and centimes Patou's efficiency department shows to him in graphic business charts. (Wilson 1925: 72–3)

Thus Lola's chic could be calculated actuarily. The mannequin, tall and slender in reality, could also be represented as a tall and slender column in a bar chart, the taller the better, as Patou's 'efficiency department' made the translation from *centimetres* to *centimes.*

Patou's run of identically dressed French and American models who opened his evening show in their thin cotton wrappers, constituted a visualisation of the very nature of the copy, embodied by the serial replication of the mannequin on the catwalk. It returns us to freeze-frame imagery of the earliest mannequins in the salon and, like them, his 'Americanisme', however voguish, was also a visualisation of contradiction. Just as Poiret was plagued by the tension between the status of the original and the copy before the First World War, so too was Patou in the 1920s. But, in the manner of the return of the repressed, what is repressed comes back through the very structures of that repression, in this case the publicity machine of fashion itself. There was thus an 'industrial aesthetic' made visible in Patou's show. Despite the luxurious setting, Patou's styling of the modernist body in the salon graphically matched the aesthetics of the industrial production line, as did Coco Chanel's 'little black dress' of 1926. The caption in American *Vogue* was 'here is a Ford signed Chanel'. The caption referred to Henry Ford's dictum that the Model-T Ford came in 'any colour so long as it's black', but it also invoked Ford's modern automated production line, the logical follower to the Taylor system. Patou's and Chanel's industrial aesthetic could be – and was, by contemporaries – linked to current types of industrial production such as Fordism and Taylorism. Patou's line of identically dressed mannequins evokes Seigfreid Kracauer's description in 1927 of the 1920s chorus line as a symbolic representation of 'the capitalist production process'; it made visible the Taylor system and the worker in the production line, thus visualising 'significant components of reality [that have become] ... invisible in our world' (Kracauer 1995: 75–6). So too did Patou's line of mannequins and his 'modern' American ways of showing; they made visible a relationship between Paris couture houses and the mass-produced fashions of New York's Seventh Avenue that had to remain concealed from the individual clients – hence the need for the two shows, one as an evening party, the other as a day-time event restaged the next morning for commercial buyers as a far more business-like affair.

The visual and commercial complexities of the mannequin's presentation had been implicit since the early 1900s, if not earlier. Couturiers had to juggle the sale and marketing of exclusive luxury gowns to a moneyed elite with the sale of model dresses to international buyers for mass-market manufacture. In this process the industrial base of haute couture had continually to be disavowed through its elite presentation and marketing. Patou's show simply made visible the connection via an industrial aesthetic that by the 1920s had become modish. Underlying economic structures, as well as cinematic tropes, were symbolically figured in the mannequin, her presentation, and her representation; in this way, the contradictions embodied in the mannequin's presentation and reception in the first thirty years of the twentieth century mirrored the contradictions of French *grande couture* itself.

Notes

1. All the evidence of the earliest British parades is tantalising but unsubstantiated. An article by Jane Barnicoat in the London *Evening Standard* for Monday 2 April 1962 on the London store Swan & Edgar claims that the store staged a 'fashion show' in 1869 but the source is uncredited and the Swan & Edgar archive is not to be found (the firm was taken over by Harrods who rebuilt

the Picadilly Circus shop in 1925–6). Alison Adburgham (1989) refers to the London dressmaker Jay as staging parades in the 1890s. And a character in George Gissing's 1895 novel *The Year of Jubilee* describes with self-loathing how she is employed in a shop to parade fashion before other women (Gissing 1987 [1895]).

2. 'Vous les voyer [les mannequins], chez "Le Grand Couturier", défiler en souple et dansant théorie ... elles avancent doucement, avec des gestes de theatre ... tournant le col avec des ports de tête malicieux, digns ou hautains.' They parade in the salon before the 'femmes du monde', 'les bras étendus, légèrement éloignés du coprs, de passer et de repasser ... et d'avancer en roulant sur soi-même, comme sur un rythme de tango, en pliant les hances, en flêchisant le genou; assurément, c'est amusant, cette danse perpetuelle' (Henriot 1913).
3. The last of the six was the sixteen-year-old Rosalind Star. The second-youngest of the six was Edwina Pru, aged seventeen in 1924 (Chase and Chase 1954: 164). See Woodhouse and Kern 1954 for an account of her, and of New York showgirls in this period.

References

Primary sources

Photographic archives

Jean Patou, company archives
Lucile, Special collections at FIT, New York
Paul Poiret at Musée de la Mode de la ville de Paris

Texts

Alexandre, A. (1902) *Les reines de l'aiguille*. Paris: Théophile Belin.
Ballard, B. (1960) *In My Fashion.* New York: David McKay Company Inc.
Chase, E.W. (1954) *Always in Vogue.* London: Victor Gollancz
Comoedia (1928) 14 September.
Creed, C. S. and E. Grant (1961) *Maid to Measure.* London: Jarrolds.
Era (1912) 24 February.
Gissing, G. (1987 [1895]) *In the Year of Jubilee.* London: Hogarth Press.
Henriot, É. (1913) 'Figures Parisiennes: le mannequin', *L'Illustration*. 27 December.
Kracauer, S. (1995 [1927]) *The Mass Ornament: Weimar Essays,* trans. Thomas Y. Levin. Cambridge, MA: Harvard University Press.
Lawson, O.C. (1925) 'Overselling Paris', *Saturday Evening Post*. 199 (16) 16 October.

Le Corbusier, (1987 [1925]) *The Decorative Art of Today*, trans. James I. Dunnett. London: Architectural Press.

Marcus, H.S. (1940) 'Future of Fashion (American Design)', *Fortune*, 22 (11) November.

Poiret, P. (1931) *My First Fifty Years*, trans. Stephen Hayden Guest. London: Victor Gollancz.

Roger-Milès, L. (1910) *Les créateurs de la mode*. Paris: Édition du Figaro. CH Eggimann.

Roubade, L. (1928) *Au pays des mannequins: le roman de la robe*. Paris: Les Éditions de France.

Taylor, F.W. (1911) *The Principles of Scientific Management.* London: Harpers.

Wilson, R.F. (1925) *Paris on Parade.* Indianapolis: The Bobs Merrill Company.

Woodhouse, P.G. and J. Kern (1954) *Bring on the Girls; The Improbable Story of Our Life in Musical Comedy, with Pictures to Prove it.* London: Herbert Jenkins.

Secondary Sources

Adburgham, A. (1989) *Shops and Shopping: Where and in What Manner the Well-dressed Englishwoman Bought her Clothes.* London: Barrie & Jenkins.

Craik, J. (1994) *The Face of Fashion: Cultural Studies in Fashion.* London: Routledge.

Crary, J. (1990) *Techniques of the Observer: On Vision and Modernity in the Nineteenth Century.* Cambridge, MA: MIT Press.

De Marley, D. (1980) *Worth: Father of Haute Couture*. London: Elm Tree Books.

Etherington-Smith, M. (1983) *Patou.* London: Hutchinson.

Geidion, S. (1948) *Mechanization Takes Command.* London: W.W. Norton & Co.

Hollander, A. (1980) *Seeing Through Clothes*. New York: Avon Books.

Kaplan, J. and S. Stowell (1994) *Theatre and Fashion: From Oscar Wilde to the Suffragettes.* Cambridge: Cambridge University Press.

Kern, S. (1983) *The Culture of Time and Space 1880–1918.* London: Weidenfeld & Nicolson.

Leach, W. (1993) *Land of Desire: Merchants, Power and the Rise of a new American Culture.* New York: Pantheon Books.

Robinson, D. (1993) *Georges Méliès*. London: BFI Publications.

Sanderson, M. (1984) *From Irving to Oliver: A Social History of the Acting Profession in England 1880–1983*. London: Athlone Press, New York: St Martins Press.

Troy, N.J. (2003) *Couture Culture: A Study in Modern Art and Fashion.* Cambridge, MA: MIT Press.

Wilson, R.G. (1986) *The Machine Age in America 1918–1941.* New York: Brooklyn Museum in association with Harry N. Abrams.

Wollen, P. (1993) *Raiding the Icebox: Reflections on Twentieth-century Culture.* London: Verso.

Response

Andrew Bolton

Since its birth in the mid nineteenth century, haute couture has been defined by the tension between the model and the multiple, between the original couture dress and the mass-produced copy. In her book *Couture Culture: A Study in Modern Art and Fashion* Nancy Troy refers to this tension as the 'logic of fashion' (2003: 4). Long regarded as a crucial problem in the history of avant-garde modernism, this tension between originality and reproduction intensified between the years 1900 and 1929, a period that saw a rapid growth in the ready-to-wear industry and a concomitant growth in the department store. Both these institutions contributed to the development of a culture of consumption that exerted enormous pressures on the boundaries between elite and popular culture, which, in turn, threatened to disrupt the unique and privileged position of haute couture.

Haute couture claims its elite status through the supposed originality or singularity of the couture dress or garment. At the turn of the twentieth century, couturiers employed various strategies to reinforce the idea of the uniqueness of the couture gown, many of which were also employed by fine artists. One such strategy was the house label, introduced by Charles Frederick Worth in the 1860s. The house label served to signify the creative individual behind the couture gown, namely the couturier himself/herself. By denoting authorship, the house label also implied individuality, in much the same way as an artist's signature did when applied to a work of art. The labels of certain couturiers such as Jacques Doucet actually bore the designer's signature. Perhaps the most notable example, however, was that of Madeleine Vionnet, whose label also bore the imprint of her right thumb in an effort to invest her dresses with an aura of uniqueness and creative individuality (Kirke 1998: 222).

In the nineteenth century, most couturiers used numbers to identify individual dresses. At the turn of the twentieth century, however, certain couturiers like Paul Poiret and Lady Duff Gordon (Lucile) began applying distinctive titles or names to their gowns. Lady Duff Gordon, who is usually credited with the innovation, became known for her rather risqué titles. 'Passion's Thrall', 'Do You Love Me?' and 'A Frenzied Song of Amorous Things' are a few examples of the titillating titles she gave to her dresses (Kaplan and Stowell 1994: 119). Like the house label, the practice of giving evocative names or titles to individual gowns was an attempt by couturiers to announce the exclusivity of their designs. Again, it was a practice borrowed from fine art and was intended to suggest that each couture dress was a unique and highly aestheticized creation, an original work of art.

While the house label and the practice of naming gowns may have given the illusion of originality and singularity, the reality was that the couture dress, as Caroline Evans points out, was 'destined for serial reproduction'. As Troy observes, 'couturiers created seasonal models that were intended to be copied or adapted either for individual, wealthy clients or for the developing made-to-order and ready-to-wear trade in department stores and other clothing outlets catering to a broader consumer market' (Troy 2003: 4). In other words, a couture dress could be reproduced any number of times for any number of clients. At the beginning of the twentieth century, couturiers sought to maintain their status as creators of supposedly unique and individual gowns or works of art while capitalizing on the potential of copies to reach a broader, largely foreign, middle-class audience.

The mannequin parade, as Evans points out, was a strategy developed by couturiers, at least in part, to come to terms with this apparent contradiction and, at the same time, to negotiate the dissolving boundaries between elite and popular culture. It not only allowed the work of couturiers to become visible (and, by extension, to circulate and to be consumed), but it also allowed couturiers to direct and control this visibility. In their own country, this visibility tended to be restricted to elite sites of fashionability such as the races, the theatre and, of course, their own private salons or ateliers. Several couturiers, such as Lady Duff Gordon, decorated their salons in the style of a drawing room in an attempt to underscore the elite nature of their ateliers and the elite status of their gowns. Lady Duff Gordon treated her presentations like private and intimate gatherings. As women were served tea and sandwiches, mannequins paraded in gowns to the accompaniment of music played by an orchestra. Belying their origins in theatre, Lady Duff Gordon's fashion parades took place on a miniature stage. Several even took the form of actual plays or thematic pageants. In 1909, for instance, she organized the ambitious *Seven Ages of Women*, a stage piece in seven acts tracing the dress-cycle of a society dame from birth to death (Kaplan and Stowell 1994: 119). By the early teens, fashion shows had become fashionable occasions in themselves. Women were going to fashion shows as they had gone previously to the theatre.

Paul Poiret similarly restricted the visibility of his couture gowns to private and semi-private spaces to 'position and promote his fashion statements as expressions of luxury and sumptuousness steeped in the cultural politics of a wealthy and aristocratic French elite' (Troy 2003: 15). Like Lady Duff Gordon's salon, Poiret's *hôtel de couture* was a discrete and highly aestheticized environment with all the trappings of up-to-date bourgeois domesticity. He staged elaborate fashion parades that, like those of Lady Duff Gordon, acquired a kind of theatrical pageantry.

They, too, were shown on a stage in the heart of his salon, specially made for him by the architect Louis Süe. Poiret also used the gardens of his *hôtel de couture* as backdrops for his fashion shows. Indeed, he seized upon the outdoor setting as an opportunity to film his mannequins in motion, which, as Evans observes, made it possible for him to take his fashion shows on the road. While Poiret, like many French couturiers such as Jean Paquin and Callot Soeurs, limited the visibility of his gowns at home to elite sites of fashionability, he extended it abroad to include such public spaces as department stores. Indeed, when Poiret went to America in the early teens to cultivate the American market for high-end women's clothing, he worked with several New York department stores, such as R.H. Macy, Gimbel Brothers and John Wannamaker, on fashion shows that closely resembled those staged in the elite and carefully controlled environment of his Parisian *hôtel de couture*. As intended, these fashion shows allowed a vast middle-class clientele to see and purchase his designs.

Beginning with Worth, couturiers had always sold models to foreign buyers who, in turn, had them copied, with or without alterations, for sale in department stores and other clothing outlets. Often, these foreign buyers paid a special price for the gowns that included the right to make and market multiple copies. These copies were sold as 'adaptations' or 'reproductions' of 'original' couture gowns and garments. What Poiret discovered on his trip to America, however, was that his designs were being copied illegally and were being sold at cut-rate prices. This discovery posed a serious threat to the elite status of haute couture, serving to destabilise the relationship between the model and the multiple, between originality and reproduction. In the world of haute couture, the number of copies produced from a single model was limited because couturiers charged high prices in order to secure the rarity of the design in circulation. Illegal piracy made it difficult for couturiers to charge high prices based on the rarity of their designs because copies were widely available at much reduced prices. Since American intellectual property law at the turn of the twentieth century did not protect couturiers against design piracy, couturiers were forced to develop new strategies that enabled them to maintain the elite status of haute couture while, at the same time, embracing and exploiting the vast American marketplace.

In pursuing the sale and distribution of his work in America, Poiret produced a line of ready-made clothing for his spring 1917 collection. Designed exclusively for the women of America, Poiret described the fourteen models as 'genuine reproductions', which he claimed gave American women the opportunity to own an 'original' Poiret design without paying the excessive price. The genuine reproduction was an attempt on the part of Poiret to overcome the distinction between couture originals and mass-produced copies. As Troy observes, 'As a hybrid devised to reconcile the contradiction between art and industry, the genuine reproduction preserved the modernist fictions of originality and authorial prerogative; at the same time it acknowledged the modern realities of industrial production and consumer demand' (2003: 302). Simple, practical and rational, Poiret's genuine reproductions reflected the needs of the new American woman who moved more freely in society. Perhaps more importantly, however, they gave aesthetic expression to the industrial and commodity character of the ready-made.

While Poiret abandoned the simplicity, practicality and rationality of his genuine reproductions after the first World War, these qualities became the hallmark of Coco Chanel's casual, loose-fitting sportswear. As Evans observes, Chanel secured her success on the basis of couture fashions that projected an image of standardisation, which, in the case of her 'little black dress' could be compared to such mass-produced commodities as the Model-T Ford. 'The simplicity of Chanel's little black dress', Troy argues, 'is surely not only that it could be adapted to suit virtually any woman but also that it would be easy to copy and distribute in the post-war ready-to-wear market' (2003: 316). However, while Chanel seemed to find a means of resolving the tension between the model and the multiple, between the original couture dress and the mass-produced copy in her work, at least aesthetically, it continued to define haute couture in the twentieth century. Indeed, the contradictory circumstances that designers like Poiret and Chanel grappled with – originality and reproduction, elite and popular culture – still resonate with the experience of contemporary couturiers today.

References

Kaplan, J.H. and S. Stowell (1994) *Theatre and Fashion: Oscar Wilde to the Suffragettes*. Cambridge: Cambridge University Press.

Kirke, B. (1998) *Madeleine Vionnet*. San Francisco: Chronical Books.

Troy, N.J. (2003) *Couture Culture: A Study in Modern Art and Fashion*. Cambridge, MA: MIT Press.

Part III
Processes of Modernity

–7–

The Fingerprint of the Second Skin

Kitty Hauser

So many things in an overcoat! – when circumstances and men make it speak.

H. de Pène, *Paris Intime*[1]

In the spring and summer of 1996 there was a series of bombings and robberies in and around the Spokane area of Washington. Police investigations led to the identification of four suspects, members of a white supremacist gang, who apparently funded their activities through crime, and who had left supremacist literature at the scene of at least one of these crimes. A successful prosecution would require positive identification, however, and these men had taken steps to ensure that this would be difficult. CCTV footage from a Spokane branch of the US Bank caught the appearance and movements of the robbers who mounted an armed raid there on 1 April 1996. A particularly clear image of one of the robbers was obtained (fig. 7.1 (a) and (b)), but any individuating characteristics of his body and face were obscured by a thick balaclava, gloves, and urban uniform of parka, denim jeans, and trainers. If the criminal's face was invisible to the camera, however, what was particularly clearly revealed in the footage were the creases and wear-patterns of his jeans.

In connection with this case, Dr Richard Vorder Bruegge of the Special Photographic Unit of the FBI has investigated the individuating properties of worn denim jeans (Vorder Bruegge 1999). Beyond so-called 'class characteristics' of jeans such as manufacturer, style and size, individuating characteristics arise, according to Vorder Bruegge, as a result both of the manufacturing process, and through normal wear-and-tear.[2] The way in which an individual washes his/her jeans, whether they iron them, what they carry in their pockets, the way they walk, and so on, will all result in particular patterns of fading and wear. In particular, it is at the seams and hems where unique characteristics appear. Puckering in these areas, an unavoidable consequence of the manufacturing process, causes what Vorder Bruegge calls 'ridges and valleys', which over time are made more visible as areas of dark and light blue, as the outer layer of the indigo denim is abraded to reveal the white cotton underneath (1999: 613) (fig. 7.2). These, appropriately enough, are likened by Vorder Bruegge to barcodes, and he suggests

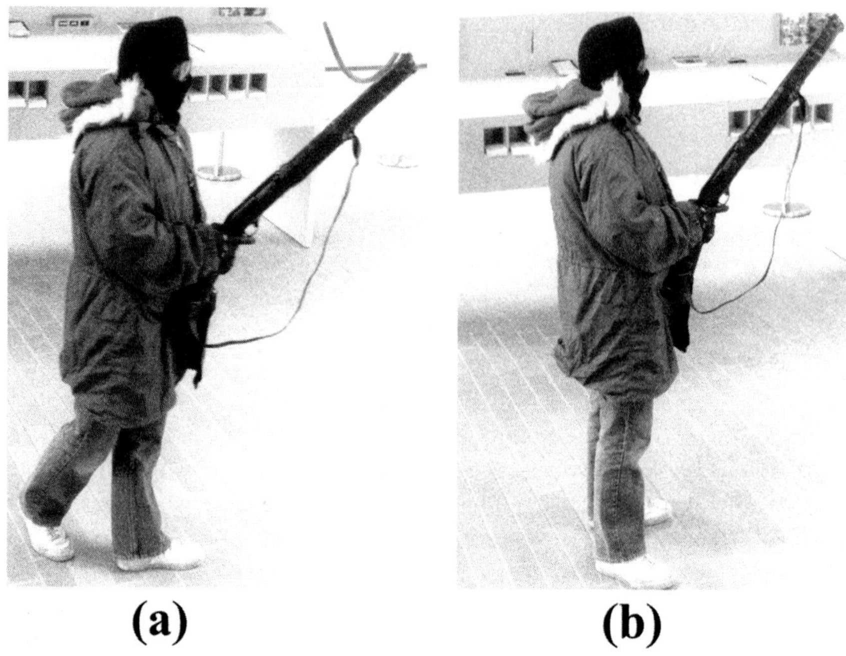

Figure 7.1 (a) Bank surveillance photograph depicting view of Spokane bank robber's left leg; (b) Bank surveillance photograph depicting view of Spokane bank robber's right leg. From Vorder Bruegge 1999. (© ASTM International)

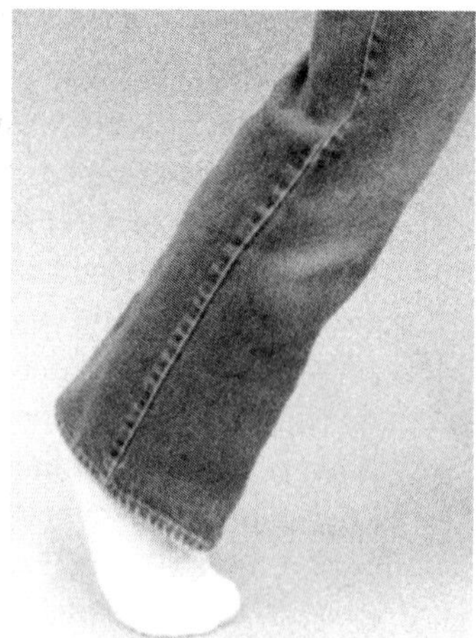

Figure 7.2 'Ridges' and 'valleys' along seam, resembling barcode. From Vorder Bruegge 1999. (© ASTM International)

– although confirmation awaits a validation study – that they may be unique to each garment (1999: 615). It is the fading propensity of blue denim that makes these 'ridges and valleys' visible, through wear, washing or perhaps pre-purchase stonewashing – and it is this fading propensity which fortuitously means that such unique characteristics are visible on CCTV footage, since the tonal differentiation of worn denim may be registered on black-and-white surveillance film.[3]

When the homes of the suspects of the Spokane robberies were searched, twenty-seven pairs of denim jeans were removed and sent to the FBI. Each pair was compared with the footage of the robbery of the US Bank – in particular, those frames in which the robber stood in such a way as to reveal particularly clearly the seams of his trousers (fig. 7.1 (a) and (b)). One of the twenty-seven recovered garments, a pair of J.C. Penney 'Plain Pocket' blue jeans, was identified as possessing characteristics matching all of those noted by Dr Vorder Bruegge on the bank film images. These, then, seemed to be the jeans worn by the robber of the US Bank; and they were used as evidence in the criminal prosecution of the suspect. In the trial the defence called on an 'exporter of used blue jeans' as an expert witness, to argue that most of the supposedly 'unique' characteristics of the jeans in question were in fact ubiquitous (Vorder Bruegge 1999: 619). The exporter produced thirty-four pairs of jeans, which, he said, exhibited the same characteristics as the bank robber's. When, as part of the trial, these pairs were examined by Vorder Bruegge, one by one each was demonstrated to lack certain features present on the jeans as depicted on the Spokane bank film. The owner of the jeans, Charles Barbee, was successfully prosecuted, and is now serving time in prison.[4]

Dr Vorder Bruegge presented his research at a meeting of the American Academy of Forensic Sciences in February 1998, and the story – including the evidence of the jeans – was widely reported in the press.[5] Whilst it emerged amidst the paraphernalia of modern technology (CCTV) and apparatuses of state control (the FBI), the case has something of the quality of myth. Vorder Bruegge's inspection of the film footage and the denim seems to hover on the well-worn line between deduction and divination, leading to accusations of 'hocus pocus' and 'voodoo' from other crime-detection professionals.[6] Based on Vorder Bruegge's 'readings' of the jeans, the successful identification of Charles Barbee echoes an entire genre of detective fiction, begun by Sir Arthur Conan Doyle and Edgar Allen Poe in the nineteenth century, in which – through slight traces and clues – an individual is successfully picked out from an apparently undifferentiated mass (see Eco and Sebeok 1983; Joseph and Winter 1996; Thomas 1999). Sherlock Holmes, in particular, could deduce things about a person from the slightest of traces: 'By a man's fingernails', he asserts, 'by his coat-sleeve, by his boot, by his trouser-knees, by the callosities of his forefinger and thumb, by his expression, by his shirt-cuffs – by each of these things a man's calling is plainly revealed' (Conan Doyle 1989 [1887]: 17).

The Sherlock Holmes stories repeatedly blur the line between rational deduction and divine inspiration, as what seems to be Holmes' second sight, as he successfully identifies a complete stranger, turns out to be the exercise of keen observation, specialist knowledge, and pure reason. As John Carey has observed, the 'appeal of this Holmesian magic and the reassurance it brings' are 'residually religious, akin to the singling-out of the individual soul, redeemed from the mass, that Christianity promises' (1992: 9). Since the nineteenth century Holmes' method has been paralleled in state practices of individual identification, which have been an essential component of tightening state control in modernity (see Benjamin 1989: 43ff.).[7] Technologies of identification employed by state bodies have gone from physiognomy and anthropometry to fingerprinting and genetic profiling (see Cole 2001; Caplan and Torpey 2001). In the Spokane case, the 'singling out' of the individual occurs where you might least expect to find it, however: not in the face or physique, and not in the fingerprints. Instead, the individual is redeemed from the crowd through his *jeans*, that most ubiquitous and apparently homogeneous uniform of mass society. Unique identity, it seems from this story, is encoded not just in the body (in the face, in fingerprints, or in the DNA encoded in an eyelash), but in its cultural wrappings too, in the very fabric of its disguises.

Taking place in the paranoid matrix of American urban modernity, the Spokane case reads like a parable of redemption. It suggests that in the eyes of one who sees (a surveillance camera, or the FBI) we are as unique as we surely are in the eyes of God, even where we seem to be most alike. And whilst this identification derives from a complex technology (CCTV, expert photographic analysis of the FBI Photographic Unit), what is particularly appealing about it is that the perception of difference ultimately depends upon nothing more than ordinary vision. The unique characteristics identified by Vorder Bruegge are visible to the naked eye; from this it would seem that just by looking we, too, might be able to perceive these minute yet significant differences. It would seem that if we look hard enough, and in the right way, we too can have access to some otherwise-hidden realm where appearance and identity concur. Moreover, the idea that worn clothing bears the individuating traces of its wearer concurs with our everyday experience, and has been well documented in literature, art and advertising. Denim is particularly well-suited to rendering visible the entropy of wear, best described, perhaps, in James Agee's astonishingly lyrical passage on sharecroppers' overalls in *Let Us Now Praise Famous Men* (1941):

> The structures sag, and take on the look, some of use; some, the pencil pockets, the pretty atrophies of what is never used; the edges of the thigh pockets become stretched and lie open, fluted, like the gills of a fish. The bright seams lose their whiteness and

> are lines and ridges. The whole fabric is shrunken to size, which was bought large. The whole shape, texture, color, finally substance, all are changed. (Agee and Evans 1941: 267)

'Each man's garment', writes Agee, wears 'the shape and beauty of his induplicable body' (Agee and Evans 1941: 267).[8] This is a conceit reinforced by our own experience and exploited by manufacturers – for example, the 1980s Levi's ad where a girl fetishistically puts on the worn jeans of her boyfriend, who has left on a Greyhound bus to serve in the army (see Finlayson 1990: 37). The motif of worn clothing of all kinds is a poetic one, and has been explored both in literary and, more recently, academic texts – especially in relation to memory, and the uncanny after-image of an absent wearer. In Thomas Carlyle's *Sartor Resartus*, the empty suits and other old clothes in Monmouth Street Market are described as the 'ghosts of life' (2000 [1833–4]: 178). Charles Dickens described the same London market in similar terms (1994 [1836]: 76–82), as cited by Elizabeth Wilson in *Adorned in Dreams*, a book which begins amongst the uncanny disembodied gowns in a costume museum (Wilson 1985: 1–2). Many of the short stories in the recent anthology *A Second Skin: Women Writing about Clothes* are concerned with the capacity of old clothes to evoke memory and cast-off identities (Dunseath 1998).[9] In the volume of essays *Defining Dress* Juliet Ash has written about the representation of 'clothes without people' in art, both as floating commodities, and as memories of absence (Ash 1999). And Peter Stallybrass, writing after the death of his friend Allon White, has eloquently considered the way in which clothing receives the induplicable smells, sweat and shape of its wearer (Stallybrass 1993).

All of these stories and academic texts focus on the way in which individual garments might be imprinted with the signature of the wearer's body, evoking or revealing the wearer's identity, character or physiognomy. At Monmouth Street Market, Dickens describes his endeavour, 'from the shape and fashion of the garment itself, to bring its former owner before our mind's eye' (1994 [1836]: 78). Second-hand clothes might eerily be imbued with the smells, sweat, or shape of their previous owners – this is the theme, for example, of Beverly Pagram's story 'Clothes Have No Memory' (Dunseath 1998: 79–83). If it has been bought new, though, a garment is, it seems, a *tabula rasa*, simply waiting to receive these impressions. James Agee describes as-yet unworn denim overalls as possessing the 'massive yet delicate beauty of most things which are turned out most cheaply in great tribes by machines: and on this basis of structure they are changed into images and marvels of nature' (Agee and Evans 1941: 267). The passage of attrition from machine-made commodity to 'nature' is complete, writes Agee, when the 'mold of the body is fully taken' (Agee and Evans 1941: 268). This transformation wreaked on denim by time and wear is evident in the photographs

Walker Evans took to accompany Agee's text (see figs. 7.3 and 7.4). New shop-bought clothes, unlike old clothes, it seems, have no particular individuality, and no memory – they are just waiting to be imprinted with ours.

But if we look closely at the unique characteristics of the jeans identified by Dr Vorder Bruegge, it is clear that the crucial individuating features do not only derive from the suspect's physique and habits, but also – and perhaps more importantly – from the manufacturing process. The analysis of the Spokane suspect's jeans focussed on the seams. When, in making up jeans, the operator pushes the denim through the sewing machine, unavoidable tensions are created in the fabric, causing a puckering along the seams, a series of 'ridges and valleys' that is effectively induplicable. This puckering may be amplified when the garment shrinks through being washed; and it is made visible over time as the raised portions or 'ridges' of the seam are worn and abraded to reveal the white core of the denim fabric, and the 'valleys' remain dark. This, as I have indicated, is referred to by Vorder Bruegge as a 'barcode' pattern. In the felled inseams of denim jeans, where the

Figure 7.3 Frank Tengle, cotton sharecropper, Hale County, Alabama. 1935–6, by Walker Evans. (Library of Congress, Prints and Photographs Division, FSA/OWI Collection, LC-USF342–T01–008154–A)

Figure 7.4 Floyd Burroughs and Tengle children, Hale County, Alabama 1936, by Walker Evans. (Library of Congress, Prints and Photographs Division, FSA/OWI Collection, LC-USF3301–031306–M5)

fabric pieces are folded over upon each other and stitched together, the seam is four plies thick. The barcode patterns on these inseams are particularly likely to be visible, since the seam stands higher than the surrounding fabric, and is therefore more subject to abrasion when the wearer walks, runs, or goes about his/her daily business (Vorder Bruegge 1999: 615).

The side seams of jeans tend to be chainstitched, rather than felled, and these give rise to a different kind of wear-pattern. A chainstitched seam is a simpler – and weaker – kind of seam, where the pieces of fabric are sewn together with no stitching visible on the outside of the garment. Inside the garment a chainstitched seam will leave two flaps of excess material. Often these flaps are pressed open flat, creating a two-ply thickness on either side of the seam. Sometimes they are sewn together, and the resultant two-ply flap will tend to lie flat on one or other side of the seam (this can occur, too, if the flaps are not sewn together). Wherever there is a greater thickness in the layers of fabric around the seam area, abrasion is more likely to occur. The flaps created by a chainstitched seam may also, according to Vorder Bruegge, generate a characteristic wear-pattern known as a 'cross-over' (1999: 615). This kind of wear-pattern is demonstrated in these two photographs of a side seam provided by Vorder Bruegge, shown inside and out, with the inside view reversed to facilitate comparison (fig. 7.5). Along the length of the seam, the inside flaps may lie on one side in some places, and then fold over to the other side in other places. The 'barcode' pattern will appear on the side of the seam where the flaps have settled, since this is where there are more layers of fabric, and therefore where wear is most likely. When the flaps fold over on the other side of the seam, the barcode pattern will appear on the other side. Where the 'cross-over' from one side to the other occurs, there will be a particularly thick section where the fabric flaps are standing on end: here there will be most abrasion, resulting in a distinctive white ridge.

These are the kinds of characteristics that Dr Vorder Bruegge was looking for in the Spokane case, when he sought to compare the jeans depicted in the surveillance film with the jeans recovered from the suspect's home, working on the assumption

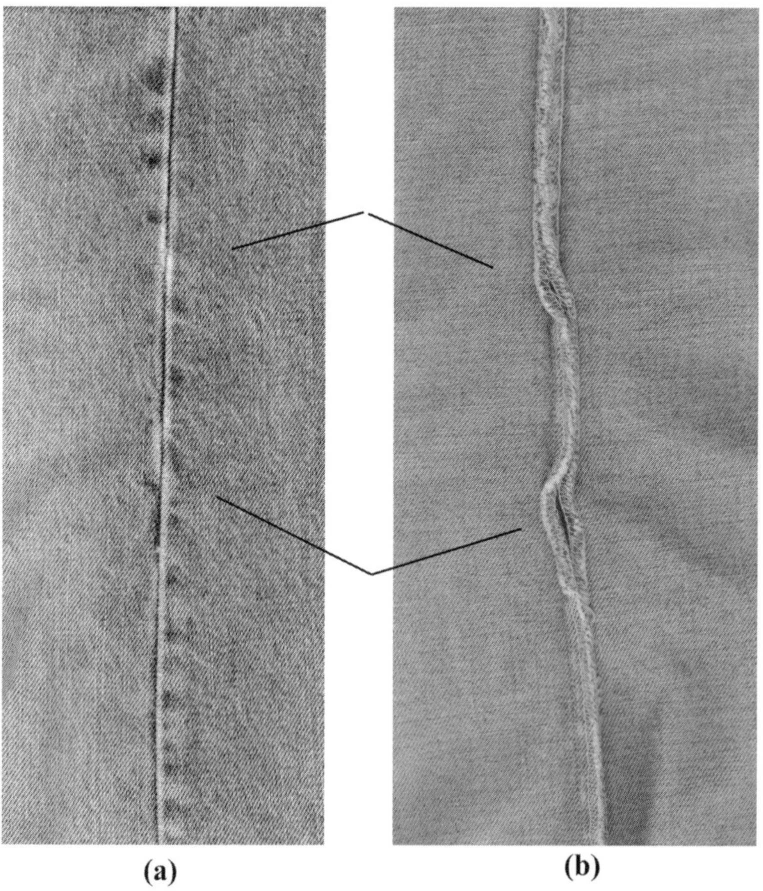

Figure 7.5 'Cross-over' pattern on chain-stitched seam (a) Exterior view; (b) Interior view, reversed to match orientation of exterior view as shown in (a). From Vorder Bruegge 1999. (© ASTM International)

– well established in criminalistics – that individualisation of a piece of evidence 'is established by finding agreement of corresponding individual characteristics of such number and significance to preclude the possibility (or probability) of their having occurred by mere coincidence, and establishing that there are no differences that cannot be accounted for'.[10]

In order to demonstrate the self-identity of the recovered jeans and the depicted jeans, when Vorder Bruegge published his results in the *Journal of Forensic Sciences*, he offered detailed comparisons through photographic means. Both legs of the jeans, as depicted on film, were compared with the same parts of the recovered jeans, which were modelled in such a way as to duplicate – as far as possible – the pose of the robber and the angle of the surveillance footage (fig. 7.6 (compare with fig. 7.1)).

Looking at the robber's inside left leg on the CCTV footage, the image was not of good enough quality, and the jeans were too much in shadow to see clearly the 'barcode' pattern on the felled inseam. Despite this, Vorder Bruegge identified

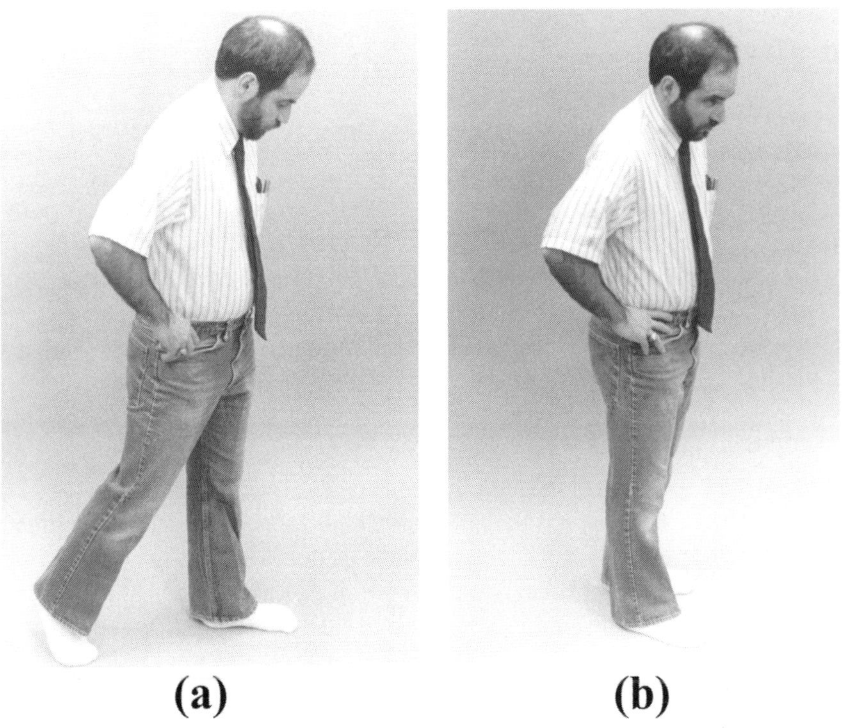

Figure 7.6 Modelling of J.C. Penney 'Plain Pocket' blue jeans, recovered from suspect's home (a) shows left inseam; (b) shows right side seam. From Vorder Bruegge 1999. Compare with fig 7.1. (© ASTM International)

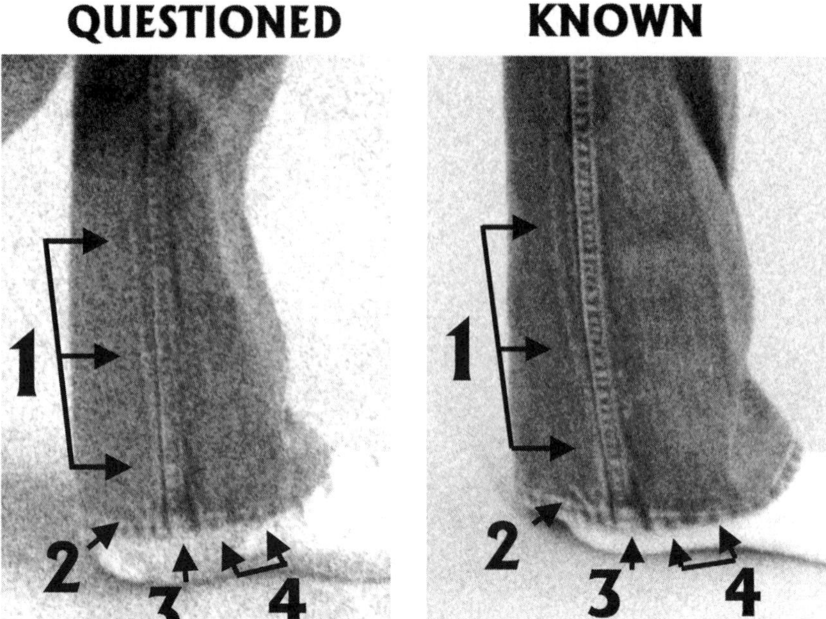

Figure 7.7 Side-by-side comparison of Spokane bank robber's left leg ('Questioned') (see fig. 7.1 (a)) and left leg of model wearing jeans recovered from suspect's home ('Known') (see fig. 7.6 (a)). From Vorder Bruegge 1999. (© ASTM International)

four key wear-features, all of which he also found on the recovered jeans (marked here as 'known') (fig. 7.7). The first of these is a 'bright linear feature' (marked '1') which runs upwards from the hem, just to the left of the inseam and running parallel to it before it angles away from it. This characteristic is also visible on the modelled jeans. The feature marked '2' is a bright 'V' shape, tilting to the left, with its base on the hemline, and its right side vertical; this, too, is visible on the recovered jeans. To the right of this, marked '3', is an 'H'-shaped set of dark patches, where the right upright part of the 'H' is broader than the left upright, which runs vertically along the left edge of the inseam. The final key wear-feature identified here by Vorder Bruegge, marked '4', is situated to the right of this 'H', and is a pair of bright features, each shaped like the Greek letter 'π' (1999: 617). Both the 'H' and the 'π' shapes can be seen on the recovered jeans (see fig. 7.7).

Turning his attention to the outside of the right leg of the robber's jeans, as depicted – much more clearly than the left leg – on the film footage, Dr Vorder Bruegge identified and enumerated a further twenty-six features (1999: 618). These were also noted in the recovered jeans, as demonstrated by the compared images (fig. 7.8: the image marked 'known' is taken from fig. 7.6 (b)). What we have here

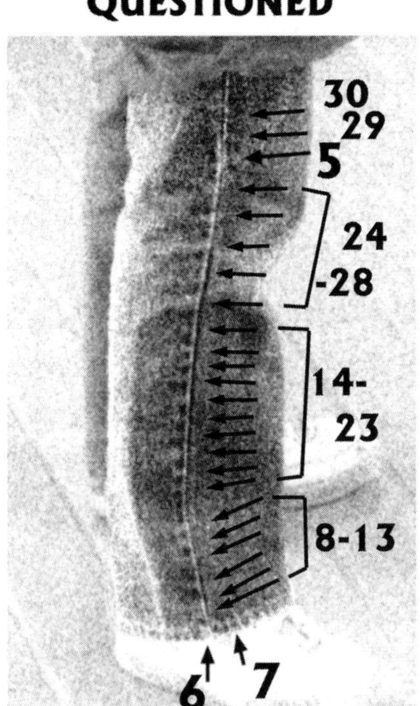

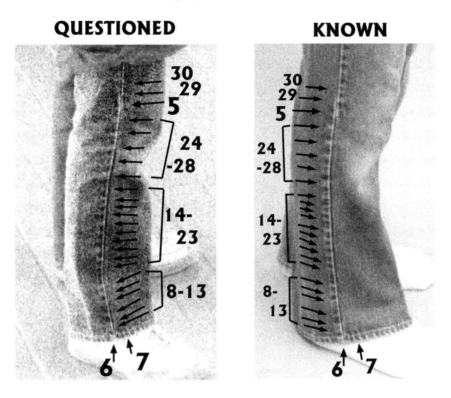

Figure 7.8 Side-by-side comparison of Spokane bank robber's right leg ('Questioned') (see fig. 7.1 (b)) and right leg of model wearing jeans recovered from suspect's home ('Known') (see fig. 7.6 (b)). From Vorder Bruegge 1999. (© ASTM International)

is what Vorder Bruegge calls 'a distinctive barcode pattern', just to the left of the seam, running from the hem to above the knee. The flaps of fabric on the inside of the trouser leg have evidently settled on this side of the seam, giving rise to the abraded series of slight ridges and furrows evident along the seam of the garment in both images. Just above the knee there is evidence of a 'cross-over' to the other side (marked '5'), as described above; for here is a bright white area, where there has been most abrasion. Above this area, the 'barcode' pattern continues on the other side of the seam. Twenty-three separate bright patches were observed by Vorder Bruegge along this seam, and two further pale areas were identified along the hem. All of these features are visible on the recovered jeans; no features on these were not borne out in the CCTV images. Hence Vorder Bruegge was able to individualise the recovered jeans as those worn by the bank robber.

Vorder Bruegge's testimony was used in the case against Barbee and his associates, but his method, as I have already indicated, was not uncontested. I am not concerned here with establishing the legal validity of the evidence, which obviously is always going to be contingent on such factors as quality of film and clarity of image, as Vorder Bruegge acknowledges. What I am interested in, are in a sense the by-products of Vorder Bruegge's research. For whilst the aim of the FBI was simply to match a garment with its caught CCTV image, in order to secure a conviction, Vorder Bruegge's inquiry at the same time almost involuntarily exposed something interesting about a worn garment. What was illuminated – inadvertently – was an otherwise hidden relationship between garment, maker, and wearer. For it is not just the traces of an individual wearer that are evident in those jeans. For the purposes of this forensic investigation, the most individuating wear patterns had themselves been primarily determined by the tensions along the seams and hems, tensions which were established by the movements of the maker's hands. These tensions result in an induplicable puckering, which, like a latent image inside the garment, waits for wear and washing to reveal it.

Vorder Bruegge's aim was primarily to individualise jeans, not individuals, and he found the key to this was in the seams. The 'ridges and valleys' could, in principle, be revealed by stone-washing just as much as by wear. Yet, as he found, the individual wearer cannot be dismissed any more than the maker. The walk, experiences and habits of the wearer have an important part to play in determining the jeans' appearance over time. Tensions on fabric and seams alike will be created by 'the mold of the body' and its habitual activities. The wearer's posture, shape and habits doubtless may determine where, exactly, a 'cross-over' may occur; these factors will certainly affect how and where a 'barcode' pattern will emerge (most quickly, and dramatically, for example, wherever the legs rub closest together on the inseams). What Vorder Bruegge's research demonstrates is that the appearance of jeans is the unique collaboration between maker, fabric and wearer. New clothes are evidently not simply waiting for our imprint to give them an identity, as poetic and literary writing about clothing might imply. Whilst we might imbue our jeans with our own shape, and mould their form and appearance through our habits, we do not do so on a *tabula rasa* – for these garments have their own unique structure, made by, and imbedded with the traces of, the actions and habits of invisible workers, in the prehistory of their existence as commodities. As James Agee suggested, it is *on the basis of this structure* that 'they are changed into images and marvels of nature' (Agee and Evans 1941: 267).

When Marx wrote, famously, about the 'fetishism of commodities', his use of the anthropological term was intended, partly, to describe how commodities appear in the world as if from nowhere, the process of their production mysteriously occluded as if they were themselves 'independent beings endowed with life' (Marx 1919: 31). A commodity is labour crystallised in an object; it corresponds to Robert Stoller's description of the fetish (in psychoanalytical discourse) as 'a story masquerading as an object' (Stoller 1985: 155). In one sense, this is tautological: surely all objects are stories in disguise. Yet for the fetish – whether of the psycho-sexual or the commodity kind – it is imperative that the masquerade be maintained. It is built into the commodity's very logic and structure that it exists *as a commodity* (retains an exchange-value) in the degree to which the social relations, and specific labour processes that caused it to come into the world, are substituted by the mysterious appearance of an object which takes its place amongst other objects in the 'phantasmagoria' of the world of consumption. 'All trace of its own production should ideally disappear from the object of consumption', wrote Adorno, reflecting here on the commodification of music. 'It should look as though it had never been *made*' (Quoted in Benjamin 1999: 670).

The fact that in *Capital* Marx's primary example of a commodity was a coat is not, as Peter Stallybrass has pointed out, accidental (Stallybrass 1998). Marx's overcoat was in and out of the pawnshop throughout the period he was working on *Capital*; without it he could not go to the British Museum to carry out necessary research – partly because of the cold, but also because it imparted a respectable air to its wearer. Marx, like countless others forced to pawn their most intimate belongings, was, according to Stallybrass, made vividly aware of how an object can again become 'a commodity and an exchange value' only when it 'is stripped of its particularity and history' (1998: 195). There are other reasons, too, why Marx should have chosen a coat as his prototypical commodity: England, as Stallybrass writes, was at this time 'the heartland of capitalism' precisely 'because it was the heartland of the textile industries'; Engels had come to Manchester to work in the cotton industry (1998: 190). What's more, the idea of the fetish in anthropological literature was from the start associated with objects worn on, or close to, the body, a proximity which in some way transformed the wearer. Such fetishes might have an affinity, then, with the much-worn overcoat, which mysteriously transformed Marx into the kind of man who could be admitted to the British Museum.

In a very real way the production and consumption of clothing still constitute, of course, a classic example of commodity fetishism at work, a fact highlighted by anti-globalisation activists who have drawn attention to the way in which multinational corporations are increasingly outsourcing garment manufacturing to cheap and unregulated labour markets around the world. The labour that has gone to make branded garments such as Gap, Nike or Tommy Hilfiger is hidden behind labels which may, according to Andrew Ross, say 'Made in the USA' even if they have been sewn on in Asia or Central America (Ross 1997: 10). Different parts of the manufacturing process may well take place thousands of miles apart. As the mass-produced garment *par excellence* of the modern world, blue jeans as much as any garment are the product of Balkanised manufacturing processes and cheap, non-unionised labour, although, of course, this may not be apparent to the consumer.[11] When we buy a pair of jeans, the identity and geographical location of those workers who have produced the fabric, cut out the pieces, constructed the seams, operated the rivetting machinery, and applied the label are not intelligible by looking at our purchase. Commodity fetishism goes deeper than this, however, for as we have seen, it is in the nature of the commodity to preclude such considerations. To ascribe to the commodity a maker, or makers, and to inquire after their identity, is to go against the grain. Denim jeans, in particular, substitute a phantasmagoric all-American myth of origins for a social reality in which they are more likely to have been made by poorly-paid migrant workers who receive 12 per cent of the retail price.[12] Denim jeans come from a mythical place called America, if they come from anywhere; they might not seem to have been *made* at all.

Looked at with this in mind, the Spokane case enacts a kind of commodity fetishism in reverse. What is inadvertently revealed in the process of individuation (of a garment, and hence of a suspect) is the evidence of the hand movements of those invisible and anonymous workers whose labour is otherwise occluded in the commodity form. It is as if it is the fingerprints of the seamstress that emerge from the dust of the criminal investigation – and it is these that help to identify the suspect. Once perceived, this reversal of commodity fetishism is not confined to this particular criminal investigation. For the FBI did not so much reveal the latent image of labour embedded in jeans, as show how this image is itself revealed as a matter of course by the jeans' wearer over time. Vorder Bruegge's research illuminates the way in which the traces of labour in jeans are themselves illuminated – almost literally – by ordinary wear. It is not so much, then, the dust of the criminal investigation that reveals the worker's fingerprints; it is the dust of wear, and this extraordinary fact is what is revealed as a by-product of the case.

It was not just the traces of an anonymous worker that were revealed as a by-product of the investigation, though – so, too, were the historical and geographical co-ordinates of the making of the seams. 'Through consultation with the manufacturer', writes Vorder Bruegge, 'it was determined that these jeans had been constructed in Clarksville, Tennessee in 1991, using standard hand-guided sewing practices common throughout the blue jean industry' (1999: 618). This kind of consultation was necessary to the investigation since it established how, exactly, the seams were constructed, and hence the observed characteristics of the jeans could be ascribed to the random consequences of hand-guided sewing. But it also established the otherwise-hidden origin of the garment.[13]

In *Sartor Resartus*, Professor Teufelsdröckh (a fictional philosopher of clothing) paces the 'Old-Clothes Market' as if it were a 'Whispering Gallery'. To him, Monmouth Street was, apparently, a 'true Delphic Avenue' (Carlyle 2000 [1833–4]: 179). So, too, with the Spokane case, where a pair of J.C. Penney jeans revealed the identity of their owner to the FBI. These jeans spoke: they were there at the US Bank on 1 April 1996; they saw the crime, they dressed the man. But they were also there at a processing plant in Clarksville, Tennessee, in 1991, where they passed through the hands and machine of an anonymous worker who left their involuntary signature in the garment, a signature which was made visible through the habits and wear of its purchaser, Charles Barbee. Like the Turin Shroud, this pair of jeans were forced to tell their story, thereby to identify the body they clothed; they told more, however, than was necessary for the criminal investigation.

Some scholars, believing the Turin Shroud to bear the negative imprint of the crucified body of Christ, think it possible to reconstruct the whole of Christ's Passion from the stains on the Shroud – the location and appearance of the shackles on Christ's feet, the shape of the crown of thorns on his head, and so on, even locating the 'saliva of the last utterance' (Didi-Huberman 1987: 53). This, as Georges Didi-Huberman points out, is a 'fantasy of referentiality' invited by stains which tell us nothing in themselves about their origins, but which as *indices* demand to be retraced to the acts that have established them (1987: 44). What's more, each act, says Didi-Huberman 'calls forth … the proper name of the actor: he who left some of his blood on this linen sheet' (1987: 44). The 'ridges and valleys' identified by Vorder Bruegge are just such indices inviting a 'fantasy of referentiality' which can be retraced to the act of sewing. These are the stigmata of labour; and we can trace them to Clarksville in 1991. The fantasy stops short, however, at the point of the 'proper name' of the machine operator; the illumination, even by the FBI, even if it were crucial to the case, could not be that powerful or bright.

Acknowledgements

Thanks to Alan Hamilton, Esther Leslie, Harro Maas, Azam Torab and Peter Wilson for their comments and suggestions, and to Dr Richard Vorder Bruegge for further information about his work. Images 7.1, 2, 5, 6, 7 and 8 reprinted, with permission, from the *Journal of Forensic Sciences*, vol. 44, no. 3, copyright ASTM International, 100 Barr Harbor Drive, West Conshohoken, PA 19428.

Notes

1. Quoted in Benjamin 1999: 223.
2. Criminalistics has long paid attention to clothing in forensic investigations. What is different about Vorder Bruegge's research is that it is concerned with ordinary wear rather than extraordinary marks (rips, blood-stains etc), and has

more in common with fingerprint or tyre-tread comparisons where forensic scientists identify and match unique patterns.

3. Vorder Bruegge points out that this is far from inevitable: the quality of the film must be taken into consideration (1999: 614). The US bank footage in question was apparently high quality 35mm, which facilitated the inquiry (Philipkoski 1998).
4. The prosecution was successful on its second trial.
5. It was reported, for example, on BBC Radio 1 and by *Wired.*
6. 'It sounds like voodoo to me', said Jack King, Public Affairs Director at the National Association of Criminal Defense Lawyers (quoted by Philipkoski 1998). King's scepticism was based partly on the ability of this type of photographic evidence to show tonal differences with sufficient clarity and resolution. For parallels between deduction and divination, see Ginzburg 1983.
7. Official state practices and the methods of fictional detectives were interestingly closely connected in fact, with borrowings both ways: see Truzzi 1983.
8. This conceit corresponds to Agee's insistence that documentary should individuate, not delineate 'types'. See Lucaites 1997.
9. See, in particular in this volume, Carol Mara, 'Divestments' (57–60); Beverly Pagram, 'Clothes Have No Memory' (79–83); and Alba Ambert, 'The Denim Jacket' (134–8).
10. H. Tuthill, *Individualization: Principles and procedures in criminalistics* (1994), quoted in Vorder Bruegge 1999: 613.
11. See 'The Big Jeans Stitch-Up', Special issue of *The New Internationalist*, 302, June 1998.
12. 'Jeans – the Facts', Special issue of *The New Internationalist*, 302, June 1998: 18.
13. In fact Vorder Bruegge is confident that these jeans were 'wholly cut, constructed and finished in the U.S.': this, he says, is 'how they do/did it at the Levi's plant in Tennessee and that's how it was described to me' (personal communication, 14 November 2002).

References

Agee, J. and W. Evans (1941) *Let Us Now Praise Famous Men*. Boston: Houghton Mifflin.

Ash, J. (1999) 'The Aesthetics of Absence: Clothes without People in Paintings', in A. de la Haye and E. Wilson (eds) *Defining Dress: Dress as Object, Meaning and Identity*. Manchester: Manchester University Press.

Benjamin, W. (1989) *Charles Baudelaire: A Lyric Poet in the Era of High Capitalism*. London: Verso.

—— (1999), *The Arcades Project*. Cambridge, MA: Harvard University Press.

Caplan, J. and J. Torpey (eds) (2001) *Documenting Individual Identity: The Development of State Practices in the Modern World*. Princeton: Princeton University Press.

Carey, J. (1992) *The Intellectuals and the Masses: Pride and Prejudice among the Literary Intelligentsia, 1880–1939*. London: Faber and Faber.

Carlyle, T. (2000 [1833–4]) *Sartor Resartus*. Berkeley: University of California Press.

Cole, S.A. (2001) *Suspect Identities: A History of Fingerprinting and Criminal Identification*. Cambridge, MA: Harvard University Press.

Conan Doyle, A. (1989 [1887]) 'A Study in Scarlet', in *The Original Illustrated 'Strand' Sherlock Holmes*. Ware: Wordsworth.

Dickens, C. (1994 [1836]) 'Meditations in Monmouth Street', in *Sketches by Boz and other Early Papers 1833–39*. London: J.M. Dent.

Didi-Huberman, G. (1987) 'The Index of the Absent Wound (Monograph on a Stain)', in A. Michelson, R. Krauss, D. Crimp and J. Copjec (eds) *October: The First Decade, 1976–1986*. Cambridge, MA: MIT Press.

Dunseath, K. (ed.) (1998) *A Second Skin: Women Writing about Clothes*. London: The Women's Press.

Eco, U. and T.A. Sebeok (1983) *The Sign of Three: Dupin, Holmes, Peirce*. Bloomington: Indiana University Press.

Finlayson, I. (1990) *Denim: The American Legend*. Norwich: Parke Sutton.

Ginzburg, C. (1983) 'Clues: Morelli, Freud, and Sherlock Holmes', in U. Eco and T.A. Sebeok (eds) *The Sign of Three: Dupin, Holmes, Peirce*. Bloomington: Indiana University Press.

Joseph, A. and A. Winter (1996) 'Making the Match: Human Traces, Forensic Experts and the Public Imagination', in F. Spufford and J. Uglow (eds) *Cultural Babbage: Technology, Time and Invention*. London: Faber and Faber.

Lucaites, J.L. (1997) 'Visualizing "The People": Individualism vs. Collectivism in *Let Us Now Praise Famous Men*', *The Quarterly Journal of Speech*, 83 (3): 269–88.

Marx, K. (1919) *Capital: A Critique of Political Economy Vol. 1*. Chicago: H. Kerr and Co.

Philipkoski, K. (1998) 'FBI Tracks the Denim Trail', <http://www.wired.com/news/technology>, 6 April 1998.

Ross, A. (1997) *No Sweat: Fashion, Free Trade, and The Rights of Garment Workers*. London: Verso.

Stallybrass, P. (1993) 'Worn Worlds: Clothes, Mourning, and the Life of Things', *The Yale Review*, 81 (2): 35–50.

—— (1998) 'Marx's Coat', in P. Spyer (ed.) *Border Fetishisms: Material Objects in Unstable Spaces*. London: Routledge.

Stoller, R. (1985) *Observing the Erotic Imagination*. New Haven: Yale University Press.

Thomas, R.R. (1999) *Detective Fiction and the Rise of Forensic Science*. Cambridge: Cambridge University Press.

Truzzi, M. (1983) 'Sherlock Holmes: Applied Social Psychologist', in U. Eco and T.A. Sebeok (eds) *The Sign of Three: Dupin, Holmes, Peirce*. Bloomington: Indiana University Press.

Vorder Bruegge, R.W. (1999) 'Photographic Identification of Denim Trousers from Bank Surveillance Film', *Journal of Forensic Sciences*, 44 (3): 613–22.

Wilson, E. (1985) *Adorned in Dreams: Fashion and Modernity*. London: Virago.

Response

Esther Leslie

Kitty Hauser's paper returns the category of labour to the study of fashion. Her investigation shows that the mode of making cannot be ignored. The specific mode of production of the jeans necessitates a pushing by hand through sewing machines, in order to fix thick seams. In Marx's terms, 'living labour' asserts itself against and in conjunction with 'dead labour'. Making jeans is apparently not a process that can be automated successfully. Machinery's dead labour cannot substitute for the physical exertion of a sewing machinist. Made alert to these processes through Hauser's tale of crime detection, we now see that these clothes, perhaps more than any others, do not mask their process of manufacture. They do not smooth away seams and materiality into magical confectionery. This is no case of unseen hands stitching invisible seams, machinically. Rather the jeans retain the specific traces of being worked on, and by human hands – be it those of the low-paid Third World machine operator or the jobbing prisoner.

Labour imprints itself on this fabric in another way. Denim was once the stuff of work clothes. But what is work? Work is transformation, or specifically, historical action upon nature or nature transformed. As such work marks itself on the jeans. Their particular unevenness, operating in conjunction with the body that is dressed in them, makes 'to wear' an active verb again. The jeans record the wear and tear of movement, of usage, of a use-value that can be consumed and exhausted eventually by someone who marks a specific selfhood on the item. This marking is not, though, on a passive receiving material, but a material that is, in turn, assertive. Both parties – wearer and worn – are involved in producing a specifically marked materiality. Perhaps the resonance here is amplified by the suggestion of an even greater intimacy between jeans and wearer, both engaged in processes of action that alters. We see it in Walker Evans' photographs, where the wrinkles on the sharecropper's face (brought about by grafting with its inevitable facial straining, exposure to sunlight and encounters with dirt), match the creases and indentations on the denim overalls, likewise occasioned by grafting with its inevitable rubbing, straining and exposure to sunlight and encounters with dirt. Jeans and face are marked by patina, by the effects of time. History and labour imprint on matter, and matter asserts its own part in the process, its particular propensity to bend or resist, to be rubbed or rub in turn, dependent on the quirks introduced by the labour process. Forcing their own effectiveness to the fore, labour and matter conspire to speak back against the fetishising socio-economic push towards invisibility. In such a process of concealment, as Adorno notes, in an echo of Marx's idea of commodity fetishism, commodification acts to confect an appearance of the never-made, by repressing all traces of labour. '[A] consumer item in which there is no longer anything that is supposed to remind us how it came into being. It becomes a magical object, in so far as the labour stored up in it comes to seem supernatural and sacred at the very moment when it can no longer be recognized as labor' (Benjamin 1999: 669).

Here though, in the jeans that make up Hauser's evidence, there is the shock recognition of human activity and material substance. Ideal forms are besmirched. With the jeans the flaws reveal: the layers of dyes that rub off under friction, fading tints, the anomalies of stitching, the scuffing of pavement at the heel, the force of the leg asserting its shape.

To generalise from this: is there something here that hits against fashion and its inextricable linkage with modernity? The complex fashion/modernity frequently implies presentness not pastness, consumption not production, expenditure not labour. Is a trend bucked here? For is not everything in modernity's and fashion's purview always to be thought of as new and ever-same, that is constant in itself and only ever at the beginning of its (shelf-)life – once passé then it passes into another state?

Here, instead, attention is drawn to the shape of the body impressed in discarded clothes, usually rendered poetically as the clothes of the dead or departed – clothes as relics, and as such almost holy, definitely sentimental. Some clothes carry so much past in them they are consigned to the past. That is to say, they become things of memory, no longer useable. At that point, clothes become anomalous, 'auratic', and never contemporaneous. That means, fashion bars them. Fashion is only of the present. A modern fabric, the fabric of capitalist modernity, cannot withstand the snarl of history (or if it can, then it is only as quotation, a cheeky reference). A fabric in modernity, and one that is so much *of* modernity, should not be able to capture history as does this one. Are the jeans, archetypal symbol of Western modernity (still work wear but so much more too), remnants of a past mode of dress, from another type of production? The past is not supposed to assert itself in the commodity that was anyway apparently never made and bears no traces of past labour or even, given the fetish of newness, the patina of use over time.

In textiles, could it be the case that modernity manifests in the efforts from the mid nineteenth century onwards to invent in laboratories synthetic dyes that did not fade when exposed to sunlight, that did not bleed when rinsed or boiled in water, that held their colours for year after year? Later, textiles were made synthetically, crease-proof, tear-proof, denying time's passage, the wear and tear of movement – though never so much that they become as indestructible, as dirt-repelling and luminous as the white suit made by the inventor in the 1951 Ealing film comedy, against which workers and bosses unite in fear for their jobs and their profits.[1] Industrial modernity's drive, in textiles and elsewhere, was the push for substitutes and synthetics, and this was felt most acutely in Germany, where chemistry attempted to concoct replacements for lacking resources from inaccessible markets or non-existent colonies. A 1938 manual from IG Farben begins with a worker's reflection on the infiltration of IG products into his company house (*Erzeugnisse Unserer Arbeit*, 1938: 7–12). The worker notes how the curtains are shining as brightly as when first bought, because of IG's synthetic dyes. His wife's dress and apron, the artificial silk tablecloth, all as bright as when first presented to her. The crockery, the butter dish, the child's beaker are all made of Pollopso plastic from IG. All chemical marvels, denying time's passing, natural decay and history's ravages. They are perfect fetishes, smooth and ever-new. And this brave new chemical world came from the same society that invented a Robotic Cloth Flaw Detector, fulfilling Ernst Jünger's fantasy of the soldier as automaton, ahuman, anatural, ahistorical and without autonomy. Olaf Nissen described this materials-testing robot in his 1943 anti-Nazi propaganda pamphlet, titled *Germany: A Land of Substitutes*. The booklet is simultaneously fascinated and terrified by Nazi-German inventiveness. Substitutes and fakes are being cooked up all over Germany as part of the war effort. This propensity to fakery and trickery comes to take on moral qualities. One aspect is an increasing denaturalisation, or a depersonalisation. Nissen writes of a robot with a steel skeleton, its flesh filling supplied by weight-adjustable sand and sawdust. This robot sits and stands in its uniform 97,000 times before the trouser cloth begins to wear. It bends its arms mechanically in like fashion, investigating how long the soldier might raise his arm and fire before his seams burst or his sleeves tear at the elbows. The robot comes with a weighing scale to measure how much cloth is lost through wear (Nissen 1943: 119). This flaw-detecting machine conjures up modernity's dream of efficiency, economy, prescribed movements, an administered society, where even the precise moment of failure hopes to be predicted in advance. Its corollary is administrators' attempts to subdue material – be that fabric or human – in order to aim at an ideal realm of ideal forms.

To conclude, the jeans are, then, simultaneously the ultimate modern fashion item and not modern, outside of fashion, because they are more a document of the past. They are documents of the past because they retain on them a record of the past (which perhaps includes their own generic past as work wear) and a chronicle of the interaction between wearer and worn, as well as the trace of labour, the actuality that subtends the fetish. Chastening though is the double action of Hauser's instance. To focus on the history, labour and activity ensnared in the material exposes the social guilt of a society, where commodity fetishism typically refuses labour any articulation or voice. But it also, in this case, under these social conditions, allows the discipliners and surveillers another means to ascribe guilt and to act with the force of law upon that.

Notes

1. This is not complete fantasy. When Indanthren colours were invented in Germany at the beginning of the twentieth century, dyers struck against the use of these permanent colours.

References

Benjamin, W. (1999) *The Arcades Project*. Trans. H. Eiland and K. McLaughlin. Cambridge, MA: The Belknap Press/Harvard University Press.

Erzeugnisse Unserer Arbeit (1938) Frankfurt/Main: I.G. Farbenindustrie Aktiengesellschaft.

Nissen, O. (1943) *Germany: A Land of Substitutes*. London: John Gifford Ltd.

–8–

Cuttings and Pastings

Alistair O'Neill

This investigation into the uses of press cuttings by creative practitioners related to the field of fashion was inspired by a project by the fashion designers Viktor & Rolf, published in the short-lived magazine *The Fashion* (see figs 8.1 and 8.2). Within the spreads the designers presented photographs of press cuttings of their recent collection as origami imitating the familiar forms of historical still-life paintings. One featured a vase of paper lilies in a paper vase, in the other newspaper articles were hung like personal letters and effects on the back of a canvas stretcher.

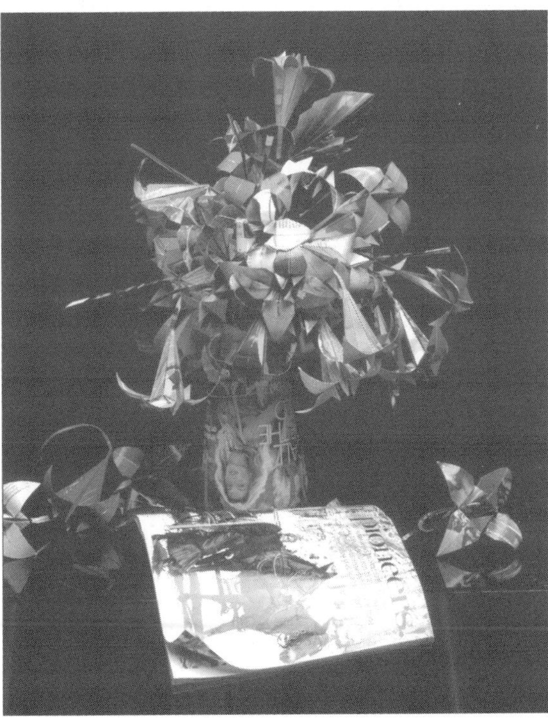

Figure 8.1 Viktor & Rolf for *The Fashion*, 3, auturnfwirter 2001–2, by Anuschka Blommers and Niels Schumm. (Photograph courtesy of Anuschka Blommers and Niels Schumm)

Figure 8.2 Viktor & Rolf for *The Fashion*, 3, auturnfwirter 2001–2, by Anuschka Blommers and Niels Schumm. (Photograph courtesy of Anuschka Blommers and Niels Schumm)

The project was unusual enough to stop my flicking and to arrest my gaze. On reflection I realised that the photographs hadn't only disrupted the flow of the fashion magazine as it turned in my hands, but that they had also disrupted its logic. By this I mean that the published project was a form of creative expression that wasn't about recycling, it was more about the status of out-of-date magazines and the things they contain. It wasn't about the imitation of art by fashion even though it might have looked like it; it was more concerned with how the themes of still-life painting can inform the purpose of fashion magazines after their shelf life. It wasn't about looking back, or harking back, as it was just all too recent. It was the kind of 'recent' that's uncomfortable to many who work for, feature, read or even buy fashion magazines. It was the kind of 'recent' we erase in the act of assimilating what's current. The photographs force us to twist our heads back ever so slightly, to perform a rewind scan that pulls us to something we've seen in the past and asks us to reconsider its worth in the here and now. They ask us what we now make of these things, fancifully presented, torn from their original context? A witty use of worthless things? A double waste of paper?

One might suppose that Viktor & Rolf used them to memorialise their work and the manner in which they are written about: a way of visually paying tribute to the tributes. But it seemed to me that there was a lot more going on here than just artful back-slapping. As photographs in a fashion magazine they claim to memorialise both a season of fashion shown and a season of fashion on the turn. Further, they pose as visual metaphors for the condition of fashion expressed in printed form: as eternal spring and as the translation of clothing into language (Barthes 1983: x). Yet the photographs point not only to the mutability of fashion, but also to the ephemeral quality of the material that communicates it. In this instance, the designers refashion the material that fashion has cast off; commemorating the moment of their own endeavour captured as printed expression.

The photographs demonstrate in visual terms the momentary fix that the fashion magazine can perform on the continuum of fashion. Yet they are rare in being able to further demonstrate a sense of loss in that moment passing, and, in their figuring of press cuttings, they present the sum of these printed materials as the memory of that moment captured. We accept that the fashion magazine is central to the articulation of fashion, even though we now accept that the fashionablilty it presents is often different to our own consumption of it. However, the experience of modernity remains unconcerned by this slippage, as the purpose of the fashion magazine is in only being the articulation of its continual state of transition. This denies another and equal aspect, as the fashion magazine is both the signifier and souvenir of the modern condition. It confirms the continual present whilst offering in material form a document of what is passing; an ossified sensibility of what was once felt.

What is marginalised by modernity is what is cast off and in this instance it's the simultaneous accumulation of material charting the fashion magazine's rolling endeavour: it's the stack of back issues, the file of tear sheets. And it is here that we find a peculiar paradox: the practice of fashion thrives as much on the material that it casts off, as on what it wishes to project. Judith Clark (2002) has identified this in the monthly collages of Anna Piaggi in Italian *Vogue* noting their ability to represent in visual form the multiple histories she fuses to form the monthly variants of fashion. Further, Caroline Evans has suggested that the repository that contemporary fashion designers draw upon is analogous to Benjamin's rendering of history not as narrative, but as composed of fragmented memory images, 'a labyrinthine relay between past, present and imagined future' (Evans 2003: 7–14). It thus becomes apparent that the repository of fragments is essential to the articulation of fashion as a phenomenon of modernity, even though it may remain on the periphery of the vision it projects.

I wish to put forward that the pile of out-of-date fashion magazines and the collection of cuttings possessed by almost every creative practitioner related to the practice of fashion are primary to the articulation of fashion as a central tenet of modernity. While accepting *bricolage* as a practical technique of fashion design and styling informed by collage, the purpose is not to concentrate on the creativity of cut 'n' paste in fashion, but rather, to consider the repository of cuttings and the logic of the magazine as informing the crafting of fashion and the experience of modernity.

This will be considered through the use of four particular examples: a printed textile design by fashion designer Elsa Schiaparelli and a collage by Dada artist Kurt Schwitters from the first half of the twentieth century; and artworks by American artists Barbara Kruger and Richard Prince from the second half of the twentieth century. The reason for using these examples it not to claim them as evidencing fashion aspiring to the condition of art, or vice versa; rather, it is because all of these practitioners have had first-hand experience in either the creation or consumption of titles circulated by fashion magazine publishing. Further, all of the examples are connected by a use of the fashion magazine's materiality as source material for reconfiguration, be it collage, transformation, representation or appropriation. In order to locate these practices it is necessary to outline the status of collage and its associated terms.

It is widely accepted that as a medium of creative expression, collage is materially driven by mass production and, in connoting the temporal and ephemeral, it is expressive of the time, speed and duration of urban experience. In fashioning fragments from what is lost and then found, collage proposes a dislocation, supplanting a representation of reality with the materiality of reality. Yet the popular nineteenth-century pastime of the scrapbook, the multiple exposure art photographs of the 1870s and the Victorian craft of decoupage, are all recognised as precedents to what is thought of as a chiefly twentieth-century medium. In her study of collage, art historian Diane Waldman proposes that: 'Both the amateur and the professional in the nineteenth century imparted to the practitioners of collage and assemblage in our era a bittersweet quality based in sentiment and nostalgia that distinguishes collage and assemblage from their peers in twentieth century painting and sculpture' (1992: 11).

Yet such a bittersweet quality is not what we might readily associate with *cut 'n' paste*, a more popular term for collage, which rather than conjuring up a sense of sentimentality denotes the menace of the ransom note spelt in letterforms cut from newspapers. The abbreviation of the word *and* in the term suggests the discordant and reductive designs that characterise this particular visual language established in the mid 1970s and associated with punk as a graphical language. As a strategy of art photography also informed by the renegade nature of punk, appropriation fostered a 'take-without-asking' approach that challenged definitions of authorship and authenticity by the practice of re-photography. This was collage without the visible seams, transformation achieved through reframing and representing. And yet *cut 'n' paste* is also an abbreviation of *cuttings and pastings*, the old-fashioned pastime of filling sugar paper pages of scrapbooks with cuttings of covetable information. By titling this essay 'Cuttings and Pastings' I wish to draw attention away from the creative practice of cut 'n' paste towards its historical predecessor, so that I am concerned not solely with the process of creativity and reconstituted meaning, but also with the process of classification and the meaning of storing printed material.

Schwitters and Schiaparelli

In MZ 180 (1921), a collage by Kurt Schwitters (see fig. 8.3), a fashion model sports an overskirt of newsprint overlaid by the artist, so that the newsprint appears as if a printed textile design. In seeming similarity, an illustration by Cecil Beaton for British *Vogue* depicts elements seen at a fashion show from spring 1935 staged by Elsa Schiaparelli (see fig. 8.4). A hat and scarf featured utilise a printed textile design formed from press cuttings of reviews of her fashion presentations. The Schwitters collage is a press clipping parading as a dress, while

Figure 8.3 Mz 180 (Figurine), 1921, by Kurt Schwitters. Collage on paper. (Sprengel Museum Hannover © DACS 2004)

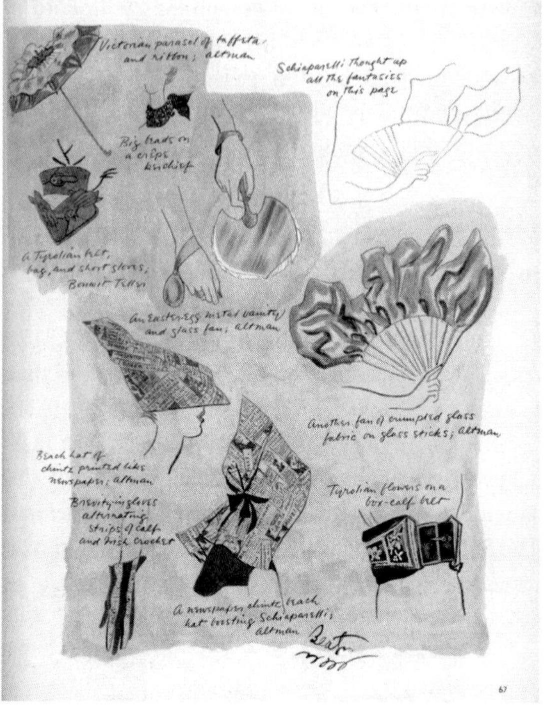

Figure 8.4 Schiaparelli hats, including one made from her 'newsprint' fabric. From Cecil Beaton, 'Fun at the Openings', British *Vogue*, 1 April 1935. Pencil, ink and gouache. (Cecil Beaton/Vogue © Condé Nast Publications Inc)

the Schiaparelli items of apparel parade as press clippings. The inverted trickery the two images propose is not unlike the painting technique known as *trompe l'ôeil*, and the implication of the one aping the other can be interpreted in many ways. The images evidence the symbiotic flow of ideas between those working in the field of art and those working in the field of fashion in the twentieth century. By their literalness they support the idea of dress as a communicative medium and by their detail they support the psychological aspect of dress as cited on the surface and readable.

As forms of collage the creations are concerned with incongruity as a principle of rendering and the pleasure of looking. In their aim to parallel the pace of fashion with the pace of daily news, the collages inscribe the one over the other on a fused surface. In doing so they point to their moment of now-time, the continual present. Yet in fixing and memorialising the time of coming into being, they point to that moment as the present passed, rendering yesterday's girl as equal to yesterday's paper. Without their own repositories of yesterday's papers, neither Schiaparelli nor Schwitter's would have had the source materials necessary to make such collages, and it seems to me that the press cuttings file in Schiaparelli's atelier is not that dissimilar to the piles of printed material in Schwitter's studio. The difference, however, is in the historical interpretation: Schwitter's pile is prized by art historians as an artwork of equal status to his collage; meanwhile, although Schiaparelli is prized by dress historians for her skill at visual quotation, her press cuttings rarely merit a mention.

In Schiaparelli's case, the printed fabric she designed was supposedly inspired by the hats she had seen women working in the fish markets of Copenhagen wearing, although the designer was herself keen to maintain that the overarching inspiration had been a cubist painting by Picasso that had used newspaper as a collaged material. The design was based on both good and bad reviews printed in a number of languages from a number of sources. As a fashion designer Schaparelli read broadly, from avant-garde journals to those of her trade. Indeed, it may well be that she got the idea for the printed textile from Schwitters himself, as she was well versed in modern art and was acquainted with many of its practitioners. A familiarity with the fashion trade journal can also be claimed for Schwitters. His parents owned a ladies clothes shop, so he would have been familiar with the kind of journals that kept the fashion retail trade informed. Indeed, a project of 1924 by the artist was to construct a personal volume of fashion, which sadly never materialised. The short inscription underneath Schwitter's collage translates as 'Paper is the Great Fashion'. Here Schwitters claims paper, his source material, as the best substance for the craft of fashioning; the cut of his scalpel blade into paper is identical to the cut of shears into cloth; the concept of fashion is defined by the activity of making. Schwitter's inscription underlines that the very material qualities of newsprint – cheap, easy to produce, bountiful and disposable – were the very properties which allowed fashion to exist at a heightened speed within the period.

Art historian John Elderfield has described Schwitters' work as 'a style not of unfolding, but stylistic accumulation' (1985: 71). Similarly, I would like to examine the recording of fashion on paper not as something which unfolds, like the turning of the pages of a magazine, but as something which accumulates, like the archives whose holdings are pasted down in cut form. This can be substantiated by returning to the two photographs by Viktor & Rolf. In 1997 Richard Martin published an article about the nature of Viktor and Rolf's creative output describing it as inverse to the recent production of art and clothing that deals with the body but maintains the division between fashion and art as oppositional visual forces:

> To present art as a collection, as opposed to the high-bred supposition of individual works of art, is immediately to accept a contemporary convention for our seeing. Culturally, we want to see thematically and often in terms larger than one. Viktor & Rolf used pre-existing fragments as the collage medium to create new clothing. Referring, of course, to the prevailing interest in deconstruction in fashion and the visual arts in

> 1993, Viktor & Rolf insisted in their intermediate world between art and fashion on the collage aspect of their work. The effect is to see, as in early Picasso collages, a new order emerging from the familiar pieces of old style. (1997: no page number)

Here Martin wishes to draw our attention to a way of seeing things informed by museological display, a way of presenting fashion through the logic of the retrospective, the academic survey of oeuvre; but in this instance it is an oeuvre which is not created by the designers, but one from which they construct their own mythology as they begin. This idea of fashion being produced as a form of thematic display that evolves by the process of accumulation, is an idea made material by Viktor & Rolf in their 1998 collection where they dressed a single model in ten outfits one on top of the other like a Russian doll. The conceptual approach of the designers means that they don't always make dresses: from a collection that consisted solely of placards painted with the words 'V&R are on Strike', to an art installation that only featured press cuttings, the designers take Warholian pleasure and fascination in knowing that printed exposure is the means by which they are understood and the means by which they continue. The photographs, however, suggest a darker and more morbid appreciation of their own notoriety.

In the first photograph a bunch of lilies mourn a double-page fashion spread lain at the base of a vase, and in the second we see the back of a canvas frame with newspaper articles draped across its wire support. As images they are overtly art historical: the flowers reference not only seventeenth-century Dutch still lifes of flora and fauna, painted to fix the continual present, but also the modernity of Baudelaire's collection of poems *Les Fleurs du Mal* (1857) where the poet discards the emotional distinctions between good and evil by seeking beauty in the perverse, grotesque and morbid. The stillness of these images, rendered by the absence of life and the absence of the material object of fashion, can only figure a printed representation on paper as the allure. The *Vogue* fashion spread exclaims 'pioneers!' at the top of the page, as if to proclaim modernity when in fact the accompanying copy underscores the use of the term pioneer as having an unequivocal historical reference: 'with mutton sleeves and broad skirts flying, our heroine joins the wagon train'. Thus it is not the historical citation made by the designers that denies modernity, but the historical citation overlaid by the magazine. And it is the stillness of the image that Viktor & Rolf have created that contradicts the endeavour to be a pioneer of fashion.

In the second image the designers hang newspaper reviews from the back of a canvas stretcher. The piece is inspired by *trompe l'ôeil* paintings of personal effects produced from the seventeeth century onwards. These would include letter racks studded with ribbons from which small, personal items could be displayed. In his study of the genre of still-life painting Norman Bryson establishes that there are two distinct kinds of painting within Western art: the first involves megalography, the study of greatness, while the second involves rhopography, the study of filth, of waste or of debris. While one is exalted the other is base. Bryson makes the following claim for the relationship of *trompe l'ôeil* painting to rhopography:

> Trompe l'oeil forms a natural alliance with detritus of every kind: scraps, husks, peelings, the fraying and discolouration of paper, or else objects taken up and looked at only occasionally – documents, letters, quills, combs, watches, goblets, books, coins. In that effacement of human attention, objects reveal their own autonomy: it is as though objects make the world, and the unconscious force stored in their outwardly humble forms – not their human users. Individual attention and consciousness are necessary or at best incidental to their independent life. (1990: 142)

So, beyond the suitability of *trompe l'ôeil* for figuring the ephemeral waste that surrounds us, these neglected things make, represent and record the world in a way that individual consciousness cannot do alone and thus the threat that paintings of things pose to the supposed greatness of paintings of people. It is the transistory detail recorded that destabilises the fixed image: a momentary punctum fixed in time, continually piercing the cultural field of authority. In the instance of Viktor & Rolf's photographs, they present their press cuttings as objects of rhopography that are situated behind the painted picture plane, behind the spectacle of what should be on show. Yet in photographing them in the style of a *trompe l'ôeil* painting, Viktor & Rolf point to the principle that, conversely, the photographs represent their creative practice more than any other aspect of their output. It is possible that they will supersede the life of the designers and the life of most of the clothing they will produce.

It would seem that in revealing what is hidden, the structural authority and autonomy of the object in question is challenged. Yet the photograph of the canvas stretcher and the press reviews suggests otherwise. It is the structural solidity of the frame that is the oppositional foil to the temporal quality of the newspaper fragments. The straplines the articles bear, 'When negative is positive' and 'This is Paris. No giggling please', although suggestive of the unease the designers may feel about the quality of the journalists who are sent to cover their presentations, are much more redolent of the mixture of the serious and the futile essential to the articulation of fashion. In sum, it is the tension expressed within empirical news about ephemeral matters that contradicts the seriousness of the creative practice of the designers, documented by word and image printed on paper.

Kruger and Prince

The visual dynamics of word and image in combination within the magazine spread became an object of investigation for the artists Barbara Kruger and

Richard Prince who were known for the practice of re-photography in the 1980s. My reason for considering their work in this essay is that they both come from a background of working with stock photographic images drawn from the holdings of magazine companies. Prince worked at Time-Life Magazines in the mid 1970s in the periodicals library, while Kruger worked as an art director for Condé Nast in the 1970s, concentrating on the layouts of its magazine titles. The working backgrounds of these artists contributed to their ability to manipulate photographic images informed by the logic of the fashion magazine. As Kruger once stated:

> it is the structuring of this idea of fashion as pervasive to the modern experience through the logic of the magazine that I am interested in . . . It's something I learned when working on magazines for so many years, that you designed a page for someone to look at, for them to look at in a relatively short time; it was important to get people's attention. If you didn't you were fired because you didn't have the competency to construct an object that was seductive enough for people to look at. (quoted in Nairne 1987: 162)

Kruger's work was concerned with the arresting of the gaze by the power of an image, aided by the slippage between the rhetoric of that image and the slogans

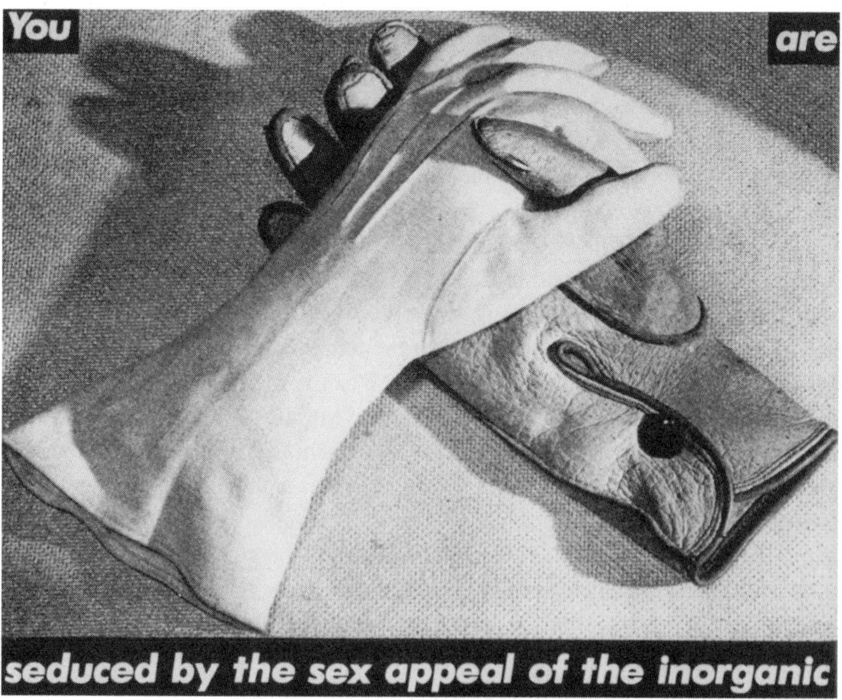

Figure 8.5 *Untitled (You are Seduced by the Sex Appeal of the Inorganic)*, 1981, by Barbara Kruger. (Courtesy of Barbara Kruger/SpruethMagersLee, London)

she overlaid. She was to demonstrate this in her artwork Untitled (*You are Seduced by the Sex Appeal of the Inorganic*) (1981) (see fig. 8.5) which suggested not only the fetishistic qualities of commodity culture and its displays, but also the rearticulation of it by a lifeless printed representation. Richard Prince was more interested in the repetitive representation of that gaze within the magazine itself.

While still working at Time-Life Prince began to stockpile photographic images from consumer magazines, many of which were fashion titles, and to re-photograph these images. With the images shorn of their copy and context, instead of selling something, they began to reappear as documentaries of something that could be considered, in Prince's terms, as aspects of life. In pieces such as *Untitled (Four Women Looking in the Same Direction)* (1977) (see fig. 8.6) Prince probed the repetitions of now-time in magazine culture to suggest not merely the stock of poses and expressions, but to hint at the generic response that these repetitions engender in the repetitions of cultural behaviour and perceptual sensibilities. Like the majority of images that one finds in an archetypal fashion magazine, the very pervasiveness of these unspectacular images proposes an ambience far more affective than one might like to admit. Art historian Jeffery Rian drew attention to this aspect of Prince's work by stating: 'What might be construed as mere image reiteration in his re-photography is indeed a form of repetition, but one that re-collects as a form of personal and cultural re-membering' (2003: no page number). In a sense Prince was creating his own repository of fragments, but fragments that concentrated on similarity rather than dissimilarity, fragments that suggested an unsettling coherence before any form of reconfiguration had taken place. In attempting to use these fragments to remember and recollect, Prince could only construct an ambient framework of familiarity rather than knowledge.

The performative implication this form of remembering infers underlines Kruger's previously mentioned observation that modern experience is invariably expressed through the logic of the magazine, but to this principle Rian adds that the cataloguing and mimicking of printed forms by individuals moves to the rhythm of magazine culture's own repetitions. In the constant reiteration of now-time, knowledge is thus understood within a framework of familiarity rather than any form of comprehensive knowledge. It is figured as a knowing, but distant, glance rather than the arched brow of concentration. It is not to know something, but to know about something. This ambient sense of knowledge, conveyed by the formal and visual aesthetics of the contemporary fashion magazine, was to be expanded by Prince, who in 1983 published his first and only novel, *Why I go to Movies Alone*. As a text that elaborates on the dislocated theme of ambient knowledge informed by magazine culture through the use of various unidentified narrators, it is strongly influenced by Stéphane Mallarmé's short-lived project *La Dernière Mode*, a fashion journal that the Symbolist poet published in the 1870s, with its use of multiple personae.

Figure 8.6 *Untitled (Four Women Looking in the Same Direction)*, 1977 by Richard Prince. Set of four ektacolor photographs, 20 × 24 inches each. (Courtesy of Barbara Gladstone Gallery)

In *La Dernière Mode* the many proclamations and utterances about fashion weave a representation of desire without referring to anything as being merchantable. The fashion object as available is replaced by a highly wrought articulation, printed on paper from which one could only imagine the experience of fashion. But whereas Mallarmé chose the vehicle of the fashion journal as a structural motif best suited to encapsulate an enquiry into the modern nature of beauty and the fugitive experience of modernity, Richard Prince uses it to demonstrate the seductive redundancy of it all.

Many of the themes the narratives in *Why I got Movies Alone* unfold illustrate the impact of the material qualities of the magazine on contemporary sensibilities: 'He had to have her on paper, a material with a flat and seamless surface … a physical location which could represent her resemblance all in one place … a place that had the chances of looking real, but a place that didn't have any specific chances of being real' (Prince 1983: 11). Similarly, the displacement of emotion in the modern subject is rectified in Prince's novel by the proposal that by repeating a single emotion as presented in the continual present of magazine culture, a sense of fullness can be achieved: 'His own desires had very little to do with what came from himself because what he put out, (at least in part) had already been out. His way to make it new was make it again, and making it again was enough for him and certainly, personally speaking, almost him' (Prince 1983: 63). Yet it is the following quotation that articulates most succinctly the idea of a condition of living informed chiefly by magazines as a measure of contemporary lore: 'Magazines, movies, TV, and records. It wasn't everybody's condition but to him it sometimes seemed like it was, and if it really wasn't, that was alright, but it was going to be hard for him to connect with someone who passed themselves off as an example or a version of a life put together from reasonable matter' (Prince 1983: 63).

The sense of a life put together, as if collaged from secondary sources characterised in the first instance by the magazine, remains a central tenet of reality for the unnamed characters in the novel: they hoard fragments to hawk a fragmentary sense of individuality. In this instance the personal archive becomes internalised and the ability to classify, store and distil 'cuttings' (the things one wishes to retain) becomes central to a fashionable condition of being. The novel proposes modern identity as shaped by an ambient form of cultural remembering communicated from the continual present of the magazine. The trick, which is the moral to Prince's novel, is that the modern individual should display it seamlessly. As one of the male narrators laments: 'his fear about hating himself for any rupture in his look was what he sweated the most. A tell-tale seam, a visibility. It was the skip that was the problem, and in any sudden jump was the kind of thing that could spread to those who talked' (Prince 1983: 63).

It appears that this is the key to the articulation of fashion when it is printed on paper as distinct from fashion's material realities: the magazine's ability to be seamless, not only in how it unfolds, from start to finish, from issue to issue, from season to season, but also how it accumulates its repetitive expressions of the continual present, keeping the pages turning but remaining immutable. And it is here that the logic of the fashion magazine unveils its essential purpose to fashion and to the experience of modernity. Even though the material accumulation of its past becomes the salvaged means through which recollecting begins, it is not for its ability to remember that the fashion magazine is prized, but for its ability to continually forget. In the need to express the continual present the fashion magazine transforms multiple disparate fragments from its past into a seamless representation. In order to be made to fit into the formal structure, to be made relevant or apparently contemporary, the fragments are filed down, smoothed off; their meanings reconfigured, their referents shorn. The validity and relevance of the continual present expressed by the fashion magazine can only be asserted by disregarding, or momentarily forgetting the continual present it replaces.

Therefore, the repetition of replacement without recall practised by the fashion magazine can only function by the equal repetition of re-collecting and recollecting. As the fashion magazine loses a sense of what has just passed, so the repository gains a remembrance of something more recent. As the popularity of the exhibition 'Unseen Vogue' (2002) at the Design Museum in London would seem to suggest, we now appear to be far more interested in the process of the fashion magazine and its archive, than its end result. However, it remains to be seen as to whether this will remain a dominant trend in promoting the logic of the fashion magazine.

References

Baudelaire, C. (1999 [1857]), *Les Fleurs du Mal.* Paris: Hazan.

Barthes, R. (1983) *The Fashion System.* New York: Hill & Wang.

Bryson, N. (1990) *Looking at the Overlooked: Four Essay on Still Life Painting.* London: Reaktion Books.

Clark, J. (2002) 'The Judith Clark Costume Gallery', Lecture, London College of Fashion.

Elderfield, J. (1985) *Kurt Schwitters.* London: Thames & Hudson.

Evans, C. (2003). *Fashion at the Edge: Spectacle, Modernity and Deathliness.* New Haven: Yale University Press.

Lacoue-Labarthe, P. and J. Nancy (1988) *The Literary Absolute: The Theory of Literature in German Romanticism.* Albany: State University of New York Press.

Lehmann, U. (2000) *Tigersprung.* Cambridge, MA: MIT Press.

Malraux, A. (1954) *The Voices of Silence.* London: Secker & Warburg.

Martin, R. (1997) no. 28, Viktor & Rolf, *Le Regard Noir*, Stedejilk Museum Bureau Amsterdam, <www.smba.nl/shows/28>

Nairne, S. (1987) *State of the Art: Ideas & Iimages in the 1980s*, in collaboration with Geoff Dunlop and John Wyver, London: Chatto & Windus in collaboration with Channel Four Television Company Limited.

Prince, R. (1983) *Why I Go to Movies Alone.* New York: Tanam Press.

—— (1995) *Adult Comedy Fiction Drama.* New York: Scalo.

Rian, J. (1984) 'Richard Prince', in *New York: Ailleurs et Autrement,* Arc Musee d'Art Moderne de le Ville de Paris.

Sciaparelli, E. (1954) *Shocking Life.* London: J.M. Dent.

Waldman, D. (1992) *Collage, Assemblage and the Found Object.* London: Phaidon Press.

Whatmore, G. (1964) *News Information: The Organisation of Press Cuttings in the Libraries of Newspapers and Broadcasting Services*. London: Crosby Lockwood & Son Ltd.

Response

Barry Curtis

Alistair starts his paper with the observation that cutting and bricolage are central to the articulation of fashion. The everyday montage of wearables which protect and project us is in a state of perpetual change and risk. Clothes are systemic and chaotic, transient, archetypal and highly individual. They serve multiple functions and perform as unruly signs. Clothes can be among the most abject and sublime of objects, and fashion can be seen as an insatiable process of satisfying desire through consumption. The term 'fashion' in English suggests an active engagement of transformation – of moulding, framing, shaping – just as 'travel' connotes the work of moving towards a destination. For artists like Schwitters, interested in the everyday and material, the process of cutting and pasting, working on the material offcuts of life, the construction of new unities and the shock of juxtaposition are close to the tactics of fashioning an appearance and provisional identities, the drama of choice, manipulation and display which are a way of life in consumer culture.

Fashion shares with much avant-garde art a priority for publicity and timeliness and, less obviously, a profound investment in the past although it is distinct from most avant-garde practice in its intimate association with performance. However, the managing of presence became an aspect of the interventionist intentions of many modernist artists and was fundamental to the self-presentation of modernism. Where claims are made on art as a way of life it finds itself with similar concerns to fashion. Modernist male artists demonstrated their priorities by style transgressions; they dressed as businessmen, engineers, sportsmen or workers. Indeed Schwitters dismayed some of his Dada colleagues by the extent to which he failed to conform to sartorial styles of revolt in spite of the highly performative programme of 'Merz'.

The collection of writings in which this text appears testifies to the centrality of fashion among the constitutive concepts of the modern. The paper I am responding to focuses on similarities in the realm of avant-garde art and high fashion. I had never thought, before listening to Alistair, of comparing Schwitters to Schiaparelli, although they clearly share aspects of the transgressive and excessive. A little known provincial, albeit much travelled, Kurt Schwitters with his aroma of home-made glue, babies and guinea pigs, an unsuccessful applicant during his stay in London for a window dressing job at Selfridges. Notorious, well-connected 'Schiap' – the fragrant, internationally renowned princess of the Place Vendome. Schiaparelli certainly wasn't the first commercial fashion designer to engage in reanimating the marginal. Both were interested in mediating between the body and inanimate objects and, in that respect, dramatising issues of choice and juxtaposition. Perhaps the fundamental difference is that Schiaparelli, like other fashion innovators, worked in a similar mode to the bittersweet and surreally disorienting nineteenth-century scrapbooks, with evocative details. Schwitters worked with fragments among which the viewer searches for comprehensible traces.

Both demonstrate in their work, as Alistair notes, an awareness of the logic of the supplement, so expertly illuminated in the work of Beatriz Colomina (1994) and Ulrich Lehmann (2000) – that fashion and publicity were not simply involved in the mediation of modernist ideas and practices but were constitutive of them. The turning of stuff into something else has always been an uneasy enterprise. The destruction of texts in the interests of transfiguration carries a troubling ideological burden – the ransom note, the slogan, the vandalised poster, the detourned ad, the worn message, all implicate the viewer and wearer in a dialectic of familiarity and surprise which characterises the operation of radical and fashionable discourses.

Fashion is the avant-garde of clothing – it feeds off the everyday, but only in the interests of creating an exclusive bridgehead in the immediate future. On the other hand it is eventually accessible to all through the mediation of the market. In many respects it constitutes a model for modernism with its aspirations to transform understanding and ultimately effect social change.

Like modernism, fashion is an exercise in subliminal acts, challenging categories and exploring boundary violations, whilst sustaining conventions of authorship and ambiance. Schwitters and Schiaparelli were unusual in that they were both concerned with the vitality of the mundane. Both engaged in ambivalent practices. Schwitters continued to paint in a realist style throughout his life. Schiaparelli conformed to the conventions of couture. For both, the artistic avant-garde provided formats for transgression which later became familiar in Fluxus and Punk.

As Alistair has suggested, these alphabetically kindred spirits are secret sharers. They both used humble materials in their work, although in Schiaparelli's case the bakelite and bug buttons, the torch brooches, tattoo patterns and synthetics, the back to front/inside out baring of devices and 'wrongness' of fabrics gained her a reputation for making the banal, even the ugly, beautiful. Some critics and historians claim that Schwitters transfigured rubbish through a sublime use of colour and formal composition into a kind of apotheosis of the ordinary, although 'Merz' seems to me more centrally concerned with matters of choice, juxtaposition and repositioning than aesthetics. One of the priorities of 'Merz' was to arrive at an equal evaluation of all materials, 'creating relationships preferably between all the different things in the world' (Schwitters quoted in Katen Husen 2000: 234), an aspect of modernism which found expression in Pop Art and was described by Lawrence Alloway as: 'a general field of communication' (1957: 28).

Certainly 'Merz' was regarded by Schwitters as: 'a tightly knit field of endeavours'.[1] 'Filing' with its original meaning of stringing things together on a thread is also an interweaving and intertextual practice, enabling access via command terms – a way of reanimating stored information. The work of Schwitters could be considered as a wilful and disorienting practice of 'anti-filing' in which the fragment is 'trained into a picture'.[2] 'Merz' has been inspirational to many artists seeking to work in a space between art and life. Schiaparelli's similar interest in reconciling fashion with the mundane has continued to influence more recent designers interested in creating meaning through inversion, misappropriation and shock. Fashion was a fascinating system for avant-garde artists who valued complexity, instability and gesture. Ironically the designers of fashionable items craved the rewards and status of a system of authorship and authority, and tried to inhabit the pre-modern artistic spaces of the 'salon'.

Modernism is a complex phenomenon incorporating, as does capitalism, a dialectic between structure and anti-structure. A persistent theme for artists was to define the limits and appropriate forms of different kinds of artistic practice and then transgress or combine them. The fashion system also similarly used tactics of imitation and play, which mediated the comic and the transcendent, often involving different models of physicality – the mannequin, the robot, the animal. Johannes Huizinga represented this dialectic as the framework for the material of play: 'In nearly all the higher forms of play, the elements of repetition and alternation are like the warp and woof of a fabric' (Huizinga 1980 [1944]: 10). The work of fashion is to refashion the past and the remote and place them momentarily at the centre as the irrefutable present – no wonder that it appealed to artists who were intent on capturing the essence of the modern world and anticipating the future.

Certainly for Schwitters and other performers of modernism, dressing up and altering appearance were appropriate forms of artistic play with identity – making something different, seeing things from a different place and employing a different point of view. The use of masks and disguises was a common modernist strategy for exploring the utopian and the grotesque. Dressing down and dressing up, showing off, acting out and making strange were, and still are, at the heart of avant-garde strategy.

Fashion also has the capacity to animate the mundane temporarily. Walter Benjamin and the surrealists were very sensitive to the enchantment of fashion and fascinated by the no longer fashionable – the particular quality of reality present in obsolescence, the aftermath of fashion's passing presence with all the frayed and irreconcilable elements no longer magically resolved into the 'look'.

Alistair makes this point in relation to 'yesterday's papers'. Fashion was a realm partly shaped by passionate interest, participation and response; it produced an assemblage of elements, which were intensely meaningful and narcotic, elements which could only be reanimated again by radical juxtaposition.

Fashion has always incorporated and idealised the sense of past time: lapels, epaulettes, corsets, ribbons and other lost devices in a dynamic system of affectionate nostalgia and irony, which has to successfully counter the phenomenological smells, wear and stains of old garments, the kind of materials so eagerly sought by Schwitters. Fashion constitutes a script for imaginatively inhabiting the past and embodying the marginal. It offers provisional subjectivities, what Max Weber has called: 'a routinisation of charisma'.[3] It also activates the archive, allowing the past to spring up at times of danger and relevance. Fashion was one of the practices which created new spaces for attention – it developed its own system of salons, catwalks, points of sale and events. It moved beyond the shop window into the spectacularised scenarios of everyday life. It turned heads and attracted gazes, created 'looks' which were anthologised in magazines and newspapers. Fashion became part of the software of architecture in ways which must have been enviable and inspirational to artists seeking to make similar interventions.

Fashion was a model for artists too, in the ways in which it constituted a system in which the point of view was constantly edited – cutting between exhibitionism and narcissism, the intimacy of touch and the abstraction of the gaze, providing a fragmented, discontinuous and mobile point of view analogous to montage and collage. Until recently fashion and art occupied different temporal worlds – even Schwitters believed that his work would persist within a system of timeless art. Alistair points to the way in which Schwitters' collages and Schiaparelli's fabrications are all archive now – hypertexts which can be reanimated and reappropriated in a perspectival history which can be infinitely recombined. They circulate within systems of conspicuous consumption, planned obsolescence and insatiable desire which, like fashion, seek to discover epiphany in the everyday.

Notes

1. This quotation is from <http://www.kurt-schwitters.org> last accessed 28 May 2003.
2. Ibid.
3. First proposed in 'The Methodical Foundations of Sociology' (1947). See Eatwell (n. d.).

References

Alloway, L. (1957) ‘A Personal Statement’, *Ark*, 19. London: RCA.

Colomina, B. (1994) *Privacy and Publicity: Modern Architecture as Mass Media*. Cambridge, MA: MIT Press.

Eatwell, R. (n. d.) ‘The Rebirth of Charisma: Concepts and Theories and the Problem of Operationalsim’ at <http://www.gla.ac.uk/departments/politics/paper8> last accessed 28 May 2003.

Huizinga, J. (1980 [1944]) *Homo Ludens: A Study of the Play Element in Culture*. London: Routledge.

Katenhausen, I. (2000) ‘Kurt Schwitters and Hanover’, in S. Meyer-Buser and K. Orchard *In the Beginning was Merz: From Kurt Schwitters to the Present Day*. Hanover: Hatje Cantz.

Lehmann, U. (2000) *Tigersprung: Fashion in Modernity*. Cambridge, MA: MIT Press.

–9–

entropy (fashion) and emergence (fashioning)

Jamie Brassett

> They give birth astride a grave. The light gleams an instant, then it's night once more.
>
> Beckett, *Waiting for Godot*

stars

Fashion produces stars: either industrially in the never-ending stream promoting the consumption of products; or personally as identities, gleaming at the locus of their own little systems. Seasons come and go, shadows lengthen and contract. Colours change with movement: psycho-cosmic Doppler shifts.

Whether fashion is uniquely a production of modernity is a moot point, considering the pinning-down of modernity is by no means easy. After reading Manuel De Landa's *A Thousand Years of Nonlinear History* (1997), we could argue that modernity began with the rise of European culture after the Chinese and Islamic cultures had dominated the first millennium of the Common Era; that the start of the modern is somehow indistinguishable from the solidification of the European city around 1100CE. Which gives us a few years to play with. Still, to stars, a millennium is small change.

The purpose of what follows is to reorientate the conditions according to which this culture—fashion—constructs its subjects. To take a parallax view of the constellations of stars; to revisit the ways that fashion culturally articulates individuals.

But why? What's wrong with stars anyway?

blackout

> ...all the lights in the universe go out. Blackout...
>
> Li'l Louis, *Blackout*

Brown shells are all that now remain of once bright stars; stars once replete in the splendour of their power, having ostentatiously worn their hearts on their

Figure 9.1 Pleiades star cluster, November 1994. (© Robin Scagell/Galaxy)

sleeves through seemingly ceaseless fusion processes; stars once magnificent and proud ... dead, cold, dark, spinning in the aftermaths of their final energetic gasps. Unfortunate enough to have missed engorging the voracious black holes at their galactic centres, these starshells will remain tokens to the power of entropy in an empty universe, if only there was anyone, anything, to see them. Dark headstones amid the blackness; no bright crosses covering the poppy fields of the Somme as a testament to an energetic youth here. Blackout. Entropy—the principle of thermodynamics which sees all energies in a closed system become heat (which would seem all right if this wasn't a 'heat' that was just a few degrees above absolute zero[1])—has prevailed. The universe has reached its heat death; there was never enough matter to effect its crunching back in on itself, so when the initial impetus of its birth has petered out, there is ... nothing. All the lights in the universe go out ... blackout.

This is, of course, a story which necessitates the identification of the universe as a closed system: its edges hard and well defined (wherever they may be) and nothing able to get in or out. A universe heremetically sealed and real only in and of itself, its existence having followed a neat linear progression from big bang to heat death. From the moment of its exultant birth its being has been only '-towards-death'.

But what happens if the system is opened? When the confidence of the teleological progress of being-towards-death can no longer be endured? When the linear becomes chaotic? To think of the universe as opening onto other arenas (universes?)—in which case, where *we* are may be like an expanding bubble in a mess of foam—seems particulary difficult at the moment (and also dependent upon one's theoretical/scientific taste[2]). Nevertheless, the image, and the question, still remains: what happens if the universe is opened?[3]

Keith Ansell-Pearson, writing in his *Viroid Life* (1997), mentions that the 'gift' of entropy has been creativity, that the promise of an 'ultimate and final heat-death' (Ansell-Pearson 1997: 167) provides the impetus to construct neg-entropic islands of life amid the sea of coldness.[4] That on the local level—of our solar system—the inexorable urge of entropy leading to nova then death of the Sun, will demand that we look for other places to which we must emigrate. Destruction=Creativity. The promise of death requires that we search for ways of living; impending systemic closure forces us to scramble for ways out. The gleam of light interrupting our headlong trajectory towards the dark grave could promise much.[5]

For Ansell-Pearson, that we have 'evolved' is proof of our ability to transform the thermodynamic process into an unstable one; making it non-linear and providing us with possibilities of creation: 'transforming stable systems into unstable ones in order to release free energy' (Ansell-Pearson 1997: 166). But once again the problem of perspective comes upon us: at what point (of view) does a system become closed/open? Indeed taking a 'global' enough perspective seems to provide the slant from which to close any sytem; so perhaps this is a false question. Maybe, instead, we should expand on Ansell-Pearson's notion and seek to promote instability in all systems; to transform the linear into the non-linear; to make the serene chaotic…?

Nomads do this, Deleuze and Guattari show in *Capitalism and Schizophrenia 2. A Thousand Plateaus* (1988). Nomads draw lines on the ground with their faces extremely close to the floor. Spread out and stroking the surface, so close to the mark that its dimensions ooze over its boundaries. Each line is slightly more than a line;[6] and each line becomes a 'line of flight': vectoral, showing a possible direction rather than a teleological joining of points.[7] So the distinctions between ground, line and face blur, and the action becomes one which affects not only the ground but the art (or cartography) and the nomad too.

Close up—using what Deleuze and Guattari call 'haptic vision' (Deleuze and Guattari 1988: 492–9)—any system has possibilities. The eye becomes an organ of touch and not one that delimits by distance purely. Lacking perspective allows for projects, projectiles, to be fired willy-nilly out of the system; becoming vectoral through aimlessness. To smooth space nomadically may also enforce the opening of closed systems; unblocking flows that have been restricted by linearity and equilibrium to trickle inexorably towards death. Impending doom, even the heat death of the universe, demands a zooming-in on systems of organisation; for in the minutiae of the molecular there may exist a way out of entropic molar states.

emergence

Emergence can be articulated very simply: it describes that process whereby the whole becomes more than the sum of the parts; or that process by which local changes end up giving global consequences. So we can get systems which can be described as exhibiting 'emergent behaviour' or as having 'emergent properties:' swarms, flocks and shoals; traffic jams, consciousness and crowds; economies and cultures... Simple. However, there is much more that we need to examine with this notion.

Emergence appears to refer to two concepts—historically different, but currently connected, as we will see. The first is contained within Chaos Theory and is best seen at work in the phrase, 'the spontaneous emergence of order out of chaos' (De Landa 1991: 229), and thus is mixed up with notions of self-organisation. In the terms favoured by such a theory, emergence describes the transition from one type of behaviour to another within a system (a phase transition), or even the transition of an entire system so that it starts to operate according to different rules (a bifurcation event).[8] To this we can add, again from Manuel De Landa, 'Roughly, we could say that phenomena of self-organization occur whenever a bifurcation takes place: when a new attractor appears on the phase portrait of a system, or when the system's attractors mutate in kind' (De Landa 1992: 138). Emergence is, then, simply change which happens without any outside input.

Under certain conditions—conditions that are far from equilibrium we should remember—the laminar flow of a liquid becomes turbulent, or apparently chaotic turbulence self-organises into a whirlpool; only for these emergences to dissipate as suddenly as they arrived. Similarly with water, at a certain temperature, its very nature will change from a liquid into a solid: at that point of becoming, we can say that a new state emerges (although the use of the term 'point' may be somewhat misleading here).

The second concept of emergence predates contemporary Chaos Theory, finding many of its theoretical elucidations in the 1920s. In his *Out of Control. The New Biology of Machines* (1994), Kevin Kelly quotes from C. Lloyd Morgan's 1923 essay, 'Emergent Evolution': 'The emergent step, though it may seem more or less saltatory [a leap], is best regarded as a qualitative change of direction, or turning point, in the course of events' (Kelly 1994: 15. Kelly's brackets). And the Web-published essay 'The Concept of Emergence' by Meehl and Sellars provides a more contemporary critique of Professor Stephen Pepper's (1926) critical essay 'Emergence'.[9] Kelly goes on to characterise these theories (or versions of the theory) thus: 'In the logic of emergence, 2 + 2 = apples' (Kelly 1994: 15).[10] According to these notions, emergence relates to a philosophical 'becoming'.[11]

In its current usage—a usage inseparable from the theories of Chaos and Complexity—the concept of emergence is bound up within the myriad architectonics of Connectionism. For example, American philosopher John Searle states:

> Because [consciousness] is a feature that emerges from certain neuronal activities, we can think of it as an 'emergent property' of the brain. An emergent property of a system is one that is causally explained by the behavior of the elements of the system; but it is not a property of any individual elements and it cannot be explained simply as a summation of the properties of those elements. (Searle 1997: 18)

The networking of billions of brain cells (neurones), their intricate interlocking of multiple connections (and, we must remember, their ability to *re*connect) is what gives rise to the possibilities of consciousness. There is nothing hidden deep within the neurone that bespeaks of thinking; however, mix a whole bunch of them together and ...

Sadie Plant shows in her essay 'The Virtual Complexity of Culture' (1996) that the term 'Connectionism' has swarmed from the specificities of Computer and Cognitive Science to infiltrate a general cultural arena; indeed, Plant's work can also be seen as influencing such an infiltration. The import of the Connectionist model, for her, goes beyond purely postmodern liberalism (as Sherry Turkle characterises the non-technical use of connectionist metaphorics).

Unlike traditional serial processing, Connectionism does not propose the linear hierarchy of information. Rather, it endeavours to connect all its parts to each other (parts that have been called 'demons' in some systems, or 'agents' in the early Perceptron system),[12] it lets relationships form where links are strong in an effort to let the multiplicity 'learn' from its 'experience'. What happens within the Connectionist arena is that information is not skimmed from the top of a hierarchic processing of pieces, but *emerges* from the entire machine working in concert. Turkle explains, albeit mystically: 'Unlike information processing AI... the connectionists did not see information as being stored anywhere in particular. Rather, it was inherent everywhere. The system's information, like information in the brain, would be evoked rather than found' (Turkle 1996: 132). Plant is somewhat less spiritual when she writes of the equation of intelligence with the workings of the Connectionist Machine:

> What is now described as an 'order-emerging-out-of-massive-connections' approach defines intelligence as an exploratory process, which learns and learns to learn for itself. Intelligence is no longer monopolized, imposed or given by some external, transcendent, and implicitly superior source which hands down what it knows—or rather what it is willing to share—but instead evolves as an emergent process, engineering itself from the bottom up. (Plant 1996: 204)

Plant shows that the Connectionist approach—especially as it is informed by the philosophy of Deleuze and Guattari (both separately[13] and in combination)—has possibilities for being emancipatory rather than oppressive.

Now we can see re-emerging some of the ideas outlined in the opening section of this paper. On one level, at its most fundamental, Connectionism provides for a multiplicitous approach to processing; in which case, the whole idea of 'processing' goes out the window, for it loses the notion of a step-by-step, *process* towards a goal (information, intelligence...) and favours something approaching a *swarm*.[14]

Not only does Sadie Plant show that the workings of Connectionism are theoretically and functionally valid within a singular discipline, but she asserts that they should be allowed to flow across disciplines too. In terms of the human (rather than the transcendental workings of theory), however, such an approach has a profound impact. We can think of these connections as occurring across species 'barriers' and material 'barriers' as well as across conceptual 'barriers'... Barriers demarcating the good from the bad, the hygenic from the diseased, us from them. To build barriers, empower territories and close systems we should remember, are necessary actions in the production of identities.

fashioning

> For among the sedentaries, clothes-fabric and tapestry-fabric tend to annex the body and exterior space, respectively, to the immobile house: fabric integrates the body and the outside into a closed space. On the other hand, the weaving of the nomad indexes clothing and the house itself to the space of the outside, to the open smooth space in which the body moves.
>
> Deleuze and Guattari, *Capitalism and Schizophrenia 2*

Is it necessary to argue that fashion is at the very least complicit—if not thoroughly responsible for—the promotion of identities? Still, we must be careful not to propose simple (and false) binary distinctions of the order Identity/Being=Bad, and Emergence/Becoming=Good. Such a process would fall into the territorial demarcation of a closed system that has been discussed above. Systems, we should have noticed by now, are much more complex than that. In his 'The Three Ecologies' (1989b), Guattari—though promoting the propagation of vectors of subjectification—reminds us that it may be necessary to consolidate these vectors, these flows, into stable positions (identities) in order to act like little militants;[15] that some instances of concrete political praxis may demand that we congeal our becomings into positions from which we can take a stand against forces of oppression and domination. There is no doubt that fashion can help us in this respect. In providing aims towards which the vectors (which determine our possible subjectifications) can point, fashion *can* be positioned either merely in opposition to, or in a blatantly antagonistic relationship with systems of oppression and domination. Most obviously, this is seen at work in subcultural groupings and the materialisation of psychosexual identifications.

Such congealings become problematic because of time; that is, when *identity* is demanded: identity—a staying the same over a period of time, a projection into the future of sameness, the promotion of stability, of stasis… Which brings to mind Bataille and his problems with 'project' in *Inner Experience*: 'And ecstacy is the way out! Harmony! Perhaps, but heart-rending. The way out? It suffices that I look for it: I fall back again, inert, pitiful: the way out from project, from the will for a way out! For project is the prison from which I wish to escape (project, discursive experience): I formed the project to escape from project!' (Bataille 1988: 59) Of course Bataille will invoke ecstacy: ex-stasis, the wrenching of a body (mind? experience?) from rest and its thrusting … away; from serenity into chaos? Bataille's problem is that project (working towards an aim) necessitates a stultification of his ecstatic urge. Which is where entropy comes back into the picture: the degradation of a closed system over time will be the result of any project thus formed. Identity is such a project: necessarily entropic. Stagnate the flows of the materialisation of psychosocial/sexual ecstacies (subcultural fashion urges) into identities—ensure that these systems articulated according to bodies and their clothing are closed, locked for ever—and entropy is all that can be promised. Bodies and fashions; dead stars lurching through a cold emptiness; shells of ash covering cores that once urged but now merely exist.

We may need to take a parallax view of what constitutes fashion itself, so that its processes do not produce points which become ends, but points which are moved through on journeys elsewhere. Promote fashion as a vector not a project; maybe not fashion, but fashioning. Get in close, look at every fold and stitch, every microcosm of texture and matter; become; and become haptic.

unravellings

> All consciousness is a matter of threshold.
>
> Deleuze, *The Fold*

Maybe, then, this is just another story about that most modern of discoveries, the unconscious. 'If, with Kant, it is objected that such a conception reintroduced infinite understanding, we might be impelled to remark that the *infinite is taken here only as the presence of an unconscious in finite understanding, of something that cannot be thought in finite thought, of a nonself in the finite self* (Deleuze 1993: 89. My emphasis). In this way the unconscious—that multiply enfolded infinite plateau—serves as the theoretical and material condition upon which any attempt at consciousness can be thought; and so it is to be understood as transcendental.

In the beginning of Greg Egan's science fiction novel *Permutation City* (1995), one of the characters—Paul Durham—is conducting an experiment on himself... on his self. He has downloaded a copy of his consciousness onto a computer and is facing himself on a terminal screen. The experiment involves changing the cycle rates at which the computer is processing the data according to which the Copy is being articulated. At first the cycle matches that of the human original: the Copy counts to ten and the original notes how long it takes (with reference to his own 'real' time). Then the cycles are lengthened up to ten thousand milliseconds; a cycle of computation every ten seconds. For the Copy consciousness of counting from one to ten seems no different from the other moments in the experiment; for the Original, the counting becomes more and more stuttered: 'One [pause]... Two [pause]... Three...' Finally, the processing of the data is not kept to a single computer but distributed across a global network of computers so that there is a spatial dislocation of processing as well as the stuttering of the frequency of computations. For the Copy, however, there is still no subjective difference: consciousness *emerges* from the multiplicity of processes, neither located nor timed. It swarms. Across boundaries, consciousness arises like a fog, like the sound of the sea or the murmur of a crowd.

Emergence always describes a relationship between thresholds: thresholds between solid and liquid, or between one and many. The threshold between unconscious and conscious must be similarly obscure. When the gaseousness of unconscious desires solidifies into the liquidity (or indeed the solidity) of consciousness is a point as difficult to mark as any threshold behaviour. That the process then becomes territorialised by binding it with notions of identity or self seems to be a massive violation, an oppression of the highest order.

Why should it be the case that fashion serves as a tool for such territorialisations? Such condemnations of ecstatic pulses to entropy? To refer back to Deleuze's *The Fold* (1993), we find him using the notion of the fold—of folding, unfolding, refolding—to describe the philosophy of Leibniz as well as some more general motifs in Baroque art, architecture and music ... and, of course, fashion. Like many of the very material images that Deleuze and Guattari use—Rhizome, Nomad, Schizo—the fold seems at once to be metaphorical and literal. Rather, it crosses—and keeps crossing—the boundaries between real and pretend. Very much, Deleuze shows us folds accentuated in Baroque clothing, rippling across Baroque architecture, fluctuating as the convoluted contrapuntalism of Baroque music; and in the layering and intertwining of the monadism of Leibniz. We could say that rhizomes spread by folding matter, by messing up the boundary between earth and air. Or, indeed, that folds are the rhizomes of material.

And so our folds and ripples in cultural phenomena bring us back to the question of entropy. Maybe the question posed earlier, 'what happens if the universe is opened?', can be further nuanced, if not answered. The continual folding of material—spacetime, fabrics, skins, sounds—could crease enough to allow openings of the system (material), allowing entry points for energies, or anything that can stir the stagnating mass of a closed system. The theoretical physicist Michio Kaku provides an eloquent account of some possible future versions of the string field theory that he co-devised, in his *Visions* (1998). Coralling notions of vibrating strings in other dimensions (either ten, eleven, eight or six so far), quantum membranes and wormholes, he wonders whether an advanced enough civilisation will be able to manipulate the very fabric of spacetime to open a way to a universe thus escaping the entropic heat death of this one. It seems, then, that the models we have navigated—fabric and felt, hapticity and the visual, swarms and identities—can work as more than 'mere' metaphors; as Isabelle Stengers writes in *Cosmopolitiques. Tome 6. La vie et l'artifice: visages de l'émergence*:

> The model must explore the disjunction [between itself and its object of study] as such, approaching it on two sides at once (negotiating the relevant internal variables in comparison with the observable external behaviour), but also approaching this external behaviour from the point of view of the *milieu* that defines it. That is, to locate the choice and values which the model requires of the *milieu*, in relation to that which it 'embodies'; to locate how, from its point of view, all *milieux* are not worthwhile. (1997: 122. My translation and italics.)

If modernity has, then, been fashioned in a way that is entropic, maybe emergence out of such identification and heat death can only come through fashioning, not as a metaphor only, but as the very action to be taken on matter.

Acknowledgements

The themes of this current paper have been bubbling around for some time. During my years as a research student studying for a PhD in Philosophy at the University of Warwick (1988–92) I encountered thermodynamics and information theory, entropy and negentropy, swarms and chaos via my supervisor Dr Nick Land. I haven't formally returned to these ideas before now and most likely what I've written about entropy, dying stars and the like is nowhere near what Nick would have; nevertheless, my work would be much drier were it not for his influence. Furthermore, some parts of this paper—particularly those discussing 'emergent properties'—appeared in the Web-published paper 'emerging cyber subjects'

(Brassett 1997). The paper benefits from the 'Fashion and Modernity' meetings of the past few years and from the editorial input of Chris Breward, Caroline Evans and Marketa Uhlirova. I would also like to thank my colleagues in BA Product Design at Central Saint Martins College of Art and Design, London, who've talked with me about these topics: Simon Bolton, Nick Rhodes, Paul Sayers, Chris Lefteri and especially Jessica Edwards. Responsibility for what's written falls, in the end, with me.

Notes

1. Which is –273.16°C. On the history of heat death see Clarke 2001: 3 and his footnote no. 2. On the philosophical power of approaching limits see Deleuze and Guattari 1991: 111–27.
2. An interesting discussion of the different consequences for the universe of differing quantum theoretical viewpoints can be seen in Gribben 1995 and is 'dramatized' in Davies and Brown 1999.
3. 'A physical system … is isolated-closed. One must understand by this that no flow of matter, no circulation of heat, light or energy, crosses the walls that define it and demarcate it in space. Under this condition and this condition only, the two laws of thermodynamics apply and are valid. With the slightest opening, the system is no longer governed by general equations' (Serres 1982: 114). This is a slightly different way of understanding an open universe than that theoretical physicists use. Michio Kaku in *Hyperspace* describes a lonely icy death as the fate of an 'open' universe—one that is open-ended and without the minimum level of matter to force a reversal of the big bang process—as opposed to the big crunch of a 'closed' universe: see Kaku 1994: 300 and Chapter 14 'The Fate of the Universe' 301–12. See also Gribben 1995: 208–14.
4. 'We willingly accept, however, the fact that the things around us do not all share the same temporality: negentropic islands on or in the entropic sea, or distinct universes as Boltzmann described them, pockets of local orders in rising entropy, crystal depositories sunk in ashes—none of these things disturb us' (Serres 1982: 117).
5. See Egan 1997. His novel *Diaspora* tells of the descendents of humanity, centuries into the future, having to find a way into other dimensions in order to escape the after-effects of an astrophysical accident.
6. 'Whereas the rectilinear (or 'regularly' rounded) Egyptian line is negatively motivated by anxiety in the face of all that passes, flows, or varies, and erects

the constancy and eternity of an In-Itself, the nomad line is abstract in an entirely different sense, precisely because it has a multiple orientation and passes *between* points, figures, and contours: it is positively motivated by the smooth space it draws, not by any striation it might perform to ward off anxiety and subordinate the smooth' (Deleuze and Guattari 1988: 496–7).

7. See Deleuze and Guattari's discussion of the 'Mathematical Model' of Smooth and Striated Space, Deleuze and Guattari 1988: 482–8. 'In each model, the smooth actually seemed to pertain to a fundamental heterogeneity ... a continuous variation that exceeds any distribution of constants and variables, the freeing of a line that does not pass between two points, the formation of a plane that does not proceed by parallel and perpendicular lines' (Deleuze and Guattari 1988: 488).
8. For a clear elucidation of this—and other Chaos Theory concepts—see De Landa 1991: 234–7, note 9.
9. Pepper's essay criticises the notion of emergence for its epiphenomenalism—'the dualistic doctrine that consciousness is merely a by-product of physiological processes and has no power to affect them' (Collins English Dictionary). Indeed, epiphenomenalism may seem to relate to some of the ideas propounded by many contemporary theorists of consciousness-as-emergent. Though this is not the place to provide another critique of epiphenomenalism, I think that in what follows we shall not find any advocation of dualism.
10. In the final pages of his *Out of Control*, Kevin Kelly explains: 'I often use the word "emergent" in this book. As used by the practitioners of complexity, it means something like: "that organization which is generated out of parts acting in concert." But the meaning of emergent begins to disappear when scrutinized, leaving behind the vague impression that the word is, at bottom, meaningless. I tried substituting the word "happened" in every instance I used "emerged" and it seemed to work. Try it' (1994: 590).
11. Both of these notions can be seen at work in the following passages: 'As soon as it is a question of emergence, the whole and the parts must thus inter-define each other and negotiate what signifies an explanation of the one by the others' (Stengers 1997: 30. My translation). 'Artaud said: write *for* illiterates—speak for aphasics, think for acephalics. But what does this "for" mean? It isn't "with the intention of...", or even "in the place of...", it is "before". It is a question of becoming. The thinker isn't acephalic, aphasic or illiterate, but becomes it. *He becomes Indian not to finish becoming, rather "in order that" the Indian (who is Indian) becomes something else and tears himself away from his agony*' (Deleuze/Guattari 1991: 105. My translation and emphasis). I discuss 'becoming' a little more fully in Brassett 1997: 282–7.
12. Manuel De Landa examines some of these in the final chapter of his *War in the Age of Intelligent Machines* (1991): 'Policing the Spectrum', 179–231.

13. See Guattari 1992 for an epistemological and systemic iteration of the political, philosophical, social and ecological issues discussed in his 'The Three Ecologies' (1989), as well as in his collaborations with Deleuze.
14. 'Emergent AI depends on the way local interactions among decentralized components can lead to overall patterns. So does the working of ant colonies and the immune system, the pile-up of cars in a traffic jam, and the motion of a flock of birds' (Turkle 1996: 138). Furthermore, see Kelly 1994, Delanda 1992 and 1997 and Plant 1996. We should also remember that Deleuze (1993) puts into play similar concepts—albeit in a more traditional philosophical manner—in his discussion of Leibniz. Herein, he notices Leibniz's examples of the sound of the sea emerging (we might say) from the connecting, the combination of the sounds of a million water droplets in motion; of the sound of a crowd, made-up of the murmurings of the individuals, though reducible to none of them (eg. Deleuze 1993: 86). See also Kelly 1994: 6–36.
15. 'There will never be a point at which feminists will be said to have committed sufficient energy to becoming-woman; nor should the immigrant population be called upon to renounce the cultural features of its being, or its membership of a particular nationality. Our objective should be to nurture individual cultures, while at the same time inventing new contracts of citizenship: to create an order of the state in which singularity, exceptions, and rarity coexist under the least oppressive possible conditions... Certainly, in the field of social ecology in particular, there will be times of struggle in which all men and women feel a need to set common objectives and act "like little soldiers"—by which I mean good militants. But there will also be periods of resingularization, in which individual and collective subjectivities will "reclaim their due", and in which creative expression will take precedence over collective goals' (Guattari 1989b: 139–40. Translation modified; Guattari 1989a: 46–7).

References

Ansell-Pearson, K. (1997) *Viroid Life. Perspectives on Nietzsche and the Transhuman Condition.* London: Routledge.

Bataille, G. (1988) *Inner Experience*, trans. L.A. Boldt. Albany: State University of New York Press.

Beckett, S. (1965) *Waiting for Godot*. London: Faber and Faber.

Brassett, J. (1997) 'emerging cyber subjects', in Simon Mills (ed.) *frAme* <http://human.ntu.ac.uk/frame/frame.html>

Clarke, B. (2001) *Energy Forms. Allegory and Science in the Era of Classical Thermodynamics.* Ann Arbor: University of Michigan Press.

Davies, P.C.W. and J.R. Brown (1999) *The Ghost in the Atom. A Discussion of the Mysteries of Quantum Physics*. Cambridge: Cambridge University Press.

De Landa, M. (1991) *War in the Age of Intelligent Machines*. New York: Zone Books.

—— (1992) 'Nonorganic Life', in J. Crary and S. Kwinter (eds) *Incorporations*, Zone 6. New York: Zone Books: 129–67.

—— (1997) *A Thousand Years of Nonlinear History*. New York: Zone Books.

Deleuze, G. (1993) *The Fold. Leibniz and the Baroque*. trans. T. Conley. London: Athlone Press.

Deleuze, G. and F. Guattari (1988) *Capitalism and Schizophrenia 2. A Thousand Plateaus*, trans. B. Massumi. London: Athlone Press.

—— (1991) *Qu'est-ce que la philosophie*. Paris: Les Éditions de Minuit.

Egan, G. (1995) *Permutation City*. London: Millenium.

—— (1997) *Diaspora*. London: Orion Books.

Gribben, J. (1995) *Schrödinger's Kittens and the Search for Reality*. London: Orion Books.

Guattari, F. (1989a) *Les trois écologies*. Paris: Éditions Galilée.

—— (1989b) 'The Three Ecologies' *New Formations*, 8, Summer: 131–47.

—— (1992) 'Regimes, Pathways, Subjects', in J. Crary and S. Kwinter (eds) *Incorporations*. New York: Zone Books: 16–37.

Kaku, M. (1994) *Hyperspace. A Scientific Odyssey through the 10th Dimension*. Oxford: Oxford University Press.

—— (1998) *Visions*. Oxford: Oxford University Press.

Kelly, K. (1994) *Out of Control. The New Biology of Machines*. London: Fourth Estate.

Li'l Louis (1999) *Blackout*, ffrr (full frequency range recordings), promotional 12".

Meehl, P.E. and W. Sellars (n.d.) 'The Concept of Emergence' <http//:csmaclab-www.uchicago.edu/philosophyProject/sellars/ce.html>

Plant, S. (1996) 'The Virtual Complexity of Culture', in G. Robertson et al. (eds) *FutureNatural. Nature/Science/Culture*. London: Routledge: 203–17.

Searle, J.R. (1997) *The Mystery of Consciousness*. London: Granta.

Serres, M. (1982) 'The Origin of Language: Biology, Information Theory and Thermodynamics' in *Oxford Literary Review*, 5: 113–24.

Stengers, I. (1997) *Cosmopolitiques. Tome 6. La vie et l'artifice: visages de l'émergence*. Paris: Editions La Découverte.

Turkle, S. (1996) *Life on the Screen. Identity in the Age of the Internet*. London: Orion Books.

Response

Ben Highmore

Jamie Brassett's 'entropy (fashion) & emergence (fashioning)' provides a glimpse of what fashion theory might gain from a perspective that is astronomical in proportions. Brassett reminds us that time and physics are not stable entities that tell us in advance what we should mean by 'history' or 'materialism'. The forms of attention we construct (historical materialism or psychoanalysis, for instance) are the heuristic devices that test out conceptions of physical and psychical life, as well as temporal existence. New physics and new understandings of duration require different heuristic devices. What (we may need to ask) is the duration of historical context? The demand to historicise, to provide historical contexts for cultural forms, is a demand routinely prescribed for cultural enquiry, specifically for forms of enquiry like fashion studies or versions of cultural studies that value the interconnections between different cultural forms. But what is this 'context', this history – what temporal forms does it take: a nanosecond or a millennium; the lifetime of a human or a planet; the beat of a heart or the length of a summer; the duration of an epoch or a government? Are 'events' (a new 'look' for instance) 'surface disturbances, crests of foam that the tides of history carry on their strong backs'? (Braudel 1995: 21). Should we 'distrust' these 'brief, rapid, nervous fluctuations' and insist on a 'history whose passage is almost imperceptible' (Braudel 1995: 20–1) (a form of cultural geology, perhaps)? Or should we take our tempo from the insistent presence of markets, from the rhythm marked out by industry?

Henri Lefebvre and Catherine Régulier, in an essay that introduces 'The Rhythmanalytical Project', suggest that time, in the *longue durée* of modernity, is always plural. Taking their point of departure from the moment when abstract 'clock time' provided the dominant form for 'measuring working time', they write:

> From that historic moment, it [clock time] became the time of the everyday, subordinating other aspects of daily life to the spatial organization of work: times for sleep and waking, times for meals and private life, relationships between adults and children, entertainment and leisure, relationships in the home. However, everyday life is shot through and cut across by the larger rhythms of life and the cosmos: days and nights, months and seasons, and more specifically still, biological rhythms. In everyday

> life, this results in constant interaction between these rhythms and repetitive processes linked with homogenous time. (2003: 190)

For Lefebvre and Régulier nature continually asserts and reasserts itself. The leaves turn brown, fall from the tree, and turn to mulch under foot. New shoots appear, gingerly poking out of the ground, tentatively taking on new shapes. Human bodies assert their tenacious pulses and proclivities, their energies and need for food and sleep. Against those who describe contemporary life as 'accelerated reality' (Virilio 2001: 47), Lefebvre and Régulier insist on the slower rhythms of the seasons and the endless and predictable oscillations of day and night. Against those who would only notice the prosthetic extensions of the human body, they remind us of the fibrillar elasticity of muscles and the circadian rhythms of our creaturely selves. But rather than simply reclaiming the material continuities posed by biology or nature, theirs is a more orchestral project that is dedicated to the polyrhythmic world. Here rhythms collide or harmonise, and the fastest movements are continually set alongside the slow stubborn pace of other aspects of material culture. This is a project that might well benefit the study of fashion culture.

Fashion, a cultural form that can register the most intense accelerations of modernity, seems tied in some fundamental way to the seasons: the spring collection, the autumn line. This regularity of pacing reminds us of clothes' intimate connections to climate, to the body's comfort and protection, as well as to the regularity of the market's demand for new products. Yet fashion is also affiliated to the most dynamic and chaotic rhythms of the culture industry, which suggests we also need to think of it in terms of other rhythms that are at odds with this sense of evenly paced change. Similarly at odds is fashion's increasing disdain for the actualities of weather and temperature (designing for a future of atmosphere-modulated environments). For Lefebvre and Régulier conflict and dissonance are at the very root of a rhythmanalysis of modernity, and it is the simultaneity of these contradictory rhythms that characterise modern life. Dissonance, especially in the conflict between the rhythms of the body and the rhythms that drive modern forms of commodity circulation, work practices, and social regulation, is both a symptom and a diagnosis of our contemporary life. As symptom it points to the lived contradictions of modernity; as diagnosis it shows how 'the inevitable shocks (stresses), disorders and disturbances' (Lefebvre and Régulier 2003: 196) that the body experiences, reveal the resistance of the organism (and the cost of that creaturely resistance) to the overreaching rhythms of commodity exchange.

Multiple rhythms animate the culture of fashion. Some coruscate across fashion's firmament, like a staccato beat picking out moments of singularity. These photoflashes highlight astonishing inventions by star designers, but also more ordinary moments when memory and desire fleetingly coalesce in the fabric and cut of clothes. Some rhythms reverberate and echo, tenaciously clinging to items long since relegated from the public sphere: 'many garments were kept long after they went out of fashion or no longer fitted, not out of a moral sense of thrift but because their owners could not bear to part with them' (Attfield 2000: 145). Other rhythms seem to ironically and sarcastically mimic the cyclical movements of the seasons: the retro-refit and the revival (clothes as quotation). Others play with direction: second-hand clothing (from charity shops and thrift stores) reabsorbed into frontier fashion industries in the shape of newly distressed jeans (faux encrustations of dirt, the ersatz patina of wear). Arrhythmic interruptions and cyclical time interwoven with the accelerations of commodity circulation and the persistence of the body: together these conjure up the dissonant rhythms of modernity.

And what of history and materialism in all this, what of context? Just as fashion's rhythmicity is plural so to are its contexts. If entropy and emergence describe the axial arrangements of fashion's force field, then between and across these axes exist a plethora of durations: the biological changes of the body; the varying conceptions of the self; the durability of fabrics; the practices of the body, of manners, of propriety; the techniques of fashion publicity; the architectonics of display and circulation; the conditions of production and the entire process of consumption (including the literal act of 'devouring', of expenditure); the persistence (or not) of memory; the competing notions of style; and so on. Listing, however, is the easy part. It points to a desire to present the culture of fashion in all its thickness. The difficulty, though, is how to orchestrate all this, how to arrange it in productive and intelligible ways. Jamie Brassett's essay offers a direction that would make such exhaustive and exhausting listing subservient to the demand to articulate the animating forces of culture. For Brassett it is energy (the force of matter) that matters. And it is this concentration on energy that points the way to a possible new physics of fashion.

References

Attfield, J. (2000) *Wild Things: The Material Culture of Everyday Life*. Oxford: Berg.

Braudel, F. (1995 [1946]) *The Mediterranean and the Mediterranean World in the Age of Philip II*, trans. S. Reynolds. Berkeley: University of California Press.

Lefebvre, H. and C. Régulier (2003) 'The Rhythmanalytical Project', in S. Elden, E. Lebas, and E. Kofman (eds), *Henri Lefebvre: Key Writings*, London: Continuum. The essay was first published in 1985 in the journal *Communications.*

Virilio, P. (2001) 'After Architecture: A Conversation [with Sylvère Lotringer]', *Grey Room*, 3.